MICROFINANCE SYSTEMS

Designing Quality Financial Services for the Poor

Graham A. N. Wright

Zed Books Ltd.
London & New York

The University Press Limited
Dhaka

Microfinance Systems was first published by:

In the UK and USA
Zed Books Ltd, 7 Cynthia Street
London NI 9JF, UK
and
Room 400, 175 Fifth Avenue
New York 10010, USA

In the Rest of the World
The University Press Limited
Red Crescent Building
114 Motijheel Commercial Area
Dhaka 1000, Bangladesh

Cover designed by Ashraful Hassan Arif
Typeset in Times New Roman by Mark Printing and Packaging, Dhaka.
Printed at Elora Art Publicity, Dhaka.
Bound by Famous Binding Works, Dhaka.

Distributed in the USA exclusively by St Martin's Press, 175 Fifth Avenue,
New York 10010.

A catalogue record for this book is available from the British Library.

US CIP data is available from the Library of Congress.

ISBN 1 85649 787 9 hb
ISBN 1 85649 788 7 pb

In the Rest of the World

ISBN 984 05 1505 5

Contents

Section 1   1

WHAT ARE WE TRYING TO DO? IN THEORY

Section 2

SO WHAT SHOULD WE DO? IN PRACTICE   127

Section 3

HOW HAS IT BEEN DONE? CASE STUDIES 161

Glossary of Bangladeshi, English and Filipino terms

40 Pesos	= $1
45 Taka	= $1
Barangay (F)	Village - typically (in the Cordillera) comprising of 100-250 households and sub-divided into 3-7 sitios
District (B)	An administrative unit with around 50-100,000 households
Dol (B)	Village faction or patron-cluster group
Gusti (B)	Patrilineal kin group
Haat (B)	A small weekly rural market, generally serving around 10-20 villages
Hartal (B)	A general strike - usually called a political protest
Kendra (B)	A group or "centre" of 5-10 groups of typically 5 members
Khas (B)	Government-owned land or ponds, which (in theory) is to be used by the poor to raise crops or fish - but which is generally occupied and used by the village elite.
Kisti (B)	Loan repayment instalment
Maund (B)	Measurement of paddy - about 37.5 kilos
Paisa (B)	Unit of currency - the smallest
Para (B)	Small sub-division of a village - usually comprising 20-75 households
Paluwagan (F)	Traditional savings device for pooling funds of the members - typically a ROSCA
Poblacion (F)	Municipal capital - usually a small market town
ROSCA (E)	Rotating Savings and Credit Association
Samity (B)	Society - a group of people - often synonymous with an MFI's groups or kendras
Sitio (F)	Small sub-division of a barangay - usually comprising 5-50 households
Shawnirvar (B)	Self-reliance
Thana (B)	An administrative sub-division - comprising 4,000-10,000 households
Union (B)	An administrative sub-division - comprising 250 - 1,000 households

(B) *Bangladeshi term*
(E) *English term*
(F) *Filipino term*

Acknowledgement

There are many, many people who deserve my deepest, heartfelt thanks. The management and staff of BURO, Tangail whose hard work and support throughout the development of the organisation was outstanding, and whose desire and commitment to push the boundaries of knowledge and practice in Microfinance continues to serve the industry well. Stuart Rutherford who has been a constant source of inspiration, insight and learning for me- it has be a privilege to work with him. Syed Hashemi who persuaded me to write this book. Mel and Tony Drexler who rescued me from a hartal-bound Dhaka airport and helped me leave Arthur Andersen & Co. for development. Philip Lacbawan, Raike Quinones and the CECAP Rural Finance component staff for their support in the difficult process of designing the CECAP system. Evelyn Bulahao, William Kiaki, Felicitas Hampuy and Filipe Comila for their hard work in implementing the CECAP system. David Cracknell, Philippe Besson, Robert Molteno, Evelyn Stark and others who were patient enough to review draft manuscripts and provide valuable comments. My Mother whose caring and commitment to helping others promoted my interest in alternative thinking, and ultimately in development. My Father, in the UK, whose kindness and understanding is remarkable, but who I have deserted for warmer climes !

Thanks to all those who reviewed the various drafts of the book and gave their valuable comments. All the remaining opinions, errors, omissions, spelling howlers and tortured grammar are entirely mine, and mine alone. This book is being published with support of the UK's Department For International Development and Swiss Development Co-operation - but the views are those of the author alone and do not in any way represent policy of these institutions.

Introduction and Overview

This book tries to put the case for providing appropriate, quality financial services for the poor, and to outline the principles and methods that could, and perhaps should, be followed to design such Microfinance Systems. The book is divided in to three sections. The first section is an extensive review of the current literature to examine the theory and what has been learned about financial services for the poor to date, and how we might go about optimising these services in the future. The second section is offered as a series of practical guides to how an organisation seeking to be come a permanent financial service provider might set about developing its services and systems. The third section comprises two detailed case studies which will be of particular interest to practitioners. The first is a detailed description of the process used to develop the Central Cordillera Agricultural Programme's Rural Finance System. The second is the history (and cautionary tale) of BURO, Tangail - a Bangladeshi NGO with extensive experience in the design and provision of flexible financial services; an institution that has put the theory into practice.

Each chapter starts with a one page summary of what is to come, printed in italics, so readers can decide if they want to plunge in and tackle the issues/ideas in depth.

The first section of the book asks "What are We Trying to do? In Theory", and begins with a chapter, "Microfinance: The Solution or A Problem ?", which discusses the benefits of providing quality financial services, and the cost effectiveness of Microfinance programmes. It argues that such programmes can have a substantial positive social and economic impact on the lives of the (in the majority of cases) women that participate in them. It also argues that well designed Microfinance programmes are a very cost effective way of helping the poor help themselves, in the way that they themselves see as the most effective.

The next chapter, "Optimising Systems for Clients and the Institution " examines some of the key problems and short comings of typical Microfinance programmes, and argues that many of these could be addressed or overcome through careful attention to the design and implementation of the system. It concludes that the more appropriate and better quality the financial services are, the greater the take up and retention by their poor clients will be.

The following chapter, "Savings: Services for the Clients or Capital for the Institution ?" reasserts the importance of focusing on savings, the "forgotten half" of MicroCredit (as opposed to Microfinance) programmes. It reviews the evidence for the willingness and ability of the poor to save both in Bangladesh and elsewhere. It goes on to argue that, in Bangladesh, the domination of the Grameen Bank credit-led systems resulted in inappropriate systems, designed more for the benefit of the implementing organisation than its clients. The chapter ends with a few remarks on the need for regulation and supervision and/or a deposit insurance scheme in Bangladesh.

The final, brief chapter of this section is entitled, "Replicating Microfinance Systems: Are Blue-Prints Enough ?" and looks at the way that the replication of MicroCredit and Microfinance programmes has been managed. It makes a plea for the design of more appropriate, better quality financial services delivered in response to the needs and opportunities in the communities the systems are designed to serve. It notes the importance of socio-cultural, geographical factors that are often simply ignored.

The second section of the book is entitled, "So What Do We Do ? In Practice", and it puts forward some principles and approaches to designing appropriate quality financial services.

The "The Principles of Microfinance" gives a brief overview of the key principles that should be generally followed when designing and implementing Microfinance programmes. These are not offered as "set-in-stone" commandments, but rather as guidelines to what seems to have underpinned successful Microfinance programmes to date.

Even once a Microfinance system is established, the implementing organisation should be consistently seeking to further improve services in order to gain and retain clients. In recognition of this, the final chapter "Beyond Basic Credit and Savings: Developing New Financial Service Products for the Poor" reviews approaches to product development. It examines how to research, design test and implement the most appropriate quality financial services for the Microfinance organisation's clients.

The third and final section entitles "How Has It Been Done ? Case Studies" reviews how two very different Microfinance programmes operating in very different environments set about designing their systems. It is designed to give a detailed account of how the systems were developed and tested through programmes of action research, and to provide practitioners on how to optimise the design of financial services and the systems to deliver them.

It opens with a chapter on "Central Cordillera Agriculture Programme: System Design Process - In Progress" which gives a detailed description of how the process of designing an appropriate, quality-oriented financial services system might be undertaken. The chapter uses an example purposely chosen from an environment and landscape very different from that of Bangladesh, the mountains of Central Luzon in the Philippines.

The second chapter in this section is BURO, "Tangail: Systems and Services Under Development", the Microfinance Institution (MFI) at the forefront of developing quality financial services for the poor in Bangladesh. BURO, Tangail is markedly different from other NGOs, in that it has consistently recognised the importance of voluntary, open access savings services for the poor and has stressed integrated intermediation as opposed to the delivery of inflexible credit. BURO, Tangail has always placed more emphasis on developing quality financial services for its clients rather than delivering quantity-driven credit to loanees. It continues to pilot test a wide variety of financial services to ensure that its clients get the best possible services. BURO, Tangail is therefore used to illustrate many of the ideas and issues presented in the book. For this reason its history, philosophy, experience and plans are discussed at some length.

The "Conclusion" is a challenge for all directly or indirectly involved in the "Microfinance movement" to constantly seek to improve the appropriateness and quality of the financial services we offer to the poor ... both our and their future depends on it.

Morsheda Akhtar
The Power of Persuasion

Anwar, Morsheda's husband, had a small grocery shop. During the 1980s, lured by the promise of high wages, Anwar tried to get a job in the Middle East through a manpower-recruiting agency. He sold his shop and its contents, and paid Tk.50,000 to the agency - and never heard from them again. After this, the family's fortunes sank and they found themselves in a miserable condition. Not only was her husband jobless, but Morsheda herself was not earning - and that year they had their first child. Soon after her mother-in-law drove Morsheda out of their family home over some trifling matter. Anwar wanted to return Morsheda to her father's house but Morsheda refused to return - the shame would have been too great for this resilient and dignified woman to bear.

She decided to take her destiny into her own hands. First, she constructed a simple thatched house on an aunt's land, and started

Contd.

vegetable gardening. Soon after, with much financial difficulty, Morsheda share-raised a cow - which she cared for like her own son, and from which she got milk in return. While struggling in this manner, she heard the name "Grameen Samity" which kindled a ray of hope in her. She joined the Grameen Bank, but very soon, she became frustrated with the organisation's regimented and inflexible rules and regulations - in particular how members could never withdraw their savings, even when they were in desperate straits. Morsheda, however, did not stop here - she saw the potential of what the Grameen Bank was doing. She decided that she would organise a samity amongst the people in her para.

"Savings are important to all of us - more important than loans," Morsheda is quite clear about this. She continues, "Before I used to try to save a few paisa in the house, but we always spent it - a guest came, the children begged for an ice-cream, or something else important came up - the money always went. Then when you really needed the money you had saved it was not there. We need a secure place to put savings - somewhere outside the house, but where we can get access to them quickly when emergency strikes."

As she was striving to do this, she came to learn about BURO, Tangail, and its open access savings system. She decided to go to BURO, Tangail for help and to ask the organisation to work in her para. She was saddened to hear that BURO, Tangail did not operate in the suburbs of Tangail where her para lay. She was told that the activities of BURO, Tangail were for poor people in the distant villages. Tenacious Morsheda still remembers her discussion with one of the managers of BURO, Tangail, "I told him," she says with a glint of triumph in her eyes, "I insisted, that the people of the suburbs are also poor human beings, and there was no reason why they should be deprived of BURO, Tangail's services. They need savings and loans as much as the people in the distant villages - and then I told him my story." Finally, she convinced the manager who reported back to the organisation and used Morsheda's story to convince the management of BURO, Tangail to start operations in the suburbs of the town.

Soon afterwards, Morsheda formed a kendra [group], and she and her fellow kendra members had the tool they needed to forge their

Contd.

Continued from: Morsheda Akhter: The Power of Persuation

own destinies. Morsheda says "We have learnt from BURO, Tangail how to save in a disciplined and regular way, how to earn money, and how to use it in order to have a decent life." Morsheda says that BURO, Tangail has provided them with a vision, and has shown great confidence in them by giving the members loans. But BURO, Tangail's management knows that it is the members who have the vision, and the confidence in themselves to use the system well and make a better future for themselves and their children.

As for Morsheda, she has transformed her vision into a reality. Her kendra is strong, and the members are self-confident and happy. "There was a time," says Morsheda, "When if I asked for Tk. 500, nobody wanted to lend it. Now if I ask for Tk. 5,000, everybody wants to lend it to me." With loans from BURO, Tangail, she has set up a small factory producing ornaments for rickshaws in her courtyard, extended the vegetable gardening around her homestead, and planted fruit saplings. Her elder son will take the Secondary School Certificate examination this year, while her younger daughter reads in Class-VI. Morsheda's mother-in-law who once drove her out from the house, is now living with her - for Morsheda understands, "It is not my mother-in-law's inhumane nature that made her drive me out of the home, but the inhumane nature of poverty."

WHAT ARE WE TRYING TO DO?
IN THEORY

Chapter 1

MICROFINANCE: THE SOLUTION
OR A PROBLEM?

Microfinance programmes are credited with an amazing array of beneficial impacts, and at the same time are accused of promoting themselves as "panaceas". With increasing donor funds being channelled into Microfinance, it is time to pause and examine these claims and concerns, and to try to separate reality from the publicity currently surrounding the Microfinance "industry".

Before examining the economic impacts of Microfinance programmes, it is important to recognise that there is a significant difference between "increasing income" and "reducing poverty". Despite the prevalent emphasis on raising incomes as the central objective of development programmes, the two are not synonymous. Clearly, the <u>use</u> to which income is put is as important in determining poverty and welfare as the level of income itself - increased income can be (and often is) gambled away. It is also important to recognise that poverty is neither linear nor static, and that today's not-so-poor may well be tomorrow's poorest - and vice versa. It is for this reason that the poor place so much emphasis on diversifying their sources of income - it reduces their exposure to catastrophic income loss. Finally, in the context of the drive to create businesses that provide jobs, the differences between the quality of formal and informal sector employment must be noted. These differences also explain why, for many, having diversified sources of home-based income is preferable to depending on exploitative employment.

Many development practitioners contend that Microfinance addresses the symptoms but not the causes of poverty, and recommend that a "community development" approach that seeks to "empower" the poor to change the structural basis of their poverty. Closer examination of community development programmes reveals their inability to develop sustainable rural organisations, their limited impact, and that their "beneficiaries" are often participating in the programmes in the hope of access to the financial services that they see being delivered by other NGOs. It is hard to escape the conclusion that "class struggle" is not 6the best way of empowering the poor, and that the poor themselves have found much more effective, non-confrontational ways of achieving the same ends.

Western feminist commentators have accused Microfinance programmes of making women even more vulnerable to gender-based conflict since they often pass on their loans to their husbands. This practice of giving loans to the husband to use is usually economically rational, but careful examination of the evidence suggests that it also typically strengthens the position of the woman in her family. Women attend the MFI's time-consuming meetings in order to conduct the family's banking, thus reinforcing and enhancing their traditional role of the family's budget manager and giving her additional status.

Attempts to examine whether Microfinance services improve the health and education indicators of participating families have been largely confined to reviewing family planning issues. What little evidence there is does indeed suggest that health indicators are improved, and certainly family planning acceptance rate in increased. However, the paucity of macro-analysis of impact on education precludes drawing conclusions about this important indicator of long-term development.

Given the positive impacts of Microfinance programmes, the relatively low cost at which they can be implemented and their ability to create permanent, sustainable institutions, it is little wonder that donor agencies are channelling increasing resources into them. But we should not lose sight of the fact that Microfinance is <u>not</u> *a "cure all" to solve all the problems of underdevelopment.*

INTRODUCTION

In the last five years, Microfinance, the provision of savings and credit services to the poor, has grown to become a much favoured intervention amongst international development agencies. There is scarcely a multi-lateral, bilateral or private development donor organisation not involved in the promotion (in one form or other) of a Microfinance programme. Perhaps it is time to examine why such a diverse set of agencies should be nailing their colours to a single mast.

The Many Flags Flying

The Consultative Group to Assist the Poorest is the multi- and bilateral donor co-ordination/policy development forum. Chaired by the World Bank, it comprises over 25 agencies including ADB, African Development Bank, AusAid, BADC, Caisse Francaise de Development, CIDA, DANIDA, DFID, EC, FINIDA, GTZ, IFAD, ILO, Inter-American Development Bank, JAICA, KfW, the Netherlands, NORAD, SDC, SIDA, UNCDF, UNCTAD, UNDP, USAID and the World Bank. Foundations and NGOs involved in Microfinance include Action Aid, Ford Foundation, NOVIB, Oxfam, Save the Children to name but a few of the thousands signed up on the Foundations and Practitioners' Councils of the MicroCredit Summit, and active in the funding and/or implementation of Microfinance programmes.

Rogaly (1996) noted the "hard selling of a new anti-poverty formula" by the "micro-finance evangelists". In the same year, Preparatory Committee Meetings for the "MicroCredit Summit" clearly showed the tensions between the RESULTS PR machine committed to publicising and promoting the "MicroCredit Revolution", and the angst-ridden practitioners so keen to discuss both its success and short-comings in order to learn how programmes might be further improved.

Many claims are made about the impact of Microfinance programmes, and an outside observer cannot but wonder at the range and diversity of the benefits claimed. Access to Microfinance is credited with reaching the poorest, increasing their income, galvanising them into collective action to resist oppression; with empowering repressed women so that they are enabled to take control of their lives, stimulating them to use modern contraceptive methods; with enabling families access to better health care, education and nutrition; and with providing a cost-effective, sustainable development model that it is applicable not just in developing countries but also among poorer communities in the developed world.

Other commentators are more sceptical, arguing that Microfinance programmes fail to reach the poorest, generally have a limited effected on income, address the symptom rather than the social cause of poverty, drive women into greater dependence on their husbands, and fail to provide the additional services desperately needed by the poor: health, education etc.. This school of thought believes that the "monotheistic MicroCredit formula ... promoted as a panacea" (Wood and Sharif, 1997) is not only inadequate to meet the needs of the poorest, but is also monopolising resources that could, and perhaps should be used for other more pressing or important interventions - health, education or "social mobilisation".

Clearly there is some dissonance here ... this chapter will try to examine the claims and counter-claims in the light of a practitioner's experience of Bangladesh, the cradle of MicroCredit (if not Microfinance), with passing reference to published research on programmes elsewhere across the globe. It is important to try to understand what Microfinance programmes can and cannot achieve, not least of all to optimise resource allocation and targeting.

The chapter has five main sections. The first examines whether we should be worried about "Increasing Income or Reducing Poverty?". It contains sub-sections on how and what we should measure ("How Do We Know, and Is Income What We Should Be Looking At Anyway?"); the importance of diversified sources of income ("Security in Diversity"); whether microenterprise development assistance or employment helps ("But What About Business Development Services and Employment?"); if minimalist Microfinance services have made a substantive difference ("So Has There Been Any Increase in Incomes With All This Minimalism?"); and finally, what about "Serving the "Poorest of the Poor"". The second section, "Community Organisation and Social Development" moves on to examine the contention of many development practitioners that Microfinance addresses the symptoms and not the causes of poverty. The third section, "Women's Empowerment and Gender Issues" looks at impact of Microfinance on these important aspects of development. The fourth section examines whether the presence of Microfinance services improve "Health and Education" indicators of participating families. The fifth section examines the current attraction that Microfinance has for donor agencies as a way of promoting "Cost-effective Development that Creates Sustainable Organisations".

MicroCredit v. Microfinance

Grameen Bank began lending operations in 1976, but has since then paid scant attention to savings (except as a source of capital and loan guarantee [Wright, Hossain and Rutherford, 1997]), an approach that has dominated thinking and practice throughout Bangladesh. The Grameen, credit-driven model is the inspiration for the "first wave" of MicroCredit programmes. The model is based on the premise that the poor need loans and that "credit is a human right".

The original slogan of MicroCredit Summit Campaign was "Working to ensure that 100 million of the world's poorest families, especially the women of those families, are receiving credit by the year 2005." This prompted many to suggest that it could be more simply re-stated as "Driving 100 million women into debt by 2005" ! A typically inelegant committee-compromise was reached and the slogan was amended to read: "Working to ensure that 100 million of the world's poorest families, especially the women of those families, are receiving credit for self-employment and other financial and business services by the year 2005."

Increasing numbers of practitioners (Robinson, 1994 and 1995; Otero and Rhyne (eds.),1994; Rutherford, 1995; and Wright, Hossain and Rutherford, 1997) are stressing the importance of offering a range of quality, flexible financial services in response to the wide variety of needs of the poor - this approach is known as Microfinance.

INCREASING INCOME OR REDUCING POVERTY?

How do We Know, and is Income what We should be Looking at Anyway ?

Rogaly notes that "Mansell-Carstens argues that direct investigation of impact is suspect, for several reasons:

- respondents may be interested in giving false information if the loans have been used for a purpose other than the stipulated one[i];

---

[i] A practice found by many practitioners and authors to be extremely common – see for example Helen Todd's discussion of this phenomenon amongst Grameen Bank borrowers where 94% did not use their loans for the purposes they had described on the loan application form (Todd, 1996).

- establishing a causal relationship to the actual loan in question involves knowledge of all the beneficiary's sources and uses of funds; and

- it is difficult to establish what could have happened if the loan had not been made (Mansell-Carstens, 1995)."

Kobb (1997) also examines the problems (practical and theoretical) arising from trying to measure impact through changes in income. He notes that incomes are heavily skewed - several high income earners distorted averages, that respondents are influenced by the way and by whom questions are asked ("Interviewees are likely to provide strategic rather than truthful answers."), and that disentangling project impact from "exogenous factors" is impossible. Kobb offers alternative measures - they revolve around PRA, case studies and qualitative techniques. "One advantage of this methodology is verifiable, observable indicators."

Despite these objections, the declared aim of Microfinance programmes generally includes a reference to "increasing the income of the target group" or some similar income-denominated objective. Implicit in this is that increased income results in a reduction in poverty. This assumption requires careful examination. On a simple, money-determined level, if increased income is simply spent in the cinema or at the tea-stall or on alcohol, there is no increase in wealth and no reduction in poverty. In addition, in the words of Sharif (1997), "Poverty, ... is not only about having inadequate income or income below the "poverty line", but is also about the inability to sustain a specified level of well-being".

A focus on "income poverty" is usually associated with seeing poverty-reduction as a process of moving households from a stable "below poverty line" situation to a stable "above poverty line" situation. This leads to strategies aimed at "raising persistently low incomes" (Dreze and Sen, 1989). In the context of financial services, these strategies, emphasise (often exclusively) the provision of credit for income-generation through self-employment. A broader, less linear, view of poverty sees income levels as fluctuating below and above the poverty line. Strategies to address poverty seen in this way seek to reduce dramatic decreases in income as a means for poverty alleviation and introduce a quite different way of viewing the role of financial services. "Protectional strategies ((Dreze and Sen, 1989) become significant: in terms of financial services this fosters a focus on voluntary savings mechanisms, emergency consumption loans and relatively low-risk income generation activities that are unlikely to create indebtedness" (Hulme and Mosley, 1997).

Here is a clear statement of the case for Microfinance programmes to provide a variety of financial services tailored to the specific needs of the clients (be they extreme, moderate or not-so-poor). The financial services should allow clients to manage their household income and expenditures more effectively. To do this, the financial services should provide options both to minimise "shocks" (arising from illness or death in the household, crop failure, theft of key assets, dramatic price fluctuations, the payment of dowry etc.), and to invest in income generation activities with risk levels appropriate to the household's basic needs security. In short they should offer a range of both savings and credit facilities.

Nonetheless implicit in this analysis is "The idea that poverty is multi-faceted has been widely accepted and, apart from material deprivation, it is not unusual to include health status, illiteracy, and several types of vulnerability, powerlessness and absence of choice. A fundamental ideational change associated with many of these restatements of poverty definition (e.g. CIDA, 1994) is the view that people's own perceptions are fundamental to identifying what poverty is" (Greeley, 1997). Once poverty is seen in these broader terms, questions as to the effectiveness of Microfinance in addressing this broader list of social issues become important. Some of these social issues will be addressed below in the sections entitled "Community Organisation and Social Development" and "Health and Education".

Security in Diversity

We should pay careful attention to Hulme and Mosley's (1997) conclusion that "A significant minority of investments fail (leading to decreases in income), while many investments that increase income soon reach a plateau (for example, operating a rickshaw, manually hulling rice, adopting HYVs and inputs on a small farm). For the latter, credit schemes give borrowers an important "one step up" in income, however, "survival skills" rarely provide the technological or entrepreneurial basis for poor borrowers to move on to the escalator of sustained growth of income."

Ironically, this commentary overlooks (or at best fails to highlight) two of the authors' own conclusions: firstly that the significant minority of investments that fail are closely associated with the poorest borrowers (see below) and secondly that the poor are generally seeking to <u>diversify</u> income sources - no single income source is expected to provide an "escalator of sustained growth of income". Todd's (1996) case studies provide interesting insights into how her "women at the centre" manage their diversified sources of income to maximise (first food and material, and then social) security for their families and themselves. For the poor it is "Less of a matter of achieving a low step on the escalator of growth than of continually inventing income strategies that ensure a modest economic lot" (Walton, 1985).

Contrary to the model implicit in traditional agricultural credit, households do not have one source of income or livelihood. Rather as Hulme and Mosley (1997) note, "depending on season, prices, health and other contingencies, they pursue a mix of activities that may include growing their own food, labouring for others, running small production or trading businesses, hunting and gathering, and accessing loans or subsidies

---

Kamala Rani's Diversified Portfolio

"Kamala Rani is an experienced borrower. She has been loans three times. The first loan was small (one thousand) and was invested in her husband's business who trades in bamboo (used as construction material). Bamboo product is also sold in his shop. Kamala provides labour input to make bamboo mats. When she obtained the second loan," (Tk. 2,000) " she invested it in bamboo product making. She makes large storage containers (used for storing crops) and other products and sells them from home, to both wholesalers and to village users. Next she borrowed another 4,000 taka, most of which she spent on buying a cow. She can repay her loan from the sale proceed of milk and profit from husband's business.

She still makes mats and other bamboo products. The mats are in greater demand after December. She therefore plans to sell at that time when the price per piece will be 20 taka. The current price is between 12-15 taka. She can utilize the price advantage because she has other sources of income to make payment of weekly instalments. Thus the choice of a diversified portfolio enables one to maximise the returns from investment" (*Rahman, 1996*).

(from the state, friends or NGOs). In terms of economic behaviour, they are closer to the manager of a complex portfolio than the manager of a single-product firm."

As Dawson (1997) notes in his review of the Sebstad and Chen (1996) and Hulme and Mosley (1996) studies, "In both of these overview studies, technical innovation among borrowers was found to be limited to a minority among those who had taken multiple loans. Much more commonly, loans were used either to increase the scale of existing activities or to diversify into related fields. Few cases of further specialisation and technological deepening were identified." Given MicroCredit institutions' careful targeting, quite why this should be either a surprise or a disappointment remains a mystery. The poor are too smart and too risk-averse to put "all their eggs in one basket" and invest exclusively and heavily in one enterprise. They are managing their portfolio of income generation activities and looking to minimise risk, so that if activity or "enterprise" fails, it only has a limited, manageable impact on total household income.

This is amplified by Hulme and Mosley's (1996) exhaustive study of 13 Microfinance institutions (including Grameen Bank, BRAC, TRDEP, BancoSol, BRI, BKK, K-REP and SANASA) which concluded that "There is clear evidence that the impact of a loan on a borrower's income is related to the level of income ... This finding should not be unexpected given that those with higher incomes have a greater range of investment opportunities, more information about market conditions and can take more risk than the poorest households without threatening their minimum needs for survival."

Todd (1996) provides a grass-roots view of this when she notes "19 out of the 27 households which have risen out of the poverty group (70%) are

---

Spreading The Risks

" ... women rarely use all their loans for one activity - even if they husk four *maunds* of paddy between one *haat* and another, the capital they need to roll over comes to less than 1,000 Taka. They spread the risks between activities which generate cash for repayment and longer-term assets. In the first loan cycles these are small assets: poultry, ducks, perhaps a calf or goats to fatten" *(Todd, 1996)*.

partnerships or are run by a dominant woman. One would expect a relationship between economic contribution of active female loanees and the success of their households. Two or three incomes are better than the one traditionally earned by the male household head. Several incomes make a family less vulnerable to disaster in any one line of business."

"It is the income from land cultivation which has pushed most of the successful GB families out of the poverty group. Land is also strongly invested with other emotions. It means food security; "eating our paddy." It is the asset which confers the most status within the village, and turns the husband from a labourer at the mercy of the landlord, into an independent farmer. It is the crucial nature of land and the critical function of the woman's capital in getting access to it that I think underlies the very strong position that two-thirds of our sample have been able to attain with their families" (Todd, 1996). This "income from land cultivation" it should be noted, is largely income from decreasing the rental costs of using land. Grameen (and other Microfinance organisations') members use their loans to lease land in preference to share-cropping - the savings on rental costs increase the net income substantially.

It is for this reason that "frontier" Microfinance programmes do not seek to put restrictions on the use of the loans they issue: the poor will generally put credit (and all elements of financial services) to the most rational (and usually economically sound) use available. And they usually have a better understanding of the issues and socio-economic circumstances facing them than the staff of the Microfinance institution providing the financial services.

But what about Business Development Services and Employment ?

BRAC believes that "The greatest potential of micro credit to improve the lives of the poor on a sustainable basis has been offset by a lack of concomitant promotion of technology. Much of such credit has been used for traditional activities, and not enough has been done to include technology along with it" (Chowdhury and Alam, 1997). BRAC has tried to address this issue by providing training to its Village Organisations and attempting to create backward and forward linkages for most of the technology-based activities, which now comprise 30% of its portfolio.

But as we have seen in the previous section, the specialisation necessary to develop a larger-scale microenterprise is not necessarily what the poor are looking for. However, profitable such a mono-focused microenterprise may be this year, its very nature increases the owner's exposure to risk in the years to come. Furthermore, from a development programmer's perspective, it is difficult to escape the conclusion that technology-based approaches are relatively expensive.

Dawson (1997); Gibson (1997) and other proponents of the "Business Development Services" school would argue that their primary goal is to create sustainable microenterprises and thus employment, and that such services can be offered on a reasonably cost-effective basis. But Harper (1997) is forced to conclude, "it is still difficult to find examples of business development services where the benefits exceed the costs". Wood (1997) in his "Breaking Out of the Ghetto: Employment Generation and Credit for the Poor" asserts that many of the poor are not natural entrepreneurs, and would like to be employed in preference to self-exploitative self-employment generating marginal returns. This is indeed true, if the employment is what Bangladeshis would call "chakri" - respectable, regular and reasonably paid (ideally in a Government office). But these formal sector opportunities are few and far between.   Most informal sector employment opportunities are insecure, irregular and verging on exploitative at best. In the words of Yunus (1989), "Unless designed properly, wage employment may mean being condemned to a life in squalid city slums or working for two meals a day for one's life. Wage employment is not a happy road to the reduction of poverty. Removal or reduction of poverty must be a continuous process of creation of assets, so that the asset-base of poor person becomes stronger at each economic cycle, enabling him or her to earn more and more." This perception is shared by many of the rural poor, Rahman (1996) citing (Hirashima and Muqtada, 1986) notes that "In the rural areas among female workers in particular and among all workers in general, self-employment is considered to be more prestigious compared to wage employment".

Yunus and many Microfinance proponents would assert that providing financial services to the poor gives them the tools to better shape their own socio-economic destiny. In the words of Bornstein (1997), "Above all, a staff member had to know when to keep silent. Grameen's collateral was largely based on its borrowers' sense of personal accountability, so it was essential that villagers come up with their own business ideas. If an idea came from their bank worker, a borrower would not enjoy the same sense of accomplishment; and if the business failed, the villager would blame the staff member who advised her. ... When villagers requested investment advice, Yunus told his staff to reply, "The Grameen Bank has lots of money, but it has no ideas"".

So has there been Any Increase in Incomes and Wealth with All This Minimalism ?

The first detailed research into the economic impact of a MicroCredit programme was Mahabub Hossain's work on Grameen Bank in 1983/4. Hossain (1988) noted, "The most direct effect of the Grameen Bank has been on the accumulation of capital by the poor. The amount of working capital employed by members' enterprises increased by an average of three times within a period of 27 months. The investment in fixed assets is about 2.5 times higher for borrowers with more than three years' membership than for those who joined during the year of the survey." He also noted in the same study that "About a third of the members reported that they were unemployed before joining the bank - almost 7 percent of the men and 50 percent of the women. With these loans, these members generated self-employment in activities of their choice." The resulting effects on income were also impressive, "... Grameen Bank members had incomes about 43 percent higher than the target group in the control villages, and about 28 percent higher than the target group non-participants in the project villages." And Hossain's analysis indicated that " ... the positive income effect has been highest for the absolutely landless, followed by the marginal landowners ..." A more recent study, conducted by the World Bank in collaboration with the Bangladesh Institute of Development Studies, and cited by Hashemi and Morshed (1997), showed that the Grameen Bank not only "reduced poverty and improved welfare of participating households, but also enhanced the household's capacity to sustain their gains over time."

Kamal (1996) noted higher rates of per capita income among MicroCredit programme borrowers compared to those who did not borrow. In 1991 Chowdhury et al. asserted that women (and men) participating in BRAC sponsored activities have more income (both in terms of amount and source), own more assets and are more often gainfully-employed than non-participants. A more recent detailed study by Mustafa (1996) confirmed this and noted that the BRAC members have better coping capacities in lean seasons and that these increased with length of membership and amount of credit received from BRAC. The same study reports growth in household assets from an average of Tk. 10,959 (for members who had been members for 1-11 months) to Tk. 23,230 (for members who had been members for 48 or more months), and increase of 112%. Similarly, household expenditure increased from an average of Tk. 419 per week (for members who had been members for 1-11 months) to Tk. 528 (for members who had been members for 48 or more months), an increase of 28%.

In their study of the impact of the Grameen Bank, Khandker and Chowdhury (1995) noted that the increase in self-employment among the poor with access to credit has resulted in an increase in rural wages, a finding confirmed by Todd's work in Tangail (Todd, 1996). This effect on local wage rates is disputed by Hulme and Mosley (1996), but Todd's conclusions may reflect the longer term impact of lending (Grameen has been operating in Tangail for more than a decade) or the widespread access of the poor to credit in Tangail where not only Grameen but also BRAC, ASA, Proshika, SSS and BURO, Tangail are all competing for clients.

Tangail is in many ways saturated with NGOs and MicroCredit/ Microfinance programmes. This is because of its proximity to Dhaka: which both makes it a pleasant day trip for donor representatives (and thus a favoured site for demonstration projects or groups), and gives farmers and producers relatively easy access to the major market in Bangladesh. As Greeley (1997) points out, we should not forget that "There is strong evidence that robust non-agricultural rural growth is closely linked to local agricultural growth, principally through consumption linkages but also through backward and forward linkages in production. Many of the activities that micro credit programmes support are dependent on this rural purchasing power, from farmers especially. If this purchasing power becomes more concentrated then there will be marked regional differences in the effectiveness of micro credit services for poverty reduction." As Grameen Bank and others have found out in remote areas like Rangpur and Pathuakali, MicroCredit is more difficult to recover when the local economy offers few income generation opportunities.

As Hulme and Mosley (1997) point out, "there is no evidence that structurally based constraints on demand for the products and services of the poor are likely to be removed by credit-induced activity: rather, they are dependent on changes in the wider economy." However, this overlooks the "Multiplier Effect" (however slight and slow), and the simple fact that it is the access to financial services that helps the poor to manage their way through "shocks" and crises so that they are ready and able (with loans if necessary) to take advantage of whatever opportunities arise. In Stuart Rutherford's terms "Rural financial services for the poor thus act as *platforms* rather than *sky-hooks*. Access to financial services enables poor rural households to secure and improve their existing situation (their current set of income sources and their capacity to exploit them), giving them a foundation on which to build. Financial services do not 'reach down' with packages of pre-digested assistance that somehow grab poor households and 'lift' them out of poverty" (Rutherford, 1997).

In his address to the concluding session of the "Poverty and Credit Workshop", Dhaka, August, 1996 Professor Rehman Sobhan expressed scepticism as to whether all the micro-level impact had had any macro-level impact on the village, union or thana level economy. This concern is in part at least answered by Bornstein's (1997) observation that: "Aleya (rich), who fits near the top of the poorest third of the population, and Aleyta (poor) who belongs, perhaps to the bottom eighth, are, to the high flyers, indistinguishable. To policy makers, they are interchangeable. On the ground, however, the differences in their daily experiences are enormous. Which is why the most vital work of Grameen Bank - which has helped millions of villagers to move from one level of poverty to a less oppressive level - is invisible at the national level." More recent work by Alamghir (1999) suggests that Grameen Bank operations have contributed between 1.1 and 1.5% of GDP. By way of comparison, the small scale industries sector contributes less than 4% and agriculture and fisheries around 3% of GDP, suggesting that Grameen's contribution is more substantial than conventional wisdom assumes.

Serving the "Poorest of the Poor"

Several authors, including Hulme and Mosley (1997) have noted that "Worryingly, both BRAC-RDP and Grameen Bank recently appear to be moving away from working with significant proportions of the hard core poor and focusing their activities on the middle income and upper poor, rather than the most desperate." This is generally attributed to the increasing emphasis on institutional sustainability which Hulme and Mosley (1996, 1997) and Rogaly (1996) see as incompatible with reaching the poorer of the poor.

But the exclusion of the poorest is recognised by both Grameen Bank and BRAC. "It seems that Grameen Bank and similar credit programs have failed to target this group [the hard core poor] effectively, resulting in most of them remaining outside the micro-credit net" (Hashemi, 1997a). "In spite of all good intentions and efforts, BRAC's success in reaching the poorest ten to fifteen percent of the rural population has been modest" (Chowdhury and Alam, 1997). And both BRAC and Grameen Bank are experimenting with other strategies to reach the poorest. In Rangpur, Grameen is experimenting with goat loans, and in what is generally viewed as the most successful approach, BRAC runs the Income Generation for the Vulnerable Group Development (IGVGD) programme explicitly to bring the poorer households into its Rural Development Programme. By 1995, IGVGD was already operating in 74 Thanas and had reached 166,918 of the poorest (Chowdhury and Alam, 1997).

As Rutherford (1995) and Wright et al (1997) would argue, the exclusion of the poorest is also driven by the emphasis on credit delivery by many organisations. For the poorest households the opportunities for productive use of loans are limited, and the risk of taking loans that are repayable on a weekly basis are unacceptably high. Furthermore, as donors and practitioners place increasing emphasis on Microfinance as opposed to MicroCredit, the poor are likely to join the Microfinance programmes in order to save. Over time the poor may also enjoy the benefits of scale that Microfinance Institutions' more affluent clients allow - in terms of interest on savings, a broader range of financial services and possibly even lower cost loans. For further discussion of this important issue, see the chapter "Optimising Systems for Clients and the Institution".

COMMUNITY ORGANISATION AND SOCIAL DEVELOPMENT

The "conscientising" community organisation and social development school used to be well represented in Bangladesh, although many (most notably ASA) have now given up the rhetoric. In the words of Rahman (1997), " ... during the initial phase the following programmes for poor households were taken up by ASA: conscientisation for social action, legal aid and awareness building program, training program to develop human potentials and occupational skills etc. During the foundation phase 50,000 members were organized into 4,000 groups and a series of social actions against oppression and violation of human rights were conducted. ...

success in this phase had been limited ... the most important reason behind the unsustainability of the phase has been operating from demand side, the acceptability of the program by the poor clients themselves. Most of these programmes did not have an immediate impact on their income and therefore did not prove to be attractive. Specifically, the other NGOs which distributed credit had an important demonstration effect on the members of ASA. They started to aspire to receive loans from ASA for investment in economic activities." (Man, or indeed woman, cannot live by words alone.)

The most prominent of the large NGOs promoting a more broad social development agenda is Proshika. "Proshika's development philosophy can be summed up as "development through the *empowerment* of the poor". In concrete terms, empowerment is achieved through raising the consciousness of the poor equipping them with organisational and practical skills, supporting them with needed resources, infusing them with the confidence and the determination necessary for taking actions to improve both their social and economic lives" (Hedrick-Wong and Kramsjo, 1997).

However, an increasing number of commentators are questioning the "conscientisation process" proposed by Freire in the 1970 classic "The Pedagogy of the Oppressed" as an approach to dealing with development issues. Too often the "conscientisation process" has resulted in a well intentioned educated elite of "community development workers" taking hours of villagers' precious time attempting to "raise the consciousness of the poor" (with the implication that somehow the poor do not fully understand the situation in which they live day to day). The implicit arrogance of this is amplified by the Hedrick-Wong's (1997) assertion that, "Gradually, the outlook and attitude of the poor are expected to change from hopelessness and helplessness to self-confidence and self-reliance." The detailed village-based socio-anthropological work of both Sarah White (1992) and Helen Todd (1996) clearly refutes this patronising idea that the poor are somehow hopeless and helpless until some beneficent NGO worker comes along.

Careful examination of the motivation of the poor lead many practitioners and commentators to conclude that "the poor" put up with the endless "dialectics" in the hope that they might eventually get access to something useful ... like access to credit. As Razia Ahmad noted back in 1983 "... we must not overlook the special conditions under which then poor are "motivated" to form groups. These people, who are on the brink of survival and in chronic capital shortage, will logically be induced to accept conditions which are even alien to them in order to obtain cash. So it may not be the "group idea" which actually attracts the rural poor, but the possibility or hopes of getting some quick cash." Therefore, "group action tends to be limited to obtaining and repaying loans" - a view confirmed by Todd's (1996) work with experienced Grameen Bank borrowers. Rutherford (1996) also noted this problem among the most committed of "social mobilization" NGOs, Proshika. "Members expect Proshika to provide loans for them. This is clear from what members told us, and from finding that *samities* whose demand for a loan is frustrated are liable to break up and to join other loan-giving NGOs." Perhaps it is in recognition of this that Proshika now operates a Revolving Loan Fund of $ 34.5 million, and projects loan disbursements of $ 89.4 million in the year to June 1999.

Rutherford's view is shared even by many of the most dedicated "conscientisers" of the 1970s, for example Shafique Chowdhury Executive Director of ASA, which has now almost completely renounced social development and turned itself into a MicroCredit organisation (see Rutherford 1995a for a fascinating description of this metamorphosis). Similarly, S.A. Khan, a Maoist of conviction who spent years organising landless associations in Comilla notes, "Given that all the landless groups thus organised (36 groups of about 400 individuals) collapsed as soon as the project ended, it would appear that the provision of credit was the main attraction. In order to gain credit, they were willing to undergo superficial "class" indoctrination. They soon realised that the more revolutionary they were in rhetoric, the greater were their chances of receive credit" S.A. Khan (1989).

In 1992 Wood decried poverty alleviation through credit, characterising it as "pernicious, even when it includes participatory rhetoric, because it suggests solutions independent of the structures which produced the problems." By 1997 he had better recognised the value of MicroCredit, but with Sharif continued to deplore "the emerging conventional wisdom that the Grameen Bank had proved the positive impact of credit upon the poor without the costly accompaniment of wider social mobilisation around common property access, wages and rent struggles, and so on." They went on to note that this has "... profound implications. It offers an alibi for donors as well as nervous host governments to withdraw from a broader analysis of poverty into a narrower, neo-liberal, conception based on people's financial liquidity. ... Clearly Proshika in Bangladesh felt especially vulnerable to this analysis. It had a large RLF" (Revolving Loan Fund) "alongside a continuing commitment to its original mission of conscientisation and mobilisation among groups of the poor in order that they can struggle more successfully for rights and entitlements in the political economy, and enter the commodity and labour markets on more even terms with other classes of social actor" (Wood and Sharif, 1997).

In the words of Hedrick-Wong and Kramsjo (1997), Proshika and the social development advocates continue to believe that, "Credit cannot challenge some of the basic and structural reasons behind poverty." They advocate "social mobilisation", "class-struggle" and "conflict" or "collective action for social justice among the rural poor" to "break the chains". There is little discussion as to whether a "quiet revolution" might achieve similar ends as effectively without the confrontation, aggravated social (not solely class) divisions and violence.

For as Todd (1996) notes, " ... these conflicts and their development and resolution over the years - with the GB members strengthened by more income, more assets, more self-confidence and the potential backing of the center - are part of a gradual and subtle process. ... Overt confrontation is too risky for the women involved. ... they work more like termites than through the tidal wave of collective action. They are adept at using traditional levers to legitimise these non-traditional actions." The recent PromPT study (1996) using PRA techniques to examine "users' perspectives" among members of Grameen, BRAC, ASA, Proshika and other credit providers noted that borrowers wanted training, but that "the biggest complaint was with what was perceived as the political motives behind Proshika's training programme. Many women and their husbands expressed objection to this and also to the expectation that the group members would join political rallies for Proshika."

Listing the "positive impacts of social mobilisation", Hedrick-Wong and Kramsjo (1997) note four main ones:

1. It raises (day labour) wages and maintains the increase achieved. But as Khandker, Khalily and Khan (1995), Khandker and Chowdhury (1995), and Todd (1996) point out, this is happening already, and besides, Todd adds, members would rather have their own enterprises or to be able to eat rice from their own fields.

2. It gives the poor access to local or *khas* resources. Some specific case studies are regularly offered by Proshika to give evidence of its success in these efforts.

3. It stimulates pro-poor legislation and/or government decisions through a popular movement at the local level. Whether much legislation or many such decisions have been "stimulated" is open to debate. With the possible exception of pre-election waivers of Government loans (which are largely captured by the richer village members), there is little doubt that what legislation has been passed and decisions taken have had very limited impact on the poor.

4. It promotes "a high level of social consciousness" necessary to challenge "vital social issues ... for example gender ones". As we shall see below, under the discussion of gender issues, increasing the access to money seems to have achieved the desired effect. In the intervening period let us turn to another "social issue" targeted by Proshika (and indeed all the MicroCredit NGOs in Bangladesh) - that of dowry.

Even for the NGOs following a more credit-based community organisation model, the challenge of creating sustainable institutions to "voice the needs of the poor ... and cater to the needs of its membership" is proving a difficult, time-consuming and therefore costly one. "Evidence, however, suggests that the VOs [Village Organisations] have yet to attain any kind of autonomy through which they will be able to move forward on their own (Mustafa et al. 1996). The challenge for BRAC and other agencies is to devise a strategy through which this can be attained" (Chowdhury and Alam, 1997). Nonetheless, through its Rural Credit Programme (RCP), and the aborted attempt to create the BRAC Bank, BRAC has recognised that its members will always need continuous and permanent access to savings and credit services. BRAC has thus jettisoned the old community organisation model of free-standing village organisations managing their own financial (and other) affairs.

Todd's work with women who had been borrowing from Grameen Bank for a decade prompted her to conclude: "What we found in these two villages are two groups of women, the majority of whom are empowered as individuals principally because of their economic contribution to their families, and to a lesser extent through their greater freedom of movement

Lifting the Curse of Dowry

Proshika rightly sees the practice of dowry as a profound and debilitating drain on the resources of the poor. For those with many daughters, it is one of the strongest life-cycle downward mobility pressures. As part of its social development programme, Proshika "conscientises" its members to resist the giving and receiving of dowry.

Todd notes that on dowry "There was universal agreement amongst the women in our two villages that dowry was an evil. There was also almost universal payment of it. ... the growing prosperity of Grameen families means they are able to pay more to get better husbands for their daughters. They certainly receive more for their sons" (Todd, 1996). But despite years of intense effort Proshika has fared little better, "Dowry and action/mobilization against dowry have been on the agenda for a long time. While Proshika members have a lower incidence of giving dowry in comparison with non-Proshika members, it has, however, increased marginally over the past few years" (*Hedrick-Wong* and *Kramsjo*, 1997).

One is tempted to suggest that a well designed savings product (say a contractual savings agreement) might allow the poor to slowly build up the funds necessary to marry off their daughters without facing the sudden (often debt-inducing) shock of having to find a large lump sum at short notice.

and interaction with other women at the center. We did not find that they were empowered through collective action. ... Of the two approaches ... the minimalist credit approach of Grameen Bank and the more integrated, consciousness-raising approach of most other NGOs, it seems that credit alone is more effective in empowering women within their families. Outside of the family, neither GB nor BRAC, according to the Schuler and Hashemi (1994) study, has succeeded in mobilising solidarity groups into collective action, against either the class enemy - the rural elite, or the gender enemy - the patriarchy" (Todd, 1996).

Whether Grameen or BRAC had ever seriously tried to "mobilise solidarity groups into collective action" is a matter that many of the "consciousness-raising/social development" school would dispute. But Todd's conclusion takes us to another key area of dispute, the effect of Microfinance programmes on women's empowerment and gender issues.

WOMEN'S EMPOWERMENT AND GENDER ISSUES

"Before, husbands used to earn and that was how wives ate. But now he gives value; I have bought a loan. I am labouring equally with him, that is why he values me more ..." (Kabeer, 1998)

Traditionally, MicroCredit and Microfinance programmes have targeted women. In most societies, women manage the day-to-day household budget, and are more likely to save regularly investing the benefits from any increases in income into the welfare of their family. Besides, they have proved themselves to be much better credit risks than their male counterparts. Hulme and Mosley (1997) noted that "81 per cent of female borrowers had no overdue repayment instalments as against 74 per cent for men (Hossain 1988). For the Malawi Mudzi Fund in late 1990, the on-time repayment for women was 92 per cent as against 83 per cent for men (Hulme 1991). In Malaysia, Projek Ikhtiar reported 95 per cent repayment rates for women as against 72 per cent for men (Gibbons and Kasim 1991)". Recently, however, concerns have been raised about the gender implications of these strategies.

A particularly useful framework within which to examine these issues in the widest possible sense was proposed by Susan Johnson (1997) in her "Gender Analysis Matrix for Microfinance", which analyses the gender implications of savings and credit programmes for the individual, the household and the wider community/national context, with regard to four key aspects: financial, economic, social/cultural and political/legal. This chapter will only consider the individual and the household, with particular emphasis on the financial, economic and social/cultural aspects.

Almost irrespective of society or culture, the status of women in households has long since been tied to their earning potential or capabilities. Dixon (1980) argued that "a woman earning half of the household income will likely have more bargaining power than the woman who earns none, even when total household incomes are the same." Mizan (1994) also asserts that "In developing countries survival of low income families may compel all members to engage in productive activities. In spite of little improvement in total household earnings a woman's status is likely to be affected by the increase in bargaining power as a result of her crucial contributions to family subsistence." She went on to explore the hypothesis of Blood and Wolfe (1960), and many other family sociologists of the 1960s, that "the power balance within marriage is determined by comparative valued resources of spouses" (Mizan, 1994).

Mizan (1994) found that "On average, women contribute 38 percent to the total household income ..." and concluded that "Grameen Bank participation has a positive and significant effect on women's decision-making both in bivariate and multivariate context. This finding indicates significant success of Grameen Bank programs in affecting women's status relative to men in Bangladesh. ... Bank participation benefits women by providing them with important monetary resources as well as non-monetary. For example, more years of participation enable women to acquire resources, including income, negotiating skills, social network affiliations, and knowledge, helping them to gain more decision-making power. ... In Bangladesh, where structural and cultural factors have hindered women from realizing their earning and household decision-making potential, Grameen Bank's contributions may be regarded as revolutionary." In the words of Todd (1996), "What gave the Grameen women more say was, according to them, the capital they bought into the household and the results of that capital in terms of increased income ... Clearly, Taka talks."

> *Did he love me before ? Well, the difference between then and now is like day and night. I did business before, but it was small business, [Tk.] 200-300, is that proper business ? Now I work hard, I earn well, I do proper business, it is worth [Tk.] 3,000-4,000; won't he love me more ?" (Kabeer, 1998)*

These conclusions re-emphasised Rahman's ground-breaking study on the gender impact on Grameen members, which concluded that even those women who let their husbands manage their loans "are in a better situation than housewives in the male loanee group though they are less important than the active loanee women" (Rahman, 1986).

"Shakeeb explains "There were so many things that I could do, but I had no Taka. Then Begum could take these loans. Each time we decided how we should use the loan and slowly our confidence grew; and our love ! I depended on Begum and together we have made progress" (Todd, 1996).

Goetz and Sen Gupta (1994) on the other hand were concerned to assess "the degree to which women actually control loans once they gain access to credit institutions". They found that "a significant proportion of women's loans are directly invested by their male relatives, with women borrowers bearing the liability for repayment, though not necessarily directly benefiting from loan use. In these cases, gender relations and the household are in effect absorbing the high enforcement costs of lending to men in Bangladesh's rural credit system because women have taken over the task of securing loan repayments from their male relatives."

63% of women had no, very limited or only partial control over the loans they received "indicating a fairly significant pattern of loss of direct control over credit. Of course, given the Bangladeshi context in which women's rights of control over productive resources are so constrained, the significance of these findings might perhaps more correctly lie in the 37% of cases in which women succeeded in retaining control over their loans" (Goetz and Sen Gupta, 1994). Many would not be surprised with the handing of loans to men for investment: it represents the decision of "economically rational woman" - a recent RD-12 study shows that the rates of return for women's income generating activities average 145%, while rates for men average 211% (Matienzo, 1993). In addition, Goetz and Sen Gupta (1994) noted the relatively high level (55%) of widowed, separated and divorced women that fully control their loans (compared to 18% in general). This prompted Hulme and Mosley (1997) to note that, "Given that such women are usually regarded as the most vulnerable in the Bangladeshi society this suggests significant advancement in their capacity to engage in economic activity."

Goetz and Sen Gupta (1994) argue that "the consequences of high degrees of male appropriation of loans can postpone the appearance of the positive social externalities expected from increasing women's control over household income. Worse, it can undermine household survival strategies where men invest loans badly, forcing women to mobilise repayment funds from resources which would otherwise be used for consumption or savings purposes. It can also exacerbate gender-related tensions within the rural household. The implications for longer-term changes in women's role in household decision-making and in gender relations may also be negative."

Todd (1996) rightly notes that, "This strand of feminist scholarship asks important questions - who uses the loans and who gets the benefit. But their stress on the negative and their ability to find it, for instance, by conflating loan use and control so that loans used for rickshaws and land cultivation are automatically classified as appropriated by males, distorts what actually happens within families". There is a perception among many commentators who have spent a long time in Bangladesh that the implicit assertion that "women giving their loans to their husbands to use in (more) productive activities is intrinsically dangerous and likely to lead to gender-related tensions" is a Western-feminist interpretation of the situation ... and a long way from the truth. This is not to dispute that in a few isolated cases, the practice does lead to some extremely difficult and profoundly undesirable situations where the woman is left trying to repay a loan squandered by her husband or son, (or possibly even mother-in-law).

Todd (1996) goes on to say, "The first thing I discovered when I raised this issue with the women in Ratnogram and Bonopur was that it was, to them, a very odd and irrelevant question. First of all, the typical village husband returned from a day's trading would give *all* his cash to his wife - not because it was regarded as hers, but because, as the one who stayed at home, it was her customary duty to safeguard the money. More fundamentally, neither husband nor wife thought in such individualistic terms. ... What is more useful is the concept of the "centrality" of the woman in the management and decision making of the family. ... Sarah White (1992) comments that this notion of centrality "focuses analysis on relationships, rather than assuming an essential individualism, [and] seems a more appropriate term than autonomy as a way of conceiving interpersonal power in the Bangladesh context"."

Kabeer (1998) also critiques the Goetz and Sen Gupta paper, noting that, "Their index of "managerial control" confuses two quite distinct aspects of decision-making related to household resource allocation which Pahl (1989) terms "control" and "management", where "control" has to do with the policy-making function (i.e. deciding how resources are to be utilised), while "management" has to do with the implementation function, putting into operation the policy decided upon." Kabir goes on to note that there are clear and varied rationales for women to transfer loans to men including attempts to diversify household income sources and hence reduce risk, to benefit from the greater range and profitability of male enterprises and as a reflection of their awareness of their reliance on men for various forms of assistance in their own enterprises and hence the need to ensure that men benefitted as well from their access to loans.

In order to describe the influence of women over the household decision making process, Todd (1996) proposes a continuum of "None, Cashbox, Cashbox plus, Partner, Banker, Managing Director." She notes, "Fully 68% (27 women) of the GB sample can be described as central to their households; they are either Partners, Bankers or Managing Directors. ...The control group by contrast are quite marginal in the decision-making process. The largest group - eight women or 36% - are Cashboxes. ... The power that GB women have in their households is closely related to their economic contribution."

Wright and Ahmed (1992) studied savings and credit programmes in the urban setting where there are relatively few opportunities for women to use loans in enterprises, and almost all the credit is passed on to their husbands. They found that in almost all cases, the women were adamant that their relationship with their husbands had improved as a result of their involvement with the savings and credit organisation. The women's job was to sit in the (time-consuming) weekly meetings and access the financial services offered there. They were the family's bankers, and this was an

> *"Lokkhi refers to the wife who is both thrifty and hard working, whose management of the household is so competent that it is never in want. Lucky is the man whose wife in lokkhi... The successful negotiations are done quietly and are harder to describe except by their results. And this is the usefulness of the concept of lokkhi. Women seeking more control did not have to be seen as breaking tradition or as challenging the authority of their husbands. If they wrapped their power up in the proper forms, they could be sanctified by custom. Lokkhi legitimised them" (Todd, 1996).*

important and appreciated role that substantially improved their status. The 1996 PromPT studies of users' perspectives also found that "women felt it was right that their husbands should use the loans" and "that their status in the family had been raised because they were key to accessing the loan".

Nor is this unique to Bangladesh, or indeed South Asia. In the MicroCredit Summit Newsletter (Vol. 1, Issue 2), Oumou Sidebe Van Hoorebeke describing the Nyesgiso programme in Mali notes, "When I go to the first village we worked with, I can see a woman whose first loan was US$ 3. Now she has borrowed US$20. When I saw that woman the first time, she was looking at us as if we were gods and had all the power. She didn't say anything ... Now, to see that woman who has grown and who has more self-confidence and who is now looking at us as a *partner* ... It's the same when she looks at her husband. At first it was her husband that had all the financial power in the household. Now she can contribute and she knows that she is useful and can do something by herself ... She now knows, "I am useful. I have money. Even without my husband I could afford my needs and the needs of my child"." In Uganda women interviewed felt that their status had been significantly improved by their involvement with an MFI. In the words of one, "Now we have learnt that a woman has a right to make some decisions in the household, and that she can make some financial contributions and take some responsibility" (Wright et al., 1999)

Nonetheless, the dynamics of gender-relationships, particularly when mitigated by catalytic cash, are extremely complex. Throughout Bangladesh there is a transformation of gender roles underway: particularly through the rapid growth of the garments industry in the cities and as a result of government and NGO credit programmes that target women in preference to men in the rural villages. In the words of Schuler et al. (1998) "Credit programmes may reduce domestic violence by channelling resources to families through women, and by organizing women into solidarity groups that meet regularly and make their lives more visible ... In some cases, however, providing resources to women and encouraging them to maintain control over these resources may provoke violent behaviour in men, because they see their authority over their wives being undermined."

Another common concern of many commentators is that so many development programmes target women that they become overloaded and responsible for everything ...from child care to contraception, from cleaning to cooking, from fetching water to feeding family and livestock, from generating to saving income and all between. It is therefore reasonable and important to ask whether Microfinance programmes targeting females are overburdening already over-worked women by asking them to use loans. However, once again we must not loose sight of the woman's reality and impose a Western world view on the Bangladeshi situation. Todd's work addressed this issue too, and she concluded, "Since this increased workload is associated with a new prosperity and particularly with a supply of food piling up in the store, it is not surprising that it is a source of pride rather than resentment amongst the GB women" (Todd, 1996).

> *"Sister, listen. It is a pleasure to do this income work. It is because of this that Taka is coming in, and since it is mostly our Taka, we become the matbar (leader). Before, after I finished the housework I used to just sit around. Now I get Taka from Grameen Bank and I use it to make more Taka. I tell you it is a joy to work hard when you are making progress" (Todd, 1996).*

Kabeer (1998) also found that, "it becomes very clear that for many women, the status of being a supplicant in relation to men is galling and humiliating … It helps us to appreciate the importance women attached to their new identities as bearers of valued economic resources and their consequent enhanced sense of self-worth. This was particularly evident in the transformation of the meaning and experience of work that many loanees reported, even where it entailed, as it often did, an increase in their workloads."

> *"Ideas of the mind are everything. If you have money in your hand, you feel joy. If you have no money, you feel pain. My labour has increased, but I don't feel it because the money is also coming in. It doesn't feel like hard work" (Kabeer 1998).*

This improvement in the socio-economic position of women is then reflected in the behaviour of the women involved in Microfinance programmes. "When you see women who have just joined the bank, they go around the outskirts and avoid people," explained Maheen Sultan, formerly one of the bank's top women field managers. "But once they've been borrowing money for a long time and they're sure of themselves, they walk through the center of the village greeting people. Before they were apologizing for being there, later they belonged. It's their, village, it's their territory" (Bornstein, 1997). Wright and Ahmed (1992) noted the same development among the members of the Concern and Action Aid savings and credit schemes they studied. "Concern Mirpur members report improved social status as a result of participation in the programme. Husbands and other relatives are described as showing more respect, members are more confident in their dealings with the outside world and are showing greater awareness of their rights. Many are learning to read and write, and there is a real sense of determination among group members to "stand on their own feet"".

Schuler and Hashemi (1994:71-73) suggest why this might be: "... credit programs affect women's levels of empowerment by strengthening their economic roles, and in other ways as well. ... Grameen Bank's weekly meetings, the chanting, saluting and other rituals are important in creating an identity for women outside their families .... The program gives women socially legitimate reasons to move about and to associate with one another in public spheres .... Ironically, Grameen Bank's more regimented approach appears to be more effective than BRAC's in strengthening women's autonomy."

Todd concludes the relevant section of her exhaustive book with a neat summary: "These then were some of the levers that women could manipulate to gain more influence and control over the lives of their families. They were the cashboxes - they keep money safe. They operated within a network of contacts which provided them with both information and economic opportunities which offset the constraints of *purdah*. Although a largely female network it was fairly porous to male kin and fictive uncles and brothers. Women could control the income of unmarried sons. Their right to separate ownership of certain assets was widely acknowledged and could be extended to major assets. Their entitlement to land leased with their loans was asserted and acknowledged" (Todd, 1996).

HEALTH AND EDUCATION

Perhaps the most common reasons cited for not living by Microfinance programmes alone is that they do not address the social welfare issues of health and education (Rogaly 1996; Wood and Sharif 1997; ADB 1997, to name but a few). Purist Microfinance advocates, Rogaly's "Evangelists", would argue that the poor's primary obstacle to accessing good health and education is money, and that if the poor have the cash, they can and would buy the services. They would argue that good nutrition is about having the money to buy adequate food, that reducing diarrhoeal disease is about having the money to install tubewells and latrines, that increasing family planning is dependent on having the money not to have to depend on many children as a "pension plan" to look after their elderly parents and so on. These arguments are attractive and not without some substance.

Nonetheless, this position, of course, overstates the issue. Many health-related problems arise from, or are aggravated by, inadequate knowledge of (say) how diseases are transmitted, or the nutritional needs of children and which foods are appropriate. Similarly, it may well be the case that if a family has taken loans and diversified its sources of income, it feels the need to keep children out of school and attending to the family's businesses.

Given the importance of this debate, it is surprising how little research has been undertaken to examine whether Microfinance programmes do have any impact on these key issues. In the context of Bangladesh, where both the Government and donors share a great interest in population, it is not unsurprising to note that what little relevant research has been done tends to relate to family planning.

> *Halimah has had six children, all before she joined the Bank, and three of them died. "None of them got treatment from the doctor, because we were too poor. Sister, I tell you, if we had Grameen Bank Taka at that time, my children would not have died." (Todd, 1996)*

Schuler and Hashemi (1992) concluded that Grameen Bank members were statistically more likely to be using contraceptives (59% of Grameen members as opposed to 43% of a matched control group). Rahman and de Vanzo reached similar conclusions as a result of their work in Tangail (pending publication). Similarly, a recent Asian Development Bank report noted that, "Contraceptive use goes up among members because they are better able to overcome the barriers to obtaining access to contraceptive services (lack of mobility, cash, information, among others). Contraceptive use goes up among non members because of the diffusion effect of changing fertility norms in the village as a whole."

Nutritional indicators also seem to improve where Microfinance institutions have been working. Hashemi and Morshed (1997) cite a study conducted by the World Bank in collaboration with the Bangladesh Institute of Development Studies, which showed that the Grameen Bank not only "reduced poverty and improved welfare of participating households, but also enhanced the household's capacity to sustain their gains over time. This was accompanied by an increased caloric intake and better nutritional status of children in households of Grameen Bank participants."

Todd and Gibbons worked with Grameen members who had been borrowing for a decade in Tangail. They concluded: "Perhaps their most significant finding was that, compared with 18 percent of non members, 58 percent of the Grameen borrowers had crossed over the extreme poverty line (defined as an annual income sufficient to provide each family member with a daily intake of 1,800 calories.) Of the 42 percent of the Grameen borrowers who failed to cross the poverty line, fully 60 percent had experienced a serious illness in the family - most commonly tuberculosis, typhoid, jaundice, and gastric ulcer. Grameen loans prevented these families from becoming destitute, but they were insufficient to overcome their crises" (Bornstein, 1996).

Todd (1996), noting that the numbers in her cohort were too small to be statistically significant, found that the children of the Grameen Bank borrowers she studied were "a little bit taller and quite a bit heavier on average than the children in the control group". She attributes this in part, to the improved household economies of the Grameen members. She notes however, "this explanation - more Taka, better food, healthier children - goes only half way towards understanding why the Grameen children are nutritionally better off than the national average. What is crucial to the welfare of these children is that at least part of this income is in the hands of the mother and that she has a powerful voice in deciding *how* the resources of the household should be used. This enables her direct the benefits of better income to the welfare of those who matter to her most - her children."

One important initiative should indeed begin to help us to understand these issues better. In the Comilla District in Bangladesh, BRAC and ICDDR,B are working together to use ICDDR,B's unique Matlab research infrastructure to examine the effects of different interventions on the population's well-being. Nonetheless, since BRAC's RDP programme includes several interventions not commonly associated with "minimalist" Microfinance programmes - for example adult functional education (including human rights and legal education), essential health care and a livestock development programme, the research design is still lacking a pure Microfinance intervention.

Results to date (Chowdhury and Bhuiya, 1998) suggest a significant decrease in severe malnutrition closely associated with the length of BRAC membership - though whether disentangling the contribution of the Microfinance services from the other BRAC interventions (particularly the functional education component) has not been attempted.

Nutritional Status of Children (6-72 months) by Length of BRAC Membership of Mothers

Length of BRAC membership	% of severe PEM (MUAC <125mm)		
1-12 months:	Male: 16.4%	Female: 22.2%	All: 19.0%
12-24 months:	Male: 7.4%	Female: 22.9%	All: 16.1%
25+ months:	Male: 5.7%	Female: 13.0%	All: 9.4%

Research on the impact of Microfinance programmes on education is even more limited, and so the question as to whether increased disposable income results in higher levels of schooling for the programmes' clients remains largely unanswered. As a result of her work, Todd (1996) notes that "When we take the crudest measure - those children over six years who have ever been to school - *all* of the girls in Grameen families have had at least some schooling, compared to 60% of the girls in the control group. Most of the Grameen boys (81%) have had some schooling, compared to just half (54%) of the control group boys."

Once again, results from the BRAC-ICDDR,B studies (Chowdhury and Bhuiya, 1998) give us an indication of positive trends. The percentage distribution of children (11-14 years) achieving "basic education" (pre-determined level of mastery in reading, writing and arithmetic, as well as "life skills") rose from 12.4% in 1992 (before the BRAC programme began in the area) to 24.0% in 1995 among the children of BRAC members. By comparison, only14.0% of the children of those who had not joined BRAC achieved "basic education". On the other hand, the influence of the BRAC pre-primary and primary schools on these statistics are not recorded.

Given the growing size of the Microfinance "industry" there is a real need to focus on the impacts of the services offered on these key social welfare indicators. Even if there is growing acceptance that Microfinance programmes offer a cost effective way of addressing a wide variety of issues, there is a pressing need to understand if, and how, they impact these key human development indicators, and over what time period. The CGAP Working Group on Impact Assessment could, and indeed should, take the lead in this work.

COST-EFFECTIVE DEVELOPMENT THAT CREATES SUSTAINABLE ORGANISATIONS

Part of the current critical backlash against Microfinance is driven by its success, both imagined and real. Critics decry grandiose claims of Microfinance as a "panacea", a solution to world-wide poverty. Although there is little evidence of such claims in recent research literature, perhaps the initial euphoria, combined with the hype of the MicroCredit Summit, gave the wrong impression.

The real success of Microfinance lies in its inherent attractiveness to donor agencies. Well run Microfinance institutions offer donors an opportunity to support organisations that will provide financial services to

---

BURO, Tangail's Plan

As of 31st December 1997, BURO, Tangail provides 45,000 clients with a range of savings and credit services. By 2003 at the latest, the organisation fully expects to be serving 100,000 clients. The capital funds for these services come from three sources: clients' savings, retained profits and donor funds. The total capital funds requested from donors is $3.9 million, with an additional $1.1 million to be invested in set up costs.

By the year 2003, BURO, Tangail could easily start to repay the donor capital funds, and indeed negotiations are on-going to try to develop a mechanism to do so. If the loan is indeed repaid, or the donor funds are used to provide capital for other replications of BURO, Tangail's methodology (as is also being discussed), the net investment of funds (including the imputed cost of capital at around 10% pa - giving $2.4 million) would be about $3.5 million or $35 per client served, to build up a sustainable and financially-sound organisation.

their clients on an increasingly cost-effective basis until in 5-10 years they become sustainable. The benefits to the clients have been discussed in detail above, and the benefits for the donors in terms of returns on investment (particularly if they <u>lend</u> the necessary capital funds to Microfinance institutions) are almost unbeatable. Furthermore as Rhyne (1994); Christen et al. (1996) and many others point out, the greater the Microfinance institution's outreach, (i.e. the more clients it serves) the more cost effective and sustainable it becomes. In most development initiatives, the more people you serve, the greater the cost becomes; with Microfinance initiatives, the opposite is true.

How else could a donor organisation invest as little as $35 per household served with a good chance of positive long-term impact, and the probability of an increasing number of households being served at no additional cost ? And ASA's stripped-down, if somewhat inflexible, system offers an even cheaper alternative. With branches breaking even within less than nine months of starting operations, and a breath-taking rate of expansion, ASA is now reaching nearly 1 million clients. Furthermore, with its new Contractual Savings Agreement scheme for richer associate members, ASA may never need donor funding again.

> *"ASA's steadfast belief in self-reliance stems from the idea that lack of control over resources is lack of control over destiny. This is as true for the organization dedicated to empowering the poor as it is for the poor themselves." (Rashid 1997).*

It is the cost-effectiveness of Microfinance programmes, together with their aim of creating sustainable institutions (thus leaving the donor free to withdraw), that makes them so attractive. It is this attractiveness that poses a threat to other development agencies hoping to access those agencies' funds. In the words of Rogaly (1996), "It may lead to a single-track allocation of resources ear-marked for the very poorest people at the cost of other potential interventions, for example, health and education."

Rogaly (1996) states that "Micro-finance cannot be assumed to reduce poverty just because it achieves high levels of outreach or almost perfect repayment rates." As we have seen this assertion may possibly be true, but it **is** fair to assume that if a Microfinance Institution is achieving a high level of outreach, client retention and repayment, it is providing a service that it is useful to and valued by its clients. In short, there is a demand for its financial services. We have also seen that simply because a Microfinance institution has not "reduced poverty", it does not mean that it has not played a significant beneficial role in cushioning and reducing the income and expenditure shocks faced by the poor. In short, the client might well have become even poorer without access to financial services ... and most will see the financial services (if they are adequate quality and flexibility) as the way that they will work their way out of poverty.

All the above is not to promote Microfinance as the panacea ... but it is hard not to believe that quality financial services are the most cost-effective form of development assistance for addressing the needs of the middle and upper poor. As both USAID (Christen et al., 1996) and the World Bank (Rosenberg, 1994) have noted, despite high demand, it is estimated that institutional finance is unavailable to over 80 percent of all households in developing countries. This, of course, includes nearly all the poor people in the developing world. In this time of limited and declining development budgets, when most national Governments seem committed to ignoring the international agreement to spend 0.7% of GDP on development assistance, this consideration takes on an increasing importance.

But relying on Microfinance interventions in isolation is like a carpenter using only a hammer to build the platform upon which the poor will stand. Other tools are essential. In the words of a recent Asian Development Bank (1997) report, "In the longer perspective, microenterprise promotion can never be a substitute for a variety of social sector programs such a primary health care, environmental sanitation, education, nutrition and family planning and child care, or "structural" changes such as land reform." While recognising and accepting this, we should not lose sight of the fact that, because of the scarcity of development resources alluded to above, the poor cannot rely on Government or NGO programmes, and are therefore busy taking care of themselves with whatever tools are made available to them. The same ADB (1997) report also noted, "In Bangladesh, between one quarter and one third of loans were used fully or partly for purposes that were not directly related to production. In rural areas, these uses included (in descending order of frequency), subsistence household expenditures on food and clothing; housing improvements; loan repayments; tubewells for drinking water; purchases of homestead land; and the release of mortgaged land. In urban areas, these uses included (in descending order of frequency) payment for medical expenses, household expenses, and the purchase of furniture. Cases of loan use for current expenditure related mostly to the extreme poor."

This capability could be further strengthened if Microfinance (and particularly MicroCredit) organisations would focus on improving the quality of the financial services they offer to their clients. Nonetheless, it is clear that Microfinance interventions, however well designed (and those of us involved in Microfinance are working on it) are still not meeting the needs of the very poorest and the destitute. Income transfers (such as food for work and similar programmes) and subsidies are a necessity if these vulnerable groups are not to be even further marginalised.

It is also clear that preventive and reproductive health services are still an essential part of the development process. Ill-health is the biggest problem facing even those poor clients involved in Microfinance programmes. For example, Matin (1998) found that 86 per cent of the crises experienced by his study households were related to illness. It is this reality that has prompted Grameen Bank to start an experimental health insurance programme, BRAC to continue and extend its health programme, and almost all Microfinance NGOs in Bangladesh to provide weekly health education at meetings and offer special loans for clients to install tubewells and latrines - they are protecting their loan investments. But Microfinance institutions are rarely, if ever, of capable of delivering other key preventive health care services like immunisation services and reproductive health care. However, it is worth pointing out that the client groups that meet regularly at the same place and time, offer a tremendous opportunity for health (and indeed most other forms of) outreach and extension work.

Education is another key development intervention that is not part of the typical MFI's service package, although once again many organisations are providing education as an additional (donor or Government subsidised) service to their clients and/or the children. Basic literacy and numeracy have been shown to be of tremendous importance to the long-term development of a nation, and it would be a foolish Government that relied purely on the impact of Microfinance programmes to provide education to their children.

Finally, as noted by many authors including Christen et al (1996), Hulme and Mosley (1997) and Greeley (1997), the economic environment within which a Microfinance programme operates is critical to its success.

Without the infrastructure and access to markets to allow the households financed by the programme to sell the goods and services they produce and offer, there is little scope for microenterprise development, and thus poverty alleviation. Thus, continued investment in basic infrastructure also remains a necessarily high priority for the more remote impoverished communities.

CONCLUSIONS

Rahman and Hossain (1995) suggest that we best understand the vulnerability of the poor as function of "downward mobility pressures" arising from: 1. Structural factors in the economy (demand for the products and services of poor people (including labour) and seasonality of these); 2. Crisis factors (household "shocks" - illness, theft of assets, natural disaster etc.); and 3. Life-cycle factors (in particular the proportion of economically active to dependent household members, but also in the context of marriages etc.).

This chapter tries to demonstrate that Microfinance services (particularly quality financial services that have been developed to address the differing needs of clients) empower the poor to cope with and overcome many of these shocks, in particular through diversifying their income sources. Furthermore, it is time to move away from the preoccupation with "raising income" to focusing on "improving net wealth and income security". But, given the current preoccupation with increased income, the chapter reviews the extensive evidence for the positive impact of Microfinance programmes on this imperfect indicator.

Some of the common criticisms of Microfinance programmes are critiqued. Wood and others concern that Microfinance programmes only address the symptoms rather than the social causes of poverty is reviewed. But it is increasingly clear that the organisations dedicated to "social mobilisation" are all slowly but surely giving up "the struggle" and electing to provide what many of their clients really want: access to financial services that they can use themselves to improve their well-being and security. Indeed, it could be argued that by giving the poor an important tool to improve their capability to manage their financial affairs for themselves, Microfinance programmes significantly "empower" the poor.

It is time to vigorously refute the Western-feminist driven concerns that women giving their loans to their husbands to use in (more) productive activities is intrinsically dangerous and likely to lead to gender-related tensions as articulated by Goetz and Sen Gupta. The paper notes that anthropological evidence indicates poor Bangladeshi women perceive the situation very differently. Indeed they find these concerns conceptually somewhat strange, and experience a very different reality. With a few tragic exceptions, the women's traditional role of family banker, and her position in the household, is significantly enhanced by participation in Microfinance programmes.

There is limited evidence for the impact of Microfinance programmes on health and education, but the conclusions seem to indicate that in the long run, the impact is indeed positive. But that there is need for further research into these important areas.

It is clear that, in these days of dwindling development budgets, the cost-effectiveness and sustainability of interventions is one of the most important criteria for programming funds. It is here that Microfinance has a particular advantage over almost (and probably) all other interventions. Microfinance offers a tremendous diversity of long-term impacts on key economic and social indicators, and can be delivered in an institutional and financial sustainable manner that permits donors to withdraw after making relatively modest investments.

This is not to promote Microfinance as a "panacea" ... there are many key areas which it does not, or would take too long to, impact. The key areas where Microfinance cannot make a contribution include: ways to assist the poorest through income transfers or subsidies, systems to provide essential health and education services, and investments in the infrastructure necessary to link more remote areas to markets, thus stimulating economic activity. These areas necessarily require separate, specially designed interventions. Microfinance should not be hyped as the cure all, but it is one of the best, most cost-effective, medicines we have in the cabinet ! Microfinance is a solution to many, but not all, of the problems faced by the poor.

Chapter 2

OPTIMISING SYSTEMS FOR CLIENTS
AND THE INSTITUTION

Members "dropping-out" or leaving a Microfinance Institution (MFI) cost the organisation dearly - both in terms of lost investments in training and "social preparation" and in terms of the opportunity costs of losing the older, more experienced members most likely to take larger loans. The surprisingly high drop-out rates experienced by Bangladeshi MFIs is probably indicative of the inflexible financial services they provide to their clients. The recent research into drop-outs strongly suggests that members leaving MFIs are usually doing so because they are dissatisfied with the quality of financial services being offered by the organisation ... or have found better services being offered by another one. Clients "shopping around" for the best services in this way has also led to prevalent "multiple membership" of the same clients with different MFIs. Clients with multiple membership are absorbing huge costs (particularly in terms of the time they must spend at meetings) just in order to get access to the financial services they feel they need - a larger loan or open-access savings facilities. Indeed, MFIs offering more flexible financial services better tailored to meet clients' needs are likely to be able to charge a premium for these services.

The old idea that members might "graduate" to survive without access to financial services is naïve. Almost everyone, and certainly every business, needs access to places to store excess cash and to borrow money in order to smooth the flows of finance through the household or business. Similarly, an institution dedicated to achieving "sustainability", certainly does not want its most successful clients to graduate (or drop-out) to become customers of the formal sector banking system. These customers, and the larger loans they take, offer the greatest potential for high-profit business, and it is therefore in the interests of the MFI to design the quality financial services that they need, and thus to retain them as clients.

Despite the rhetoric surrounding "group guarantee", neither peer pressure nor peer support are as effective as their advocates suggest - particularly after the first two or three loan cycles have been completed. Amongst older groups, in the case of default, group guarantee is soon replaced by group fund guarantee, and individual follow-up by the MFI's staff. On the other hand it has become increasingly clear that the single most effective deterrent for defaulters is the prospect of losing access to financial services - follow-on loans and savings facilities. It follows, therefore, that the better the quality of the financial services provided, the more clients want to maintain their access to those services, and the less likely they are to default on loans from that quality financial service provider.

Although Microfinance programmes are often credited with reaching "the poorest of the poor", there is increasing recognition of the fact that they consistently fail to attract the bottom 10-15% of the population. There has been a great deal of interest in and research into this in recent years, trying to differentiate exclusion by the members themselves and exclusion by the MFI and its staff. This division is arbitrary since it is the systems and (in particular) the financial services of the MFI which will determine whether members "self-exclude" or not. An MFI's ability to attract the poorest depends on the financial services it offers, and whether they have been designed to be appropriate for the poorest - in short the quality of its financial services.

MFIs are paying increasingly close attention to the nature and quality of financial services they offer. The trade-off between the quality of the services and cost of providing the services is a clear one. Nonetheless, there is evidence that, to date, MFIs in Bangladesh have put too much emphasis on trying to implement standardised, inflexible low-cost, credit-driven systems when their clients are asking (and willing to pay) for a better quality and broader range of financial services.

"However, it is now widely recognized that not all poor households have been able to benefit from Micro credit programmes. There are three groups of such households: those who are active members but who are not improving their economic condition; those that initially join but subsequently drop out or become inactive as loan recipients; and those that never join" (Greeley 1997).

GROUPS

This chapter tries to examine the dynamics of groups formed to access financial services, and specifically, groups who agree to guarantee fellow group members' loans. It should be noted, that while this is the prevalent model in Bangladesh, and has proved remarkably successful, group-based systems are not the only way of delivering financial services. Most of the international Credit Union movement serving millions of members in a wide variety of settings throughout the world, the immensely successful Bank Rakyat Indonesia (BRI) which serves nearly 14 million clients, and many other financial service institutions do not use groups or group guarantee mechanisms at all. Nonetheless, this chapter will focus on groups, and their implications for those who leave them or are unable to join in the first place.

DROP-OUTS

The number of drop-outs a Microfinance programme experiences has profound implications for the viability of the institution and reveals a great deal about the quality of the financial services it offers to its clients. High drop-out rates cost the organisation dearly. The groups from which members drop-out are destabilised and must recruit new (less experienced) members, who will qualify for smaller loans thus reducing the overall interest income for the institution. The members who have been with the organisation longer qualify for larger loans, and the newer, replacement members can only get access to smaller ones. Despite this, the newer members have to take a disproportionate risk and guarantee the larger sums taken by their fellow group members, adding further stress to the group guarantee principle (this is examined in more detail in "Defaulters" below). Furthermore, each drop-out is a lost client who has undergone lengthy, expensive training ("social preparation"). The new replacement members must either also be given this training on an individual basis, or join the system without the initial training regarded as so important by many MFIs. The former option of *ad hoc* training is extremely cost ineffective, and the latter, if indeed "social preparation" is so important, threatens to undermine the system. In addition, in the face of frequent or multiple drop-outs, some of the groups may disintegrate entirely. Finally, drop-outs often leave because they cannot (or do not want to) manage loan repayments. These drop-outs no longer attend the group's regular meetings, and freed of the group guarantee, and of the incentive of continued access to financial services (be they loan or savings facilities), are more likely to leave behind an outstanding, unpaid loan.

High drop-out rates often indicate a dissatisfaction with the financial services being offered by the institution. Members choosing to leave a financial services organisation generally do so either because the organisation is not providing good enough services to warrant the (social and financial) costs involved, and/or because they have identified a better alternative.

Members expelled from a Microfinance programme (for, of course, not all drop-outs are voluntary) are likely to be indicative of an even more complex bundle of factors. These factors include: client selection (or better said "de-selection") either by fellow members and/or by staff (as we shall see in "The Excluded" below), the clients' ability to pay loans or even savings (again examined in "The Excluded") and clients' motivation to repay loan, which is in part, a proxy indicator of the level of satisfaction with the services (as we shall see in "Defaulters" below).

The increasing awareness of the importance of the number of drop-outs a programme experiences has prompted a series of studies in recent years. In 1992, BRAC lost 102,814 (or 15.3%) of its membership, and another 78,725 (or 10.9%) of its membership the following year. Clearly, even when they are replaced, such client turnover may compromise the sustainability of a programme, particularly when the drop-outs were relatively long-standing members eligible for larger (and therefore for the Microfinance institution seeking sustainability, more attractive and cost-effective) loans. Khan and Chowdhury (1995) collected information on the drop-outs' length of membership and concluded, "The average years for which they had been members before leaving was 4.7 for males and 3.8 years for females." This strongly suggests that BRAC was indeed losing many of its older, more experienced, and cost-effective clients, and that only a part of the drop-outs arose from villagers joining on a test basis before concluding that BRAC's system was not meeting their needs or expectations.

It should, however, be noted that in these two years BRAC was undertaking a membership restructuring exercise. As Khan and Chowdhury (1995) stress "In order to extend services to larger number of households, only one member from one household was allowed to retain VO membership. In RDP's emphasis on women, the male members were asked to vacate their membership, which also resulted in disproportionately high dropout among male membership as reported in this study." This is, nonetheless, in marked contrast to the same study's observation that "Over three quarters of the respondents from among the discontinuing category reported that they voluntarily dropped out while a quarter was expelled. The proportion of those expelled was higher among males, while the proportion of those dropped out voluntarily was larger among the female members" Khan and Chowdhury (1995). We can therefore probably conclude that only a small proportion of the drop-outs arose as a result of the membership restructuring underway. More fundamental issues were driving members to drop-out of BRAC's programme.

As can be seen from the above, the reasons for drop-out are, in the words of Mustafa (1996), "multidimensional". Indeed, the unifying theme of the studies on the subject is that the reasons for drop-out are complex. Sixteen reasons for drop-out were catalogued by Hassan and Shahid (1995). Of these, four related to social pressure (peer pressure over loan repayments, family disapproval/problems etc.), four to resource constraints (inability to finance weekly loan repayments, group fund not refunded, savings not available for withdrawal in emergency etc.), and four to the organisation (BRAC) itself (unpaid loan instalments resulting in the expulsion of the client, low interest on savings, member unable to count and sign her name and cancellation of membership while away). The remaining four were migration, death, joining another NGO and no access (as hoped) to Vulnerable Group Development cards.

Mustafa et al. (1996) noted in particular causes related to lack of easy access to savings, the excessive emphasis on credit discipline, the frequent policy changes and conflict among Village Organisation members. ASA's (1996) study noted "negligence of the staff/lack of staff quality and efficiency" which was identified in 56 (27.72%) of cases, low loan ceiling and "absence of multiple credit" identified in 151 (74.75%) of cases, and an additional 47 (23.27%) "members withdrew their membership as they disliked the savings rules".

Khan and Chowdhury (1995) also present an interesting table on "Reasons frequently cited for dropout and expulsion by gender" which shows a very high proportion of voluntary drop-outs being driven by the inflexibility of BRAC's system - in particular its savings facilities.

	% of dropped out members mentioned		
Reasons for voluntary dropout	**Male**	**Female**	**Total**
Group fund is not refunded	63.2	70.4	68.0
Savings not withdrawable in emergency	55.3	59.2	57.3
Other NGOs provide better facilities	36.8	52.7	49.8
Family Problem	11.8	45.0	29.3
Failure to repay loan	33.6	38.5	36.6
Reasons for expulsion			
Failure to repay loan	44.8	56.1	59.6
Irregular attendance in meeting	17.2	41.5	27.3

These high levels of drop-out prompted Hulme and Mosley (1997) to conclude, "Given the scale of "dropping out" (15 per cent per annum for the Grameen Bank, which is 300,000 members a year; 10-15 per cent per annum for BRAC, or 181,700 members, in 1992 and 1993) there may well have been significant under reporting of credit-induced crisis in most studies of finance for the poor". But although this may well be important for a minority, examination of the studies reveals a common dominant theme among the three quarters of drop-outs who leave voluntarily: dissatisfaction with the financial services being offered, and a belief that other NGOs offer better facilities (including crucially, how the organisation's staff behave with their clients). The majority of voluntary drop-outs are leaving their Microfinance providers as a result of dissatisfaction with the services and products being offered.

One of the key determinants of drop-out, often lost in the category "failure to repay loan" by these studies, is the insistence by field staff that clients take loans[1]. Irrespective of what official Head Office policy says, there is a clear understanding among most field staff that they should push out loans - often with little care for whether the clients need or can use them. In the words of one BRAC Zone Manager, "If we do not disburse loans how can we cover costs ?" (personal field notes, 1996). Similarly, PromPT's (1996) study of the perceptions of Grameen, BRAC, Proshika, ASA and other MFIs' borrowers, (using participatory rural appraisal and focus group discussions), found that many borrowers felt pressurised or sweet-talked into taking loans. Matin (1998) also notes, "MFI lending technology is insensitive to variations in household conditions. Most MFIs put all households on a treadmill of continuously increasing loan size and insist on a fixed repayment schedule."

Additional evidence for this can be easily seen in the percentage of clients with outstanding loans at any one time. BURO, Tangail offers credit on an entirely voluntary basis, as and when the client wants it, and (subject to graduated ceilings) however much the client wants. As a result, at any one time only about half of BURO, Tangail's clients have a loan outstanding - although as we shall see in the chapter "Savings: Services for the Client or Capital for the Institution?" most do choose to take a loan at one stage or other. By contrast, at any one time, almost all Grameen Bank, BRAC and ASA clients have loans outstanding. In the extreme case, ASA's loan policy dictates when the clients must take a loan and how big the loan must be with absolutely no reference to the need of the client for credit at that time. This policy has lead to a remarkable ability of ASA clients to manage their way round the system by on-lending, reciprocal agreements and cumbersome storage arrangements (Rutherford, 1995a). But clearly, managing one's way around an inflexible, credit-happy system is not ideal, and so clients will begin to look at the services offered by other Microfinance Institutions (MFIs).

It seems clear from the above that clients are "shopping around", "switching bank accounts", in search of flexible, quality financial

---

[1]   Although there are suggestions that these practices may now be declining.

services. In the words of Khan and Chowdhury (1995), "Other NGOs (Grameen Bank, ASA, Proshika, etc.) working side by side with BRAC in the same areas provided extra facilities to VO members. These included: less deductions from loan, higher loan ceiling, low interest rate, quick disbursement, etc. The study revealed that a good proportion of dropouts had enrolled themselves with other NGOs for better terms and opportunities." The MFI that wants to reduce its level of debilitating drop-out should carefully examine the services and products it is offering its clients and seek to improve them on an on-going basis.

Clients "shopping around" for the best services (or at least ones that meet their needs) has also lead to prevalent "multiple membership" of the same clients with different MFIs. In the Districts such as Manikganj and Tangail where many MFIs and NGOs are operating, villagers may be members of several organisations. Indeed, some estimates suggest that 40-50% of people in these Districts have multiple membership, and certainly PromPT's (1996) study found it a common phenomenon. Many MFIs and NGOs have reacted negatively to clients taking services from several organisations by trying to prohibit multiple membership. The reasons for this vary, it depends on who you talk to. The common official explanation is the fear that clients will take several loans from various organisations, use one loan to pay off another loan, and "over-stretch" their ability to repay. The less common, unofficial explanation is the MFIs' desire to maintain a monopoly over providing financial services to their clients, and a fear of competition.

But this all requires careful thought. In affluent societies, and indeed among the richer classes in Bangladesh, having several accounts is common (meeting a variety of savings and credit needs - current and fixed deposit accounts, housing or building society accounts, shares, hire-purchase accounts for appliances, a mortgage, credit cards and so on). This occurs because these different accounts or financial services meet different needs, and there are only limited additional costs associated with having multiple accounts and membership with these financial service organisations.

For the rural (and indeed urban) poor multiple membership has high cost. Multiple membership necessitates complying with multiple sets of rules and sitting in multiple (usually) weekly meetings, taking precious time away from pressing household and income-generation activities. In addition, many of the MFIs have membership and loan application fees. In short, multiple membership is not something to be entered into lightly

- it costs time and money. Few clients will voluntarily take out multiple membership unless they are not getting all the services they need from a single organisation. In the same way that much drop-out is indicative of dissatisfaction with the financial services being offered, multiple membership also suggests that the client is looking for more, or that some MFIs/NGOs are offering services not available in others and vice versa. For example, several of its clients only save with BURO, Tangail which offers open-access facilities, while taking their loans from another MFI (say ASA or Grameen Bank) which offers credit at a lower interest rate (Abdullah et al., 1995). One of the most common complaints about the services on offer from MFIs is that the loan ceilings are too low for many members' businesses (Abdullah et al., 1995; Todd, 1996; PromPT, 1996; ASA, 1997). So these potentially good and lucrative clients are compelled to take out multiple membership in order to access two or more loans to make up the amount they feel they need. They then not only have to handle two (or more) sets of rules and meetings, but also the varying loan disbursement schedules. Once again clients find themselves forced to manage their way round inflexible systems.

Of course, in some individual cases the MFI managers are right to worry about "over-stretching" of clients' ability to repay, and over-ambitious clients. Indeed Matin (1998a and 1998b) found many households deeply in debt to local money-lenders (another form of multiple participation in credit markets) in order to maintain their weekly repayments to MFIs through the lean season and other periods of stress and cash shortage. Matin (1998a) notes, "Some degree of cross financing is inevitable because of seasonal fluctuations in income and when coping with shocks (Wiig, 1997). But it can have a deleterious effect in the long run if households continuously manage loan repayment without having the ability to repay." Those interested in promoting open-access savings facilities would note that such facilities would provide a much better, cost-effective method for households to meet these short-falls and maintain the weekly repayment discipline.

In 1992-93, under pressure to respond to rising wage costs and achieve increased sustainability, Grameen Bank suddenly introduced seasonal loans on top of the traditional general loans, thereby doubling of the value of loans to (or debt burden of) its members. Matin (1998b) examined the effects of this move, and found that the "non-defaulting group have significantly lower multiple credit NGO participation, lower loan burden measured in terms of: a) proportion of borrowers having loans in addition to general and seasonal [loans], b) total outstanding due as a proportion of income and c) total instalment size." As noted above, there is some indication that these loans were being forced on members both from studies conducted (PromPT, 1996) and from internal correspondence within Grameen. For instance in 1993, a Grameen Bank branch manager in one of his monthly reports to the Managing Director wrote (quoted in Rahman, forthcoming): "Recently there is an intense competition among different managers to increase their loan disbursement. Increasing disbursement is important for the bank, but we must not forget the capabilities of our members. If we continue with our present attitudes, the result will be serious."

However, there is an additional problem posed by offering client-determined loans. One of the most effective mechanisms used by MFIs to screen credit-worthiness is to insist that clients build up a credit history, becoming eligible for larger loans only when they have paid off smaller ones - it would probably be unwise to change this. Nonetheless it is clear that excessively inflexible systems may well be forcing clients into multiple membership. This presents a tremendous opportunity for MFIs committed to a more flexible, quality financial services approach.

On the credit side, if MFIs were able to better identify clients' needs, and those clients who could manage and effectively use larger loans, they could attract and retain those valuable clients, while also better supporting their businesses. Similarly, if MFIs were able to better understand and respond to clients' needs for savings products, they could attract more capital to fund the larger loans. When an MFI offers a package of quality financial services that respond to all the needs of its clients, they are much less likely to take out multiple membership, and more likely to be willing to pay a premium for the convenience of having all their needs met by one institution, in one meeting. It is this comparative advantage of BURO, Tangail's client-responsive system that allows the organisation to charge an interest rate on loans that is effectively almost double that of Grameen Bank or ASA - and still attract clients. Indeed BURO, Tangail experienced a drop-out rate of only 3% in 1997 - the majority of these drop-outs are likely to have been driven by migration (particularly as younger women members get married and move to their new husbands' villages).

GRADUATES

One of the reasons that is notable by its almost complete absence from these listings of grounds for drop-out is "graduation". A few years ago, there was a belief that credit programmes would give such a boost to the income of "beneficiaries" that they would "graduate from poverty". The dynamics of poverty were discussed at length in the chapter "Microfinance: The Solution or A Problem", and it is clear that the route out of poverty is neither linear nor absolute.

There were two schools of thought on "graduation". One held that after a limited number of benign (subsidised) loan cycles, the beneficiaries' businesses would no longer need credit. In retrospect, this was supreme naiveté, for there is scarcely a business in the world that does not use overdraft facilities to manage its way through the cyclical nature of the supply of its inputs and demand for its products or services. And vast international financial markets have developed round the need of businesses for capital for expansion. The other school, more plausibly, believed that poor clients could "graduate" with enough wealth and self-confidence to become the clients of formal sector banks. Indeed there are many Microfinance programmes throughout the world seeking to establish Self Help Groups, Credit Unions or Village Banks and link them to formal sector financial service institutions. This is a more viable and desirable option for those NGOs (for example foreign ones) or Government projects/agencies not intending to stay and establish a permanent banking institution.

But (as we saw in "Drop-outs" above) for those NGOs seeking to establish permanent MFIs, these richer, more self-confident, potential "graduates" are the most valuable clients. For it is these clients that will often take the larger loans to expand or maintain the working capital of their business, or to finance asset acquisition. It is these larger loans on which the MFI will make the most profit since the cost of administering the loan is almost exactly the same irrespective of its size. Indeed these longer-term, richer, more self-confident clients should be the better credit risks - although this is subject to debate (as we shall see in "Defaulters" below). And crucially, it is these clients taking larger loans that allow the MFI to finance the provision of smaller loans to poorer clients. The last thing that an MFI with its sights set on financial sustainability wants to see is these precious larger clients "graduating". Instead, MFIs should seek to retain them as clients by seeking to meet their needs through a range of client-responsive financial services.

DEFAULTERS

"Peer pressure and peer support", "group guarantee", "joint liability", or "social collateral" are viewed as one of the cornerstones of "solidarity group" credit programmes. It is this part of the Grameen Bank system that has been most discussed and replicated as the basis for MicroCredit programmes all over the world. In some respects, the "success of group guarantee" is seen as "the magic of Grameen". But there are increasing numbers of commentators and practitioners who have come to the conclusion that while "group guarantee" may be important and work for the first few loan cycles, thereafter, it weakens and becomes largely irrelevant (Yaqub, 1995; Sharif, 1997). Other factors have been identified as critical, and amongst these, the continuing access to repeat loans (which is of course, implicit in the group guarantee system) is probably the most important (Berenbach and Guzman, 1994; Rhyne and Otero, 1994).

What is Behind GB's Success ?

1. *Close Relationship*

   The close relationship that is developed between the bank and the borrower, and among the borrowers themselves, is a very important factor in the success of GB.

2. *Peer Pressure and Peer Support*

   Formation of small five-member groups of the members' own choosing and federating the groups into centres, helps create the right kind of peer pressure at the time when a member tries wilfully to violate GB rules, and peer support at times when a member falls into any difficulty in pursuing his economic pursuit."

   (Professor Md. Yunus, in Gibbons, 1992).

The idea that Grameen, or indeed any other "solidarity group", members are likely to offer much peer support to one another has already been explored in the context of community organisation and social mobilisation in the chapter "Microfinance: The Solution or a

Problem?". If peer support is likely to work anywhere, surely it must be in the mature (ten plus years old) Grameen groups in Tangail. But there Todd's (1996) work showed that, "Members did help one another out with repayment, since default of one member threatened the new loans of the other members in her group and the good name of the whole center. But this help had distinct limits. More general help for members in trouble was rare. ... In these villages, the groups and centers pulled together in unity when their access to loans was a stake. Otherwise more primordial loyalties and support networks of family, gusti, and even dol usually took precedence."

Even if peer support only works in order to ensure continuing access to loans, could it be that peer pressure and the group guarantee principle, is more effective ? Are the group members ensuring that defaulters pay ? Jain (1996) notes that in the case of Grameen Bank, the group guarantee principle was the subject of much training and discussion, but that members who fell behind on repayments were usually visited in their households on an individual basis by the Bank staff.

Matin's (1997) work in old Grameen kendras (established in 1980) in Madhurpur found, "In all the centres in these four villages the repayment rate has fallen drastically and the numbers of inactive borrowers have risen. ... Many of the borrowers who have overdue loans have stopped repaying altogether, some are repaying part of their dues as and when convenient, and a few remain good payers. Those who still remain good repayers are getting new loans. Staff pressure and concomitant peer pressure is almost non-existent. The whole system is now operating on the basis of individual liability. ... Thus the only way in which joint liability works is via the staff pressure induced peer pressure which is directed at the centre to solve "kisti problem". This works as long as the "kisti problem" is manageable, that is when there are a few with "kisti problem", and when the "kisti" is small. But this is not sustainable. ... A point could be reached where eliminating the "problem borrowers" which is often to "clean" the centre becomes difficult as a borrower's overdue amount far exceeds her Group Fund contributions. As numbers of on-time repayers decrease, an "unzipping" effect is likely. This would render staff pressure induced peer pressure increasingly ineffective."

The "unzipping" effect[2] Matin refers to is when the entire group, and indeed often the entire kendra, burdened by excessive or multiple default, sees no further hope for continuing loans and elects to default en masse, thus causing the group or kendra (and the group guarantee that held it together) to "unzip". It is this risk that drives MFI field workers to continue to give loans to the good payers in the longer established groups or kendras - after all they have developed a long credit history - and thus to negate the group guarantee principle. And it is for this reason that, despite all the rhetoric, the effectiveness of the group guarantee principle is limited to the first few loan cycles.

In addition, from Matin's work, we can see that not only must staff induce "peer pressure", but also that "group guarantee" has a declining influence over time. Furthermore, the study also demonstrates that the "Group Fund" is playing a significant and important role as a "loan guarantee fund", and indeed, some commentators have suggested that it is better, honestly, labelled as such (Wright et al., 1997). We will return to the importance of the Group Fund and other compulsory savings systems in the chapter "Savings: Services for the Client or Capital for the Institution?"

Yaqub's (1995) work on BRAC found other, related, problems with the group guarantee system. The longer members had been with BRAC and the bigger their loans, the less likely they were to accept the group guarantee principle. Yaqub attributes this to the fact that "GBF [Group Based Finance] relies ... substantially on the borrowers' lack of alternative sources of credit and social powerlessness." Yaqub goes on to conclude (as discussed in the chapter "Microfinance: The Solution Or A Problem") that clients involved in Microfinance programmes gain experience, self-confidence, (and in some cases, like BRAC, education), and increased income and wealth too. These attributes enable clients to seek and find better alternatives and to absorb whatever sanctions are threatened by the MFI (or fellow group members) in the attempts to recover the loan. And so the group guarantee principle, which depends on the financial and social weakness of those involved, is compromised by the very positive outcomes that access to financial services and the MFIs' services promote.

There is one other area in which the "joint liability" may be stressed to breaking-point, and this too may offer explanations why "group

---

[2]   A term first coined by Rutherford during 1992

solidarity" and "peer support" instead of increasing over time, appear to decrease. The problem is different loan sizes. As groups mature, in those MFIs that do not force their clients all to take larger and larger loans, different members take differing amounts of credit. In extreme cases, some members of a guarantee group may be taking loans ten or more times larger than those of their fellow group members. The members with smaller (or in some cases, no) loans must then assume joint liability for much larger loans than they are ever likely to take - and may be unwilling to do so. It is likely that their desire for continuing access to credit facilities will mean that they will assume joint liability in theory, but that they will feel little obligation to "group guarantee" in practice. Hence Jain and Matin's observation that with more mature groups, the joint is transmuted into individual liability - a reality recognised and acted upon by the Grameen field staff.

Rogaly (1996) also notes that, "Peer group monitoring has not proved necessary to other institutions seeking to do away with physical collateral. Chaves and Gonzalez-Vega (1996) document the use of character references and locally recruited lending agents by government-sponsored banks in Indonesia. The degree to which Grameen Bank employees themselves implement peer-group monitoring has recently been questioned, with the suggestion that the key to its high repayment rates are the weekly public meetings (at which attendance is compulsory) to collect loan instalments and savings deposits. These induce a culture of discipline, routinised payments, and institutional accountability (Jain, 1996)."

Once again, there is a consistent theme running through these apparently diverse studies. In common with the work of Todd (1996), Matin (1997) and Yaqub (1995) stress the importance to clients of continuing access to loans, while Jain (1996) puts emphasis on the disciplined weekly repayments as well as the transparent accountability of Grameen's staff as providers of financial services. It is not unreasonable to suggest therefore, that the more clients value and appreciate the financial services being offered to them, the more they will do to protect and sustain their access to those services, and therefore the less likely they are to default. And the better the quality of those financial services (both credit and savings facilities, and the manner in which they are delivered), the more the clients will value them.

It may be for this reason that BURO, Tangail, which has introduced innovations that are popular with its clients and more flexible financial

services than the hundreds of other MFIs operating in Tangail -
including Grameen, BRAC, ASA, and Proshika (Rutherford and
Hossain, 1997) - has a remarkably low default rate. As of December 31,
1997, only 1.05% of loans had repayment instalments more than 26
weeks overdue - of which many date back to the old BURO days.
BURO, Tangail's clients appreciate the organisation's flexible financial
services (and in particular its unique savings facilities and entirely
optional loans), and therefore protect their access to these by repaying
the loans they take on time.

THE EXCLUDED

The rhetoric surrounding Microfinance remains extraordinary, and
almost shameless. For years (and indeed, in many cases, still now)
programmes blithely asserted that they were serving "the poorest of the
poor". Part of this (as we see in the chapters "Microfinance: The
Solution or A Problem" and "Replicating Microfinance Systems: Are
Blue-Prints Enough?" is because of the efforts to promote Microfinance
as a "cure all". But any Microfinance Institution seriously claiming it
reaches the "poorest of the poor" is either not monitoring its clientele
properly, or simply being economical with the truth ... unless that is, the
institution is offering revolutionary quality financial services that attract
the poorest and destitute. Certainly none of the larger MFIs operating in
Bangladesh are serving the poorest of the poor through their mainstream
credit and savings activities.

> "... *Habibah's criteria for the selection of new members explicitly
> excluded the poorest women in the village. "They should not be
> landed, but they should have some land - some house land and some
> vegetable land. They should not be extremely poor. Most important,
> they should be hard working, not just the wife, but also the husband.
> They should be experienced in goats and poultry and grow some
> vegetables."*
>
> *Conversations with the Branch staff put them closer to Habibah's
> definition of the rules. One told me: "We look for people who   have
> some profession. They must have a source of business, like trading, or
> tailoring or cows. Landless, yes; but not hopeless.""* (Todd, 196).

> *In the words of Hashemi (1997) "It seems that Grameen Bank and similar credit programs have failed to target this group [the hard core poor] effectively, resulting in most of them remaining outside the micro-credit net. For the most part these people are so destitute that they consider themselves not credit-worthy. They do not feel that they have enough resources to generate incomes to pay back loans. They therefore "self-select" themselves out of credit program membership."*

There is a large-scale debate underway as to why MFIs are failing to attract the poorest. It is a debate that is particularly important in the context of the on-going efforts to achieve institutional sustainability, for many are concerned that the donors emphasis of financial self-sufficiency may be prompting the MFIs to go up market to serve richer clients more likely to take larger loans. In the words of Hulme and Mosley (1997), "Worryingly, both BRAC-RDP and Grameen Bank recently appear to be moving away from working with significant proportions of the hard core poor and focusing their activities on the middle income and upper poor, rather than the most desperate." As we saw in the chapter "Microfinance: The Solution Or A Problem", both BRAC and Grameen have recognised this as an important issue and have developed special programmes in an attempt to address the problem.

In addition, most of the larger MFIs are studying this problem to examine the causes of the exclusion of the poor. "An exercise was conducted in four villages where Grameen and BRAC were active to determine the reasons for target group households not joining credit programs. It was found that out of 498 target group households only 284 (57%) joined Grameen and BRAC as members. The major reason for not joining (49%) was because people felt they would be unable to pay back the loan money and would therefore be stuck with debt for which they would eventually be forced to sell off what little possessions they still had. They refused to be burdened with still another debt. A quarter of the women did not join because of social and religious sanctions that dictated that joining credit programs would be a violation of social norms. Only 13% of the women said that they had actually wanted to join but were not accepted because other program members felt that they were high risks (their husbands were gamblers and would waste the money; they would migrate out of the village; they were not good money managers; they did not get along with others)." (Hashemi, 1997)

In view of the accusations that MFIs are increasingly forsaking the poor for the better off as the drive for sustainability gathers momentum, the studies conducted tend to try to differentiate between "self" and "programme" exclusion. In fact, as we shall see, the difference is limited: not only do programmes exclude clients, potential clients also "self exclude" on the basis of programme design.

Greeley asserts that "Programme-driven exclusion is of three types. First, it may be a response by other new members at the time of group formation to perceived risk of default which, if it occurs, may affect their own access to credit under joint-liability provisions. Second, it may result from programme staff who perceive that their targets and performance indicators will be more easily attained by focusing on "good" credit risks; they may also find it easier to start operations by utilizing the services of village leaders and this may result in effective exclusion for some because of local social and political factionalism. Thirdly, it may result from the limited size of the programme; too many people interested and not enough places available (Greeley, 1997)." But in the same article, the author notes that colleagues (Evans et al. 1995) found no evidence to support these interesting propositions. He concludes (perhaps somewhat wearily), "Despite this, one frequently hears the view that, with the renewed emphasis on accountability as programmes scale up and donors have more at stake, some form of programme-driven exclusion does occur" (Greeley, 1997).

Grameen Trust's research reaches broadly the same conclusion, "Only 13% of the women said they actually wanted to join but were not accepted because other program members felt they were high risks" (Hashemi, 1997a). But another, related, paper goes on to make the not unreasonable observation that, "Actually what this is indicative of is not so much that Grameen is unable to bring all poor women into their fold but that micro credit may not necessarily be the way out for all the poor. Successful micro credit operation is strongly dependent on strict screening to ensure that money that is borrowed can be repaid. .... Thus, in order to ensure increasing disbursements and high repayments (the targets that are set up by programs) NGO field staff and group leaders may therefore end up screening the destitute out" (Hashemi, 1997b).

Greeley (1997) notes "Some ... anecdotal field evidence (Montgomery, 1996) does suggest that both staff and other members do seek to enforce exclusion for members who are in arrears and that these are the poorer members." One can scarcely be surprised that staff, who are evaluated on the basis of (inter alia) loan portfolio performance, and must take the time to follow-up defaulters, choose to exclude those they view as unlikely to be able to repay. And it would certainly be unreasonable to blame clients for choosing to exclude those who are seen as being unable to repay loans, but for whom they must assume joint liability. Would you formally guarantee a loan for someone who you viewed as a credit-risk ?

The ASA (1997) study of 626 respondents (drawn from a mixture of ASA staff and clients) revealed different perspectives, perhaps as a result of focusing on the exclusion of the absolutely destitute. Almost all (98.88%) of respondents, and all the clients, said that lack of minimum clothing (to leave the bari and attend a public meeting) excludes the "hardcore poor". 87.06% (including all the unit office staff) said that the local elite (moneylenders, religious leaders, union chairmen etc.) play an important role in the exclusion of the hardcore poor. 77.16% of respondents noted that ASA's age limits on membership (18-50) exclude the hardcore poor. Finally, analysis of the responses of the unit staff suggests that they themselves often screen out the hardcore poor as too risky clients ... this is in contrast with the HO staff's responses which assured the researchers that staff were not screening out the poorest. 62.5% of respondents thought that hardcore poor had joined and been discharged from groups for poor repayment/attendance.

Alamghir, (1997) also reviewed this issue from the potential clients' perspective. He estimated that there were 1,553 members poorer than the members who had already joined the groups in the command areas of his 296 study samities. He then investigated why these poorer families did not join the groups, finding that of these, 391 persons (25.17%) did not join because they would not be able to pay regular weekly savings, 228 (14.68%) did not join because they would not be able to pay regular loan instalments, 114 (7.3%) did not have any interest in receiving loan, and 108 (6.9%) did not like to attend weekly meetings. It is interesting to note that none of the explanations for not joining documented by Alamghir involved MFI's staff screening out the poorer families.

Thus while credit-oriented MFIs' staff may be screening out some of the poorest (for entirely pragmatic and legitimate reasons), it is the MFIs' policies that seem to play a particularly important role in the exclusion of the poorest. Not only are they unable to attend weekly meetings, and fear for their ability to make the weekly repayments, but also they even cite the weekly savings requirement as a mechanism that excludes them from risking taking membership in MFIs. Once again, there seems to be an opportunity to examine still more flexible financial services (for example entirely voluntary, open access savings accounts, without the weekly deposit requirements) to attract the poorest. This is an area worthy of operations research by the MFIs committed to quality financial services. But such a service would be expensive to implement, and whether it would be a cost-effective strategy for an MFI with its sights firmly set on financial sustainability is open to question.

Perhaps cross-subsidies are the answer. As the MFIs' clients become more experienced and take larger loans, and as the MFIs reach out to serve the not-so-poor, they may be able to use the profits made through this business to finance services for the poorest. Indeed, it might be argued that such a strategy might be an effective "loss-leader" to cultivate potential clients for the future in exactly the same way that the formal sector banks accept relatively small deposits from clients with potential in the future (for example students). Christen et al. (1996) certainly believe in this approach, "Some observers have argued for an exclusive focus on the poorest clients, with the objective of poverty alleviation. The data assembled here and arguments for financial leverage suggest that mixed programs serving a range of clients can also be highly effective in reaching the poorest. It is scale, not exclusive focus, that determines whether significant outreach to the poor is achieved."

CONCLUSIONS

There is compelling evidence to support the contention that a significant majority of "drop-outs" occurs because MFIs' financial services are inadequate or inappropriate to meet the needs of the very clients they are trying to serve. Drop-outs are expensive for MFIs, both in terms of money already invested that is lost as the member leaves, and in terms of lost potential future business from the member. MFIs seeking to develop permanent sustainable organisations should seek to improve the financial services they are offering in order to reduce client dissatisfaction and thus drop-out. Such a strategy is likely to prove cost-effective.

For those MFIs committed to creating permanent financial service institutions, "graduating" the more experienced and affluent clients into formal sector banking system is not a desirable strategy as it implies the loss of the most valuable and cost effective clients. Indeed, MFIs should be looking to tailor their services to ensure that they retain these high value clients.

It is also clear that distinctions between "self-" and "organisation-driven" exclusion of the very poor are largely arbitrary, for it is the nature of the financial services and the programme rules that accompany them that exclude the poorest from joining. In preference to "targeting the poorest" and trying to persuade them to join organisations offering inappropriate financial services, it is the services themselves that require revision and tailoring to meet the needs of the poorest, and thus to attract them into Microfinance programmes.

There is also increasing evidence that the "group guarantee" system, while probably useful in the initial loan cycles, has a declining ability to secure repayment of loans. Continued access to follow-on loans has long been viewed as one of the most important incentives for clients to repay. Given the value that the poor place on having access to financial services (both credit and savings facilities), it is clear that the better the quality of these financial services, the more the poor will value access to them, and thus the more likely they are to continue to meet their obligations (including repayment of loans) to the MFIs that provide them.

For all these reasons, MFIs should pay (and indeed are paying) increasingly close attention to the nature and quality of financial services they offer. The trade-off between the quality of the services and cost of providing the services is a clear one, but getting the balance right is difficult. There is evidence that, to date, MFIs in Bangladesh have put too much emphasis on trying to implement standardised, inflexible low-cost, credit-driven systems when their clients are asking (and willing to pay) for a better quality and broader range of financial services. But, as we shall see in the next chapter, "Savings: Services for the Client or Capital for the Institution?" this is now changing.

Different Clients Differing Needs

On the basis of his work in Madhurpur, Matin (1998) counsels, "For instance, MFIs should consider individual liability lending to long time borrowers with good repayment record[s] and who now borrow large sums. Many of them are likely to have a large credit needs, greater risk-bearing capacity, an ability to provide collateral, and the necessary entrepreneurial skills to invest in productive enterprises. For them i) the group contract and the jointly liability system can be dispensed with, ii) different repayment schedules devised, and iii) loan applications screened after detailed project appraisals. While these measures are likely to reduce the overhead costs of lending more importantly, they would create right incentives for larger and regular borrowers to maintain high repayment rates. On the other hand, MFIs should mimic the informal sector when lending to poorer target group households by accounting for seasonality and providing i) repayment flexibility, ii) a ceiling on loan sizes, and iii) in kind loans."

It is perhaps Safe*Save*'s programme that has come furthest in Bangladesh, and probably the world, in terms of delivering flexible, high quality financial services to poor people.

*Safe*Save is a financial services provider for poor slum dwellers based on a daily deposit collection service. It is registered as a Co-operative (registered number Dhaka 119) which gives it the right to mobilise deposits from the general public and investors[3]. It began work in August 1996 in two slums in Mohammadpur, Dhaka. By January 1999 it had sixteen full-time staff and 2,407 active client accounts in six slums.

*Safe*Save demonstrates:

- that poor slum dwellers have a strong desire and capacity to save, especially if they can turn those savings into usefully large lump sums

---

[3] *The Co-operative Societies Ordinance, 1984*, chapter IV, section 32, page 11: "A co-operative society shall receive deposits and loans from persons who are not members only to such extent and under such conditions as may be prescribed in the rules and bye-laws."

in flexible and convenient ways (through withdrawals or by borrowing)

- that savers need a discipline to help them save, and that a frequent *opportunity* to make small savings out of day-to-day cash resources provides that discipline

- that this discipline of *frequent opportunity to save or repay* is as powerful as the discipline of *obligation to repay* that is used by Grameen Bank and others who offer the poor loans which are essentially advances against future savings

- that this service can be offered successfully to men women and children

- that this service can be delivered to individual households without group formation

- that this service can cover its costs even at a modest scale of execution

*Safe*Save offers its clients a daily opportunity to transact with it. Each day, clients may save (as much or as little as they like) or may choose not to save. They may withdraw savings (up to the limit of their savings balance) or choose not to withdraw. They may borrow (within limits) or choose not to; and if they have a loan they may repay (as much or as little as they like) or choose not to. The only thing they *must* do is pay their monthly interest on any loan they have - this they can do any time during the month, and they can do it in instalments if they wish.

*Safe*Save is experimenting with various ways of offering this ultra-flexible service. The current most popular product of this type is described in a flyer below.

*Safe*Save's experience so far is that slum dwellers, when offered such an opportunity, can and do save. Many use the service as a 'current account', withdrawing small sums as and when they need them. Most clients also take the opportunity, quite early, to take loans secured against their savings. There are many small-scale opportunities to use modest amounts of capital profitably in an environment like the Dhaka slums and loans of up to 20,000 taka (about $450) have been issued, though the average loan is much smaller. Some clients repay their loans by continuing to save and then cutting the loan sum from their savings balance, though most choose instead to repay the loans without dipping

into their savings balances. Many clients take and return loans quickly -
a loan life of three to six months is common.

A summary *balance sheet* for January 31st 1999, and a summary
income and expenditure table for the year to January 1999 follow.
US$1 = taka 49 in early 1999

Summary balance sheet: Jan 31 1999	Taka	Assets	Taka
Liabilities		**Assets**	
Client savings	2,375,846	Loans outstanding	3,722,575
Borrowings (i.e. loans taken by *Safe*Save to run the programme)	2,675,335	Cash in hand / at bank, and debtors	924,189
Income and Expenditure Account c/f	-294,577	Fixed assets	109,840
	4,756,604		**4,756,604**

Borrowings have come from one of the two *Safe*Save founders, and,
later, from an international NGO. Fixed assets consist of computers and
office furniture. *Safe*Save now has two branches operating, the second
having opened in October 1998.

Income and expenditure: Jan 1998 to Jan 1999	+	–	Taka
Interest earned from loans	628,188		
Consultancy & other fees, and bank interest	151,402		
Running costs		839,307	
Depreciation on equipment		37,280	
Loan losses		29,295	
Previous Income and Expenditure Account b/f	168,284		
Income and Expenditure Account			**-294,577**

Receipts consist mainly of interest earnings on loans and began with
the first loans in November 1996. There have also been some small
earnings from consultancy services sold to SafeSave replicators.
Payments have to date been largely wages, rent advances and office
equipment and furniture, including computing equipment.

*Safe***Save** is now covering its operational costs each month, and making
a small surplus so that the costs of capitalisation are being gradually
met. Other costs such as loan losses, and provision against inflation, are
not yet being met in full, but with further growth these costs should also
be covered within a few months.

Growth rates: Charts showing growth rates for key indices follow:

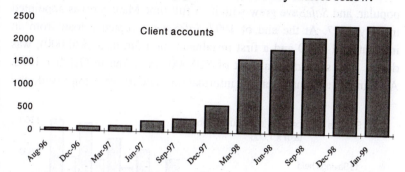

*Safe*Save focuses on poor households. Since a means test for each household would be expensive and intrusive, *Safe*Save maintains its poverty focus by selecting certain slums and recruiting clients within those slums. This ensures that the vast majority of clients are poor. Recruitment is done by workers, called 'Collectors', who themselves live in the slums. These Collectors make the daily rounds of all clients.

Clients earn the automatic right to a loan and the rules for loan eligibility and value are clear to everyone. Thus, although loan disbursement responsibility is delegated to the Collectors (who disburse loans on the spot), the Collectors have no discretion. This reduces the risk of their indulging in rent-seeking behaviour.

Overview of first two years of trading: *Safe*Save began life as a private experiment of the two founders. Stuart Rutherford is a writer and practitioner of microfinance, and Rabeya Islam a housewife and experienced manager of traditional ROSCAs and other savings clubs. They agreed to set up *Safe*Save as an attempt to use the learning gained from studying and practising informal finance to create a formal institution that would provide high-quality financial services to the poor and very poor. The principle of daily collection was adopted from the very start.

At first (August 1996 to May 1997), we were overwhelmed by the amounts of savings that the first 250 clients made. Because we had set the permitted ratio of loan size to savings at a generous level we soon ran short of capital. This led to two main changes: a redesign of the instrument with low-but-rising loan sizes, and a decision to professionalise *Safe*Save.

The revised instrument (as outlined below) proved stable and popular, and *Safe*Save grew with it. A full-time Manager was appointed in May 1997. At the end of 1997 *Safe*Save accepted a loan from an international NGO and a first instalment, of 1.3m taka ($30,000), was drawn. The second instalment of $20,000 was taken in October 1998. Accounting and management information systems were improved, and

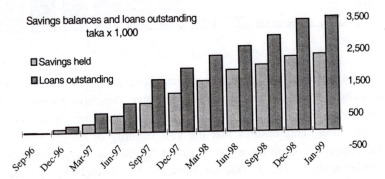

Savings balances and loans outstanding
taka x 1,000

□ Savings held
▣ Loans outstanding

Sep-96, Dec-96, Mar-97, Jun-97, Sep-97, Dec-97, Mar-98, Jun-98, Sep-98, Dec-98, Jan-99

3,500, 2,500, 1,500, 500, -500

an audit was done. At the end of 1997 *Safe*Save moved out of Rabeya Islam's drawing room and into a small branch office, and then in October 1998 into a second branch.

As we moved into successive slums, we selected ones that were progressively poorer. By early 1998 we reached 'Beri Bad' - an area where very poor people squat on a flood embankment and break bricks for a living[4]. 'Beri Bad' was badly hit in the 1998 floods: about one third of clients there had to move when their homes went completely under water. During that period their transactions - savings and withdrawals, loans and repayments, reached record highs.

Loan portfolio performance has also been good so far. For example, at the second branch, now more than one year old, there were, at the end of December 1998, 477 loans outstanding, with a total value of taka 857,559. Of these, only six loans were in arrears in interest payments.

---

[4] Brick chips are used as aggregate for concrete in a country that lacks stone. In the embankment community many households are woman-headed. Women earn about 20 taka (50 cents US) a day for from four to six hours of breaking bricks, often perched up on a pile of bricks under a makeshift sunshade and with a baby strapped to their back.

The total value outstanding of these loan accounts in arrears was 12,245 taka, or 1.4% of the total loan portfolio outstanding. Only one loan was more than one month in arrears. However, at our first branch, we lost contact with some clients as a result of the floods, and a few loans have had to be written off.

*Safe*Save has been replicated by several organisations, some of whom have simplified procedures and grown quickly. Another replicator is testing *Safe*Save principles in the rural area.

Prospects for the third year (1998-1999): A third branch will be opened and client numbers are targeted to grow to 4,000 by mid 1999. A further modification of the instrument will be introduced and tested in selected areas.

Since SafeSave's replicators have shown more interest in rapid growth than in product diversification, SafeSave will remain small but act as a centre for the innovation and development of high-quality savings, loan and insurance products for the poor. As they mature, the technology for these products will be made available to replicators. Replicators will themselves be assisted to adopt these products by another international NGO.

More information on *Safe*Save including regular updates is available on its web site:

http://www.drik.net/safesave

translation of a flyer:

EARN 250 TAKA FOR EVERY 1,000 TAKA YOU SAVE WITH *SAFE*SAVE'S NEW FIVE-YEAR ACCOUNT!

*Safe*Save's new *five year account* **is a savings collection service for poor people.**

*Safe*Save's new *five year account* allows you to build up your savings with speed, safety, and convenience. Every time you save 1,000 taka you earn 250 taka interest. Then at the end of five years, you get back all your savings plus all the interest. In the meantime if you need money you can take a loan and repay it in any way that suits you. You can withdraw some of your savings if you want. You can close your account early, or extend it.

Here is a summary of the rules: (please ask our worker for details)

SAVINGS: When you open your account we give you a savings passbook. Our worker will call on you every day, or every few days, according to your wishes, to collect your savings. Just give your savings to her and she will write the amount in the passbook.

As soon as you have saved 1,000 taka you earn 250 taka interest and this is written in your passbook. Then when you have saved another 1,000 taka you earn another 250 taka interest. And so on for five years. After five years you take back all the deposits plus interest. For example, if after five years you have saved a total of 20,000 taka you will take back that 20,000 taka plus 5,000 taka interest.

If you want to close your account before five years you can do so but you will not get as much interest. If you want to keep your account running for more than five years you can do so - and we will pay you up to double the interest as a bonus!

If you want to withdraw cash from your account you can do so but we do not recommend this as you will loose the interest you earned on the amount you withdraw.

LOANS: When you need money we recommend that rather than withdrawing taka from your account you should take a loan. Our loans are easy to use. You pay us back when you like, in instalments or at a time - but you must pay us the interest on the loan each month.

Your first loan can be up to the size of your savings balance plus an 'extra' amount of 1,000 taka. So if you have saved 700 taka then your first loan can be up to 1,700 taka. As you take each successive loan so the amount of the 'extra' rises by 500 taka. If you have saved 1,300 taka your second loan can be 2,800 taka (1,300 plus 1,500 'extra').

You pay only two taka per hundred per month for the loan, plus a handling fee of 100 taka when you take the loan (200 taka if the loan is more than 5,000 taka). When you have a loan, you can't withdraw savings or close your account. You might consider holding more than one account if you want to go on withdrawing from time to time.

So if you save more, then you earn more interest, and you can take a bigger loan.

JOIN *SAFE*SAVE TODAY AND START SAVING FOR A BETTER LIFE!

Chapter 3

SAVINGS: SERVICES FOR THE CLIENTS OR CAPITAL FOR THE INSTITUTION?

Savings have risen to the top of the Microfinance community's agenda. Previously Microfinance Institutions (MFIs) viewed savings as a less important service than credit, and typically extracted savings from clients through compulsory systems. There was a prevalent and powerful perception that "the poor cannot save", thus compulsory savings systems often required members to deposit small token amounts each week and levied more substantial amounts at source from loans . Evidence from the remotest of Bangladeshi villages and indeed from all over the world suggests that the poor want to save, and indeed <u>are</u> saving in a wide variety of ways. What has been lacking until very recently among most MFIs in Bangladesh are the facilities to allow the poor to save in a way that helps them to meet their current needs and opportunities, as well as to save for the future. The large MFIs have instead concentrated on providing credit facilities at the lowest sustainable interest rates, and on capturing compulsory savings in order to do so.

There is a clear preference amongst the poor for voluntary, open-access savings, although compulsory minimum weekly deposits (particularly when they are client-defined) are also often welcomed since they provide savings discipline and an opportunity to safeguard savings from "trivial" spending. This preference, when met with flexible and responsive savings facilities, can result in large-scale savings mobilisation. However, the larger, longer established MFIs in Bangladesh have resisted introducing voluntary, open-access savings facilities since they have used compulsory, locked-in savings as loan collateral and a source of capital. Nonetheless, voluntary, open-access savings schemes can generate much more net savings per client per year (and thus greater capital for the MFI) than compulsory, locked-in savings schemes ... and provide a useful and well used facility for clients while doing so. As a result MFIs' compulsory, locked-in savings systems have come under increasing pressure not only from the professionals involved with financing, managing and reviewing MFIs and but also from the clients themselves. This is driven by the fact that, in the words of Marguerite Robinson (1995), "There is substantial evidence from many parts of the world that: (1) institutional savings services that provide the saver with security, convenience, liquidity and returns, represent a crucial financial service for lower-income clients; and (2) if priced correctly, savings instruments can contribute to institutional self-sufficiency and to wide market coverage."

Effective (but not restrictive) regulatory systems and (ideally) depositor protection schemes should be in place to provide security for the introduction of large-scale savings mobilisation schemes. The basis and options for such schemes are described. With such safeguards in place, MFIs that believe in serving the poor (and particularly the risk- and credit- averse poorest) and in generating indigenous capital funds, should move ahead with the development of voluntary, open-access, savings facilities. For open access to hard-earned savings, is not just a human right, it also makes business sense.

> *"As one villager commented, "My investment opportunities are not the same throughout the year. I need a place to store money safely while I look for the right openings"" (Robinson, 1994).*

INTRODUCTION

Professor Yunus has consistently (including recently at the MicroCredit Summit in Washington, February 1997), argued that "credit is a human right". What has been often over-looked by many Microfinance Institutions (MFIs) programmes operating compulsory, "locked-in" savings systems, is that savings, and particularly open-access to savings, is also a human right. And that voluntary, open-access savings also make business sense. This chapter examines: 1. whether there is a demand for voluntary open-access saving services amongst MFI clients and 2. the implications for the capitalisation of MFIs if they were to make these services available.

Recently savings have risen to the top of the international development community's agenda. There has been a sudden realisation of, and interest in, the savings side of savings and credit systems. Previously MFIs viewed savings as the poor relation, Vogel's (1984) "forgotten half", and typically extracted savings from clients through compulsory systems. There was a prevalent and powerful perception that "the poor cannot save", thus compulsory savings systems often required members to deposit small token amounts each week and levied more substantial amounts at source from loans. These compulsory savings were then often "locked-in" until (or in the case of Grameen Bank until 1995, even if) members left the organisation - thus denying them access to their own money. Until recently, compulsory, locked-in savings systems, in one form or other, were an extremely prevalent model throughout Asia, and the dominant one in Bangladesh (which we examine in detail below).

However, these compulsory, locked-in savings systems came under increasing pressure not only from the professionals involved with financing, managing and reviewing MFIs but also from the clients themselves. The Consultative Group to Assist the Poorest (CGAP) in its Note 2 of October 1995 stressed "Possibly the greatest challenge in microenterprise finance is to expand the provision of savings services to the poor." This is driven by the fact that, in the words of Marguerite Robinson (1995), "There is substantial evidence from many parts of the world that: (1) institutional savings services that provide the saver with security, convenience, liquidity and returns, represent a crucial financial service for lower-income clients; and (2) if priced correctly, savings instruments can contribute to institutional self-sufficiency and to wide market coverage."

But for MFIs with a history of credit-driven services, which have levied compulsory savings as part of the package, the shift to flexible financial services including (even stressing) savings products is often hard to effect. Staff can take time to make the transition from enforcing compulsory savings to encouraging voluntary savings, as Banco Caja Social (BCS), Columbia (and many, others making this difficult transformation in business practices) have found out. "The shift from a forced to a voluntary savings model is still not reflected in the practical, daily work of branch staff. Some branches are still reluctant to sell voluntary savings products and prefer to offer a credit + savings package. To some degree, this is due to the long tradition of using forced savings as an entry ticket for credit ..." (GTZ, 1997a).

Nonetheless, once the shift is made, the rewards for both the MFI and its clients are immense. Bank Rakyat Indonesia (BRI), with which Marguerite Robinson has worked for over a decade, has mobilised over $ 2.7 billion in voluntary savings through 16.1 million savings accounts and provides services to 30% of Indonesia's households. And BRI <u>does</u> attract the poor: a 1993 BRI study found that over 30% of BRI members had a monthly income of $78 or less (now, after the Rupiah's fall, substantially less). At any time, for every borrower, there are five savers, and their savings provide the capital for all of BRI's loans. To achieve this extraordinarily level of market penetration and capitalisation BRI offers three savings facilities:

1. The liquid which permits unlimited number of withdrawals,
2. The semi-liquid with a restricted number of withdrawals per month, and
3. The fixed deposit.

These products were developed on the basis of research on savings motives and preferences of rural people that demonstrated that a savings facility should combine:

1. Safety/security,
2. Convenience,
3. Liquidity, and
4. Positive return (GTZ, 1997b).

Thus as with traditional banking, these facilities offer clients the opportunity to balance liquidity and returns.

The SANASA Thrift and Credit Cooperative Societies in Sri Lanka offer both open access accounts and higher interest term deposits. These have proved successful not only at providing a service that is much in demand and mobilising savings from which SANASA can make loans, but also in meeting the needs and optimising the participation of the very poor. Richard Montgomery (1995) argues that SANASA's flexible repayment terms, open access savings facilities and instant consumption loans provide vitally important coping mechanisms for the poor in times of stress. Indeed it is this flexibility of financial facilities offered by SANASA that allows it to attract the poorest as clients. But as we shall see, the same arguments may well be applicable to Bangladesh.

Certainly Todd (1996) notes in her Tangail-based research, "Several women in the control group who did not even have enough to eat, amazed me during the year by producing "secret savings" and investing them in assets."

SOME DETAILED ANALYSIS FROM BANGLADESH

In Bangladesh - largely as a function of the all-pervasive influence of the Grameen Bank system - until recently most NGOs were implementing systems that involved compulsory savings that were then locked-in and only available to clients when they renounced their membership and left the organisation. Details of the Grameen Bank and BRAC systems and commentary on the results and implications of these are attached at the end of the chapter as Appendix 1.

THE CLIENTS' PERSPECTIVE: ABILITY AND DESIRE TO SAVE

The importance the poor attach to savings is also demonstrated by the many (and often costly) ways they find to save. These include investing in assets that can be sold in emergency (for example corrugated iron sheets or livestock), lending between family and friends, or even by taking a loan from an MFI. Stuart Rutherford argues that such loans are often "advances against savings" (see box below).

Loans as Advances Against Savings
(an important digression)

When Rubhana bought the calf with her first loan, she knew it would be a struggle. Not only would she have to find the Tk. 70[1] for the weekly repayments, but also she would have to buy food for the calf so that it grew and fattened quickly. But by taking a little more care with the meagre household budget, and selling the eggs from their few chickens, she felt that she could manage. Feroza was confident that, if by the grace of God, her husband was well enough to cycle his rickshaw throughout the year, she could pay off the loan she had used to buy jewellery for her daughter's wedding, and a few sheets of corrugated iron to replace the leaking thatch on their home. (Of course,

contd·

---

[1] Tk. 44 : US$ 1

Continued from Loans as Advances

---

she had told the NGO's field worker that she was using the loan for "rickshaw business" to keep him happy.)

Rubhana and Feroza share one thing in common with millions of other MFI members throughout Bangladesh, they are making their weekly loan repayments not from income arising from the loan, but from the normal family household income. This pattern is extremely common not least of all because of the typical MFI repayment schedules. These schedules normally require 50 weekly instalments (no grace period), and thus require investments that generate an immediate and rapid rate of return if repayments are to be made from the enterprise's income. Therefore, savings from household income are usually the primary source of the money used to make loan repayments.

Thus loans can, and indeed should, be seen as "advances against savings". And when they are seen as such, the ability of the poor to save, and the latent demand for savings becomes even clearer.

Despite the clear importance of undertaking market research to optimise MFI's systems and financial services, work to examine the client's perspective has been extremely limited in Bangladesh. Extensive discussions with clients on savings and perceptions of BURO, Tangail's savings facilities held as part of the Wright et al. study (1997), provided some interesting insights.

The Wright et al study (1997) showed that for women, saving (making *shonchoi*) is now very closely identified with membership of an NGO, to the point of being almost synonymous with it. Other forms of saving such as saving at home in bamboo or clay "banks" or by forming user-owned *samities* are now either discontinued or seen as trivial or second-best; the temptation to spend savings kept at home was repeatedly cited as a problem. Almost all older women confirmed that before the NGOs came they saved at home (and sometimes in local *samities*). Some younger women said that before the NGOs came they did not think about or understand savings and that the NGOs had taught them.

Virtually every woman denied that they or their fellow-members "save only to get loans". Several said they joined BURO, Tangail to save and later found themselves facing needs or opportunities that made the option to borrow useful. (It is interesting note that only half of

Shamima, Rokeya and Anwora all agreed, they had always made savings by putting aside a few taka from the sale of eggs and fruit - after all "a good wife saves". The savings had been useful for school fees, clothes and other small-scale expenses. Before they had kept their savings in clay money banks - shaped like fish - but there was always the temptation not to put money in, or to take some out for little treats for the children or visiting guests.

But Rubia and Nurjahan disagreed, they had not saved before: Rubia because she "had no place to save", and Nurjahan, because she "did not think about saving". They all liked BURO, Tangail's savings account system, the ability to withdraw their savings and the discipline of having to save each week. "Now we save more, much more", they chorused.

BURO, Tangail's members are borrowing at any one time, although almost all of them choose to do so at one stage or another - in response to need or opportunity).

Minu smiled confidently and assured us that "everyone" is saving more these days, and that this is "part of the progress and development in the whole area". People are busy buying cows, raising poultry and working hard - almost everyone is in an NGO group.

Considerable sensitivity to interest rates was expressed by many respondents, and they are aware of the different rates. Several pointed out that NGO rates on savings fall well below what can be obtained in the village from lending out. There is a good case for a MFI experimenting with a relatively high interest rate on a liquid savings scheme, even if that means maintaining loan interest rates at a high level. In such a scheme, more members might save and fewer borrow: good for them as it would lower their costs and their risk levels, and raise their self-reliance; good for the MFI because it would earn more from fewer loans.

Savings was, and largely still is, seen as a female activity. As such its source is associated with traditionally female occupations such as poultry raising or other *bari*-based production, and the use of savings is often associated with female-controlled work such as child rearing: the most common use cited for savings was schooling costs. This view is shared by men, women and school children. One group of women laughed outright at the suggestion that men could save out of their earnings. This may reflect the men's partiality to tea and cigarettes, films and cards, or may mean that saving is still seen as a small-scale matter. Before the NGOs came women saved at home in sums up to Tk. 500 or perhaps Tk. 1,000. Now, they do not appear to be unhappy with the fairly small size of their NGO savings balances. However, with open access savings facilities there is some suggestion that this may be changing.

Using savings as more than a store for trivial amounts of "female" money is giving way (in some households) to using savings as part of a household-wide strategy for economic growth. This represents a challenge and an opportunity for often female-focused MFIs to attract potentially larger "male" savings.

> *Hashimon is a poor BURO, Tangail member from Sit Kazipur village. She and her husband have agreed on a plan. She saves heavily out of energetically-pursued poultry keeping and, though they have two small sons, she saves from Tk. 30 to Tk. 50 a week regularly and has built up a large balance. She has taken two loans (Tk. 2,500 and Tk. 4,000) which he uses for trading in rickshaw parts and he repays these from his normal income from rickshaw riding.*
>
> *The idea is that they will soon stop taking loans and rely instead on savings regularly drawn down on and replenished. She has an unusual record as a saver - once, before the NGOs, she saved as much as Tk. 3,000 over three years at home in a clay bank. Her neighbours in this very poor-looking bari see her as something of a role model and are proud of her. They told me she is "doing something new". They do not see her as a miser, she says, "rather they praise me".*

The study showed that the more typical uses of the members' most recent savings withdrawal can be grouped into "quality of life" uses (household consumption, improving housing and health care - 38%), investments (acquiring land, expansion of business activity and education - 31%) and social (marriage and other functions and acquiring gold/jewellery - 16%). Only 7% used the withdrawal to make a loan repayment. In contrast, the members had planned to use their savings in a markedly different manner. 50% of the members planned to use savings for social purposes, 30% for investments, and 13% did not know.

In a subsequent study of BURO, Tangail's operations research programme (which is looking at introducing new even more flexible financial services), Rutherford and Hossain (1997) note that, "Depositing spare cash in a safe home like BURO, Tangail protects savings from trivial uses and the demands of children, husbands, neighbours and relatives, and provides some profit too. This is important for women mainly because in Bangladesh culture the maintenance of the household (including the ability to produce cash out of the air when an emergency strikes, and the ability to contribute to known bulk expenditures like a daughter's marriage) falls on women's shoulders."

THE CLIENTS' PERSPECTIVE: COMPULSORY VS. VOLUNTARY SAVINGS

From the above analysis, it would appear that the poor require little compulsion to save ... they simply want a reasonable mechanism to do so, and (as we shall see below) the assurance that they can access those savings when they need them. Indeed, there is evidence that compulsory savings, particularly those that are deducted from the loans issued, are simply viewed by clients as part of the cost of the credit. Indeed, it seems clear that the common system of compulsory deduction of 4 or 5% from the loan at source is almost universally disliked by clients (PromPT, 1996).

Nonetheless, until recently Grameen Bank, and many MFIs following its principles and modified versions of its *modus operandi*, assured everyone that members liked the compulsory savings schemes since the schemes allow them to set aside funds for longer run purposes, for insurance against emergencies or as a provision for old age (Jackelen and Rhyne, 1990 and Lovell, 1992). One is tempted to observe that well designed open access savings accounts and contractual savings agreement schemes[2] could give the clients the *option* of setting these funds aside.

---

[2] Contractual savings agreements (CSA), commit clients to save a specified amount, every specified period, for a specified number of periods in return for a pre-determined pay out on successful completion of the CSA. Thus for example a woman with a 14 year old daughter that she expects to marry off at 19 years of age might undertake a CSA to save 10 Taka a week for five years in return for a lump sum of 3,500 Taka on successful completion of the CSA.

Weekly compulsory savings schemes seem to be more acceptable to the clients (particularly when the amount to be saved is client-defined and the savings accounts are open access - see below), since they enforce a discipline of saving. Indeed, the discipline of <u>having</u> to find a specified small amount each week or month is not only valued in Grameen Bank-inspired schemes, it is the basis of Rotating Savings and Credit Associations (ROSCAs), savings clubs and many other more traditional indigenous schemes throughout the world (Miracle et al., 1980). For a description of 58 varieties of financial service systems for the poor see Rutherford, 1996a. Of course, once again, this need could also be met by voluntary contractual savings agreement schemes.

But clients also greatly value facilities that allow them to save <u>more</u> than the minimum compulsory amount whenever they have disposable lump sums (a not so uncommon occurrence in poor households, on the sale of assets - livestock etc., after harvest and so on). When BURO, Tangail increased their maximum weekly savings deposit from Tk. 50 to Tk. 200 at the weekly meeting, and unlimited deposits at the branch, this facility was welcomed by the clients who noted that it suited the real cash-flows of poor people, and (as Rutherford and Hossain (1997) observe) makes BURO, Tangail more popular than its competitors (banks and the many other NGOs operating in Tangail).

THE CLIENTS' PERSPECTIVE: OPEN ACCESS V. LOCKED—IN SAVINGS

In years up to 1996, Grameen and BRAC members became increasingly vocal about their dissatisfaction with the denial of access to their savings, and many mature members were leaving the organisations in order to realise their (often substantial) compulsory savings. By the end of 1995, there was a widespread strike among Grameen Bank members in Tangail District in support of demands for access to their locked-in "Group Funds" (generated through compulsory savings). The financial consequences of this strike were profound. According to an unpublished Grameen Bank internal report (1996), in Tangail District there were nearly 60,000 general loanees with repayments more than 25 weeks overdue, and the cumulative un-repaid amount had climbed to over Tk. 82 million or $ 2 million. In 1995, Khan and Chowdhury noted that nearly 57% of membership discontinuation in BRAC's programme is attributed to the lack of access to group savings during emergencies.

In 1993, BRAC introduced a savings experiment in ten branches, which were instructed to introduce open access or "current" accounts for

---

Evidence from City Slums
(Wright and Ahmed, 1992)

In the words of one of Concern's Chittagong group member, "Before, our economic situation was very bad as we had debts with others. Now, when we need to, we can take money from our group savings, and meet our needs."

The poor value the opportunity to make regular savings extremely highly, as one Action Aid group member explained: "In a poor family, it is not possible to save regularly, but because of the shomiti's system, and group pressure, we are now saving regularly."

Action Aid members planned to use their savings for the acquisition of tangible assets (56%), and for health and education (19%). A recurrent aspiration among members was buy land and/or a house in the village. This was seen as the best security available in an uncertain economic climate, and was not generally motivated by romantic notions of pastoral life, or the desire to leave the city slums behind.

Concern - Mirpur members planned to use their savings for the acquisition of tangible assets (36%), and for meeting their HSD housing purchase instalments and other emergency payments (24%). This reflected the prevalent concern among all group members in the camp, to maintain the HSD instalment schedule and to amass savings to pay the final registration fee that would give them ownership of their houses in 7-9 years time. Members also planned to use their savings to meet health and education expenses (14%), to extend business activity (13%) and to meet social obligations (11%).

Concern - Chittagong members planned to use their savings for the acquisition of tangible assets (39%), business activity (22%), and to meet social obligations (17%)

---

the members. The design and implementation of the experiment was not rigorous enough to draw any operational conclusions, but an indisputable finding of the study was that the clients greatly valued the scheme. "The Village Organisation members' attitudes towards BRAC

... have significantly improved due to this new facility" and "The villagers on the whole stressed that they would prefer that BRAC maintain an open savings account even if it meant that lower interest was paid on deposits ..." (Zaman et al., 1994) Indeed, the authors of a follow-up study assert, not to allow members open access to their savings "runs counter to the fundamental organisational goal of BRAC" — the empowerment of the poor (Deeba and Ara, 1995).

THE MICROFINANCE INSTITUTION'S PERSPECTIVE

> *"By insisting on savings, "new wave" micro-finance institutions screen out some potential defaulters, build up individuals' financial security, increase funds available for lending, and develop a degree of identification with the financial health of the institution among members." (Rogaly, B., 1996)*

So why had powerful and poor-sensitive institutions such as Grameen Bank and BRAC persisted with locked-in savings systems in the face of the clearly expressed desires of the very members they were serving ?

The answer lay in institutional financing needs and an erroneous assumption: Grameen and BRAC faced the apparent dilemma confronting all of the larger MFIs in Bangladesh. By the end 1995 Grameen Bank members had generated a cumulative Group Fund savings of $ 105.4 million, or over 70% of the value of all grants received from donor and other institutions, and were meeting a very important part of Grameen Bank's capital requirements (Grameen Bank, 1996).

And in the words of the BRAC savings study, "However pertinent it may sound to have a differentiated savings scheme with a provision for complete withdrawal access, at present it is not feasible for BRAC to operate in such a way due to the interdependence of savings and credit programmes, and the operations of the Revolving Loan Fund. In BRAC Rural Credit Programme members' savings partially serve as an insurance mechanism against loan default. Furthermore, BRAC relies on members' savings for its Revolving Loan Fund" (Deeba and Ara, 1995).

Not only had the locked-in "Group Fund" savings acted as *de facto* loan guarantee reserves (although this is formally covered though Emergency Fund contributions in many MFIs) but also years of enforced group savings had allowed the larger MFIs to develop a huge capital fund for their lending operations. It was feared that allowing open access withdrawal of those savings could result in massive outflows of funds as the members use these large balances - possibly in preference to taking loans.

And Grameen Bank's initial experience in Tangail, where they experienced a massive outflow of funds when they finally relented and allowed members to withdraw their locked-in savings, would seem to confirm this (see Appendix 1 for a description of this). But we should not lose sight of the build-up to the change in policy that allowed members the right to withdraw from their substantial Group Fund savings: a right won after years of protest and, in Tangail, a strike during which many groups did not meet. It may take a while for the members' confidence to be rebuilt. Informal discussions with the Pathorail Branch Manager in late 1997 suggested that both confidence and the members' savings were indeed returning (personal field notes, 1997).

In view of the demand for access to Group Funds, in 1995 BRAC introduced loans-against-savings schemes very similar in nature to that of the Grameen Bank Group Fund (which to its credit, Grameen has always operated). These schemes allowed members to make a limited number of withdrawals from their own savings subject to the usual rigorous weekly loan repayment conditions. Such schemes are unlikely to attract those who want to save to buy capital items or fund children's education. Nor those who want open access to their savings in the event of emergencies or opportunities without the prospect of having to add another repayment instalment to their weekly household expenditure. (Indeed as early as 1988, Mahabub Hossain was finding it "difficult to understand why a large proportion of the Group Fund remains unused since the poor tend to be in constant need of credit"). The schemes are hardly the recipe for massive savings mobilisation or for meeting the needs of the members. But these loans-against-savings schemes had been developed more on the rationale of the MFIs' institutional necessity to secure and safeguard capital funds than on the members' needs or desires.

But the basis of the rationale that limited access to the Group Funds will indeed better secure the capitalisation of the MFIs in Bangladesh had not been adequately explored.

Wright et al. concluded in 1997 that "The programmes of BURO, Tangail suggest that voluntary open access savings <u>can</u> raise funds not dissimilar to those levied through the mainstream MFIs' compulsory savings schemes. And do so while offering an important service to the poor. Nonetheless, it also appears from BURO, Tangail's work from 1991-96[3] that:

a. the poor (quite rightly) take time to develop confidence in an organisation and its ability to repay savings - they like to see loans being made available on demand and to test the withdrawal facility to ensure that it operates as advertised. Banking is all about confidence; and

b. the very poor (for whatever reasons) have not become members to date.

However, BURO, Tangail's programme is not adequately established to see if <u>even more</u> savings will be mobilised as the members gain confidence in the system, or as it becomes more fully open access."

This conclusion was underlined and amplified by the remarkable upsurge in BURO, Tangail's annual savings deposits in 1996 and 1997, which jumped by 102% from US$ 111,425 in 1995 to US$ 224,974 in 1996 and by another 97% to US$ 442,440[4] as of December 31, 1997. Clearly, these figures are somewhat distorted by the rapid growth in BURO, Tangail's membership, which grew by 56.5% in 1996 to 32,744 as of December 31, 1996 and by a further 37.4% to 45,003 as of December 1997.

Detailed analysis of the ten oldest, more established branches (which experienced more limited (24.2%) membership growth in 1996 and 2.9% membership growth in 1997) demonstrates that all the indicators of savings activities have surged in 1996 and 1997. The net savings balance per member rose from Tk. 382 to Tk. 517 in 1996, and by another 64% to Tk. 848 in 1997. Furthermore the savings deposited during the year per member rose by a total of 126% from Tk. 247 in 1995 to Tk. 559 in 1997. The overall rise in savings deposits and net savings was spectacular, while the modest growth in withdrawals also shows the clients using the open-access facilities actively. (See the graph *BURO, Tangail: Savings over Time - First Ten Branches* below).

---

[3] To May 1996.

[4] Converted at the prevailing rate of: 1995 Tk. 40: US$1, 1996 Tk. 42: US$1 and 1997 Tk. 44: US$1

Effective April 1st 1998, BURO, Tangail took the final step and removed the requirement to have 15% of any loan taken deposited in the

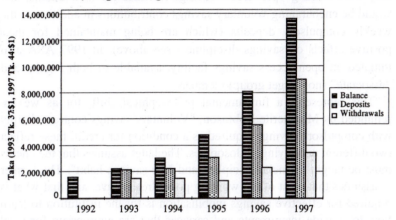

BURO, Tangail: Savings Over Time - First Ten Branches

loanees' savings accounts. With this, BURO, Tangail moved from a partially to a fully open-access system. Initially, as had been expected, members made large-scale withdrawals and total net savings in the ten oldest branches declined by 18% in April and a further 12% in May. The net balances increased marginally in June, before the advent of the floods in July (discussed in detail below) knocked savings down again. The large scale withdrawals in April and May reflected the members adjusting to and testing the completely open access system as Grameen and BRAC experienced during their experiments with such systems. By the end of the year there was an up surge in savings deposits and a dramatic reduction in withdrawals. In December 1998, despite the devastating floods, net savings in the oldest branches increased by 13% and was quickly moving the net savings position to its December 1997 level.

Thus it is fair to conclude that in its mature branches BURO, Tangail has indeed demonstrated that voluntary open-access savings schemes can mobilise <u>more</u> net savings (and thus capital) per member, per year, than compulsory locked-in savings schemes ... and provide a valued, and well used, financial service while doing so.

It was perhaps this realisation that has resulted in the predicted "beginning of a new era in Bangladesh when the large MFIs provide a wider range of financial services to a broader spectrum of people and thus improve the indigenous capitalisation of their systems" (Wright et al, 1997). In 1995 Grameen Bank, and in 1996 BRAC, announced that they were starting open-access savings facilities for their clients, and would be encouraging voluntary savings contributions in addition to the weekly compulsory deposits (which are being maintained for their positive effects on savings discipline - see above). In 1997 ASA also initiated an open access savings facility, available to both regular and "associate" (non target group) members.

This represents a fundamental philosophical shift, for as we are reminded by Marguerite Robinson, "Voluntary savings contrast sharply with compulsory savings required as a condition for credit; these reflect two different underlying philosophies. The latter assumes that the clients must be taught financial discipline and "the savings habit". The former ... assumes that most of the working poor already save, and that what is required for effective savings mobilisation is for the institution to learn how to provide instruments and services that are appropriate for local demand" (Robinson, 1995). And as noted above,   staff training, attitudes and practices, book-keeping and monitoring systems and many other aspects of the organisation must also change - a transformation that is not easy to effect.

Now that MFIs in Bangladesh have come to accept that there is a large scale of demand for open access savings facilities, we must ask "are MFIs in Bangladesh in a position to start mobilising voluntary savings from the public ?" In terms of the history and performance of many of the MFIs in Bangladesh, they are unquestionably organisationally capable, and now it seems they are ready to start with voluntary, open-access savings schemes. However in Bangladesh at present, despite many examples the precious savings of the poor being lost (usually through both benign incompetence but occasionally through criminal intent), there is no regulatory nor insurance mechanism to safeguard all the savings being mobilised. There is a clear need for the MFIs and others interested in the well-being of Microfinance in Bangladesh to be proactive in developing regulatory mechanisms and depositor protection schemes.

In the particular context of Bangladesh, the constant threat of natural disaster seemed to necessitate that MFIs work together to develop second tier re-financing arrangements. Disasters such as floods, cyclones or tornadoes were considered likely to result in a massive draw-down of open-access savings (indeed such emergency needs may be one of the most important motivations to save in open-access accounts). The MFI must be able to respond to this demand to draw-down savings in order to maintain the clients' trust and confidence in the institution, and were therefore considered to need re-financing support. Localised natural disasters seemed to present less of a threat to larger MFIs with nation-wide coverage (since they could simply move surplus savings from other unaffected areas), but were expected to have a profound impact on smaller district or thana-based MFIs. And there were fears that nation-wide disasters such as the 1987 and 1988 floods could place severe stress on even the largest MFIs now that they have moved to open access savings-based operations. These concerns were tested in practice by the 1998 floods which, according to the world Bank, were "the worst in living memory" and covered two thirds of Bangladesh for a period of nearly three months.

The results were surprising. Hassan Zaman's work on BRAC revealed, "Having [special and extraordinary] access to [half] their savings was welcome during the crisis but recourse to it was less than one would have expected. The reason for this is that clients know that larger savings deposits within BRAC means access to larger loans. Hence they perceive withdrawing money from their savings accounts as a de-facto interest-free loan as they may need to 're-deposit' some or all of the amount they withdrew in order to be eligible for the loan size that they require" (Zaman, 1999). BURO, Tangail with its completely open access savings accounts experienced a similar pattern of deposits and withdrawals.

As noted above, BURO, Tangail had already removed their requirement that 15% of the loan taken should be held in the members' savings account, thus the reaction of the members was an acid test of the durability of an open-access savings system under the stress of natural disaster. Furthermore, in contrast to many of the larger MFIs, BURO, Tangail remained open for business almost without interruption – even the extremely badly flood affected groups met regularly and transacted again after a suspension of activities of only three weeks. Surprisingly, a remarkably small proportion of the flood affected members' open access savings were withdrawn, and indeed deposits kept flowing in, albeit at a reduced rate.

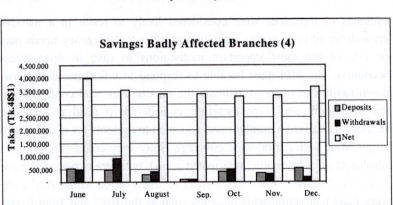

Savings: Badly Affected Branches (4)

In July, as the flood waters rose, in badly affected branches, withdrawals doubled to around 25% of the net savings balance, and in the same month savings deposits halved. In the areas unaffected by the floods, withdrawals also increased by about 34% and deposits also declined by 27%, probably suggesting that seasonal factors were influencing members' savings activities. Even in the most badly affected branches, savings deposits were exceeding withdrawals again by November, the month after the flood waters had finally receded. By December, monthly deposits had returned to their pre-flood levels and withdrawals had dropped to 6% of net savings balance – members were building their savings balances once again. These trends are shown in the graphs below drawn from a sample of data taken from four badly affected and the two unaffected branches.

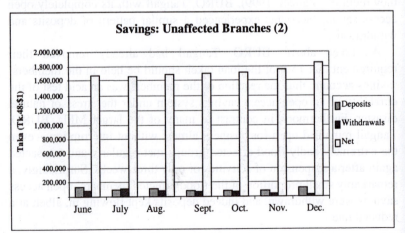

Savings: Unaffected Branches (2)

It is therefore reasonable to conclude that natural disasters have a smaller than hitherto expected impact on savings balances (a phenomenon also noted by CARE-Bangladesh in an informal communication on the Development finance Network in December 1998 and SafeSave in its monthly progress reports for 1998). This somewhat startling conclusion is also reflected in recent research conducted in Uganda where in response to crises, MFI clients preferred to run-down their trading stocks, sell assets or take informal loans from relatives in preference to making large-scale withdrawals from their savings accounts (see Wright et al. 1999).

REGULATION AND SUPERVISION

> *"The primary reason for ... covering microdebt institutions with regulation and supervision is to allow them to mobilize deposits. Now I'm all in favour of expanding the opportunities for more poor people to increase deposits, but I continue to be uneasy about an industry that is dominated by altruistic motives getting into deposit-taking. ... Allowing many NGOs to start mobilizing deposits may delay the collapse of many of these organisations, but it will also augment the costs of the ultimate collapse, especially the costs imposed on poor depositors"* *(Dale Adams on the on-line DevFin Discussion Group at Ohio State University 1998).*

DEFINITION OF TERMS

"*Prudential financial regulation* refers to the set of general principles or legal rules that aim to contribute to the stable and efficient performance of financial institutions and markets. These rules represent constraints placed on the actions of financial intermediaries to ensure the safety and soundness of the system" (Chaves and Gonzalez-Vega, 1994).

Thus financial regulation should serve macroeconomic goals by ensuring the solvency and financial soundness of all financial institutions. In addition regulation should provide the client (in particular those making deposits) protection against excessive risks that may arise from failure, fraud, or opportunistic behaviour on the part of the financial service institution. Finally, regulation should also promote efficient performance of financial intermediaries and competitive markets.

"*Financial intermediary supervision* consists of the examination and monitoring mechanisms through which authorities verify compliance with and enforce either financial repression or prudential financial regulation. Supervision includes the specific procedures adopted in order to determine the risks faced by an intermediary and to review regulatory compliance" (Chaves and Gonzalez-Vega, 1994).

Financial intermediaries could put deposits at risk by, for example, investing in excessively risky loans at high interest rates. Savings deposits usually offer fixed interest rates, and so the owners of the financial institution would benefit and take the profits if the risky loans turn out well, but have only a limited exposure to the potential losses from the risky loans. The institution would simply go bankrupt and the owners would be able to walk away from the losses. This is referred to as *moral hazard.* Moral hazard is the incentive for someone who holds an asset belonging to another person to risk the value of that asset because the person holding the asset does not bear the full consequence of any loss.

In the case of MFIs, particularly those where neither the Executive Committees nor the Board of Directors have any substantial investment in the institution, there is clear moral hazard. In the event of poor repayment rates, it is the savings of the depositors (be they compulsory and locked-in or voluntary and open-access) that are at risk. Indeed arguably, the risk to depositor's savings is greater when they do not have access to withdraw those savings when they perceive that they are at risk

With ASA already mobilising savings from nearly a million members and "associate members", and BRAC and Grameen slowly moving towards taking the plunge to liberalise their savings facilities, the mountains are finally on the move. It is now more than high time to recognise the financial risk and introduce appropriate regulation and supervision of the MFIs in Bangladesh. The options are many and varied but the international debate is currently centred around a central bank-driven conventional view.

OPTIONS FOR REGULATION AND SUPERVISION — THE CONVENTIONAL VIEW

External regulation is but one of several important elements to create well-managed and permanent financial institutions. Elements of "self-regulation" are probably even more important as they are permanently imbedded within the institution's systems. Supervision should be undertaken by several different parties representing the interests of either shareholders, management, or the clients.

The main instruments of regulation and supervision are:

1. The *Executive Committee/Board of Trustees* (or in the case of publicly owned institutions, the Annual General Meeting) which meets to review the progress of the institution and its strategic planning;

2. The *Board of Directors* that establishes good business, financial, and risk management policies and procedures, and holds management accountable for the effective implementation of those policies;

3. The *internal controls and internal audit* department which operates to ensure that policies and procedures are implemented promptly and effectively;

4. *External auditors* who are knowledgeable and competent in Microfinance as an objective check on institution's policies, procedures and systems of control and audit to protect against fraud and mismanagement; and

5. *External supervision* by a central bank or its agent to ensure that management does not misuse its power to use depositors funds for its benefit and maintains industry standards (usually in terms of "CAMEL", Capital adequacy, Asset quality, Management capability/systems, Earnings ratios and Liquidity).

The authors argue that the regulatory environments in most countries need to be changed to transform their fragmented financial markets into cohesive continuums thus making it easier for MFIs to pursue a process of progressive institutional transformation.

In this context, Carpenter (1997), in her case study of Bangladesh laid out the options for regulation:

"Designing an appropriate regulatory framework requires consideration of several factors; the financial condition and structure of local micro-finance institutions; their roles within the financial services industry; and the capacity of the regulating entities to administer external regulation and supervision effectively.

With those factors in mind, the five main options for regulation include:

A Liability-Based Continuum of Mandatory Regulation

Van Greuning et al. (1998) of the World Bank's Financial Sector Development Department use an analysis of MFIs' liabilities to highlight distinguishing features of different types of MFIs and focus on risk-taking activities that need to be managed and regulated. A continuum of MFIs, these experts argue, can be classified into three categories. The authors propose thresholds of financial intermediation activities that would trigger a requirement for an MFI to satisfy external or mandatory regulatory guidelines:

1. MFIs that depend on other people's money (donor grants, small scale compulsory savings as loan collateral) to be self-regulated; and those that depend on other people's money (commercial paper and large certificates of deposit) to be regulated by Companies' Registry Agency, Bank Supervisory Authority or Securities and Exchange Agency.

2. MFIs that depend on (common bond) members' money to be regulated by the Cooperatives' Authority or Bank Supervisory Authority.

3. MFIs that leverage the public's money (savings deposits) to be regulated by Bank Supervisory Authority.

---

1. *No external regulation*: This is the current environment for most MFIs (and effectively for the Grameen Bank) and it has produced an innovative and strong micro credit industry in

Bangladesh. However, some regulatory oversight is needed now that MFIs are putting member's savings at greater risk.

2. *Self-regulation*: This would require individual MFIs to strengthen their institutions and share financial information on a consistent basis. For an MFI to regulate itself, it requires three elements: 1) an independent board with the technical expertise and authority to hold management accountable; 2) well-formulated and properly implemented internal control and risk management policies; and 3) high quality auditors who are educated about micro finance. Self-regulation is only possible if these three elements are combined with transparent disclosure.

3. *Hybrid approach of part self-regulation, part supervision by a third party*: Under this blended approach, MFIs would be held responsible for meeting higher standards of financial reporting and performance analysis, and the regulatory authorities would contract to a third party to monitor their compliance with those standards. For example, to ensure consistently presented financial information, the regulating entity could contract with an accounting or consulting firm to conduct routine financial audits of MFIs, including standardised financial presentation and ratio and trend analysis. Full disclosure would allow investors and depositors to make rational choices, however this presumes that they have choices of financial services providers.

4. *Regulation through the existing legal and regulatory framework*: MFIs could apply for a standard banking license if they met all requirements for a commercial bank, such as BRAC attempted to do in 1994. To date, the Bangladesh Bank has resisted granting bank charters to MFIs. Since some development financial institutions in other countries have thrived under the regulatory oversight imposed by commercial bank status, this option should be given greater consideration.

5. *Regulation through MFI-specific regulation*: Some countries have created a distinct legal status and regulation for non-bank MFIs, such as Bolivia and Peru ... In some cases, these institutions are supervised through a separate unit within the

central bank or delegated supervisory authority. In Bangladesh, this mechanism was used to create the Grameen Bank charter, but the central bank does not currently plan to use this approach again.

In general, the greater the financial risk and the more money at risk by depositors, the more important external regulations becomes to avoid what economists call "moral hazard" by management and owners. This suggests the need for separate tiers of regulation and supervision based on quantitative measures."

However, despite extensive efforts, few countries have been able to introduce appropriate and effective systems of regulation and supervision systems. It is time to consider the alternative options and approaches.

OPTIONS FOR REGULATION AND SUPERVISION — THE UNCONVENTIONAL VIEW

Increasingly Microfinance Institutions (MFIs) have come to recognise the need to provide savings services – both as a much valued service to their clients, and as a long-term source of capital that is more dependable (if a little more costly) than donor grants. In recognition of this significant shift from microcredit to microfinance, donors, microfinance gurus and increasingly central banks are expending a great deal of time and energy trying to dream up systems of regulation and supervision that will protect depositors' savings while allowing MFIs to take (and intermediate) deposits.

While recognising the need for some basic rules designed to maximise the security of deposits, on the face of it, it appears to be naively optimistic to think that a system of central bank regulation and supervision will secure poor people's deposits. In developing countries, central banks often struggle to regulate and supervise the urban-based commercial banking sector. In Kenya, Tanzania and Uganda, for example, the central banks each have typically little more than two dozen formal sector commercial banks to supervise, and despite this apparently limited task, there has been a series of bank collapses, often due to corrupt practices or mismanagement. The record in the developed world is marginally better, but hardly the model of security. The Bank of Credit for Commerce and Industry collapsed despite being under the strict regulations and supervision of the Bank of England, the Japanese banking sector is currently in turmoil despite the best efforts of the central bank, and few need reminding of the Savings and Loan scandal in the USA[5]. This latter case is instructive since the Savings and Loan institutions were subject to central bank regulation and supervision in one of the world's most technologically developed societies with one of the most sophisticated and comprehensive regulation and supervision

---

Bangladesh Bank: A Notable Exception

The central bank in Bangladesh is an important and illuminating exception to central bankers' entrenched obsession with regulating and supervising all financial institutions. The Bangladesh Bank has the vision and understanding to be extremely reticent about getting into regulation/supervision of the MFIs. The Bangladesh Bank has recognised three important issues that prohibit it (and indeed most) central banks from getting involved in the regulation/supervision of MFIs:

1. the poor state of the formal financial sector and the role the Bangladesh Bank is playing in the reform process leave little institutional capacity free to support this rapidly growing sector;

2. microfinance is radically different to the financial sector which Bangladesh Bank supervises and would require considerable resources to devise a supervisory framework; and

3. the sheer size of the microfinance sector in terms of number of institutions poses logistical problems for supervision.

In short, the Bangladesh Bank wants to focus on its central mandate and strengthening the formal financial sector – no small task.

---

systems, backed in turn by first class auditing companies. Some claim that the Savings and Loan scandal occurred because the savers' deposits were guaranteed by the government, and thus the owners of the Savings

---

[5] A lesser known statistic is the estimation that in the USA alone, around 2,000 banks have collapsed in the last 200 years.

and Loan institutions were less-risk averse and more willing to take on high-risk and high return investments – a case study in moral hazard. And one that cost each and every US tax payer about $2,000. Bert Ely, a US-based banking consultant, notes that moral hazard and information problems that make it impossible for government regulators to price deposit insurance efficiently (J.D. Von Pishke- personal communication).

Despite this sub-optimal record, the donors and developed country-based microfinance gurus seem intent on developing central bank-driven systems of regulation and supervision. It is ironic to think that central banks struggling to supervise a handful of commercial banks should be expected to supervise dozens of small-scale MFIs. One cannot help but worry that the central banks, lacking the resources and capability to supervise the formal commercial banking sector, might be stretched beyond reasonable limits if required to supervise large numbers of MFIs running a business for which central bankers usually have scant regard, and of which they have less understanding. But conversations with many central bankers reveal that they view it as their sacred mandate to protect depositors and avoid systemic risk ... and so they believe, the central bank must be involved.

Donors, defensive and risk averse by nature, would hate to be associated with poor people losing their savings, and therefore seek the most conservative approach – usually some form of government deposit guarantee which in turn "necessitates" central bank regulation and supervision. For some strange reason the gurus of microfinance have chosen to support this approach. One cannot believe that the fact that they are (generally) based in developed countries blinds them to the short-comings of developing countries' central banks, and even if it did, the history of supervision by central banks in their own countries scarcely inspires confidence.

The result of the coalition of sophisticated-system gurus, risk-averse donors and control-concerned central bankers has been a strange paralysis ... for few, if any, central banks have been able to develop appropriate regulations and systems of supervision – they remain a dream. Endless research has been conducted, study-tours and participatory workshops have been held and earnest papers have been produced, but progress has been limited. And the poor have been left hanging, waiting for the day when they might be allowed to access to savings services.

The need, desire and capability of the poor to save is increasingly well documented (e.g. Miracle and Cohen, 1980; Adams and Fitchett, 1992; Steel and Aryeetey, 1994; Rutherford, 1998; Wright et al.,1997; and Rutherford, 1999). The need for MFIs to offer credit and savings

---

Informal Self Regulation: RoSCAs and Other Savings Clubs

The informal sector is, by definition unregulated ... at least in the formal sense. However, it is important and possibly even instructive, to note that RoSCAs and many other types of savings clubs (for example Christmas clubs) have a built-in and extremely efficient system of self-regulation. These savings and loans systems are time-bound and self-liquidating. That is to say that people (usually informally) contract to participate in the association or club for a specified cycle, and on completion of that cycle they are free to join the next cycle or to opt out. Successful, well-managed RoSCAs and savings clubs generally continue and start a follow-on cycle, but members are unlikely to re-join poorly-managed associations and clubs, and particularly those from which they did not recover their savings.

---

services is also well documented (e.g. Robinson, 1994; Otero and Rhyne, 1994; Wright et al. 1997; and Hannig and Wisniski, 1999). But the quest for perfect security of deposits prevents these two complimentary needs from meeting and resolving. And so the poor are forced to rely on (unregulated) cost-ineffective, often insecure and unreliable, systems to save. These include roving savings collectors who often charge 3% a month to provide the service; livestock that must be fed, housed and protected from illness; jewellery and hidden stores of money held in the home that must be secreted from thieves and marauding family members; and RoSCAs that provide an efficient but inflexible and limited savings mechanism.

Perhaps the time is to learn from the anarchy of benign neglect in Bangladesh where hundreds of unregulated and unsupervised NGOs are offering savings services with impunity. In this environment many poor people <u>have</u> lost their savings either to incompetence or fraud (as they have in many regulated and supervised environments) ... but they still keep looking for safe MFIs which will offer them savings services. Now the poor of Bangladesh are increasingly coming to recognise MFIs which have been operating in the area for a long time, or who are well

---

One Alternative: A Savings Guarantee Foundation

In the light of the Bangladesh Bank's enlightened reticence to get involved in supervising MFIs, Henry Jackelen has suggested an innovative approach. He proposes a "Savings Guarantee Foundation" with the central purpose of to certify organisations and provide financial backing to guarantee client deposits. To obtain this guarantee organisations would pass through an intrusive review of their operations and would also have to be continually monitored. Certified organisations would be required to pay an insurance premium for this service. Two basic types of guarantees would be provided: i) certifying that NGOs place the amounts raised from clients in identifiable accounts in banks and are not used for on lending, or ii) for NGOs deemed to have appropriate capacity - certifying that the financial condition, lending policies, procedures and management of the institution are of a quality acceptable to use member savings in on-lending activities.

---

known in the country, and are entrusting their savings to these institutions in preference to the small lesser known NGOs. The market, information dissemination and brand recognition are working ...

But it is time to recognise that central bank regulation and supervision systems are only attempts at oversight of the issues at the core of deposit-security: ownership, governance and management. Perhaps we should seek to define a regulatory framework that sets very basic requirements in terms of capital adequacy, asset quality, management systems, earnings and liquidity (CAMEL). If these basic standards are met, and the MFI has a clear ownership and effective governance structure, it should be entitled to offer savings services to its clients – without the backing of a deposit guarantee scheme or the supervision of central banks.

Ownership and Governance
(from Carpenter, J., 1997)

There are several key components of clear and effective ownership and governance systems. These include the following:

Involved outside investors and a for-profit structure creates an important group of stakeholders: shareholders. This group complements management and staff, the board, and the clients by focusing on the bottom line and the health of their capital investment in the organisation. For NGOs an "equity-equivalent" investment for an NGO might be a long-term subordinated debt instrument with equity-like terms, or other instruments that might attract private investors. The right "investors" will probably bring value to the organisation through access to financial resources, some protection from government interference, and management experience from a like-minded financial institution.

Although NGO-MFIs often have weak boards and dominant executive directors, a strong Board of Directors, with appropriate representation of the investors, is a central component of an effective governance system. Boards should identify competent managers, approve strategies and policies for business activities, risk management and internal controls, and should hold management accountable for implementing those policies. Boards should set clear and measurable goals, monitor the progress towards these, and confront weaknesses or short-comings where and when they are detected. Finally, Boards must also be able to regulate themselves, to maintain continuity while ensuring renewal and a constant process of self-evaluation. Boards should focus on the big picture, yet be aware of details so they can identify potential problems. Board members should be drawn primarily from the private sector, including resource people who complement management's skills. By thinking of themselves as the stewards of the MFI's capital, board members can assume greater responsibility to

contd·

Continue from Ownership and Governance

identify organisational development and strategic priorities. Board representation by clients may keep the organisation focused on the end-customer, but those representatives are unlikely to push the MFI to address financial and organisational issues. (See also Rock, Otero and Salzman, 1998 for an excellent discussion of the role of Boards).

A frequent criticism of MFIs is the questionable accuracy or completeness of their financial statements and reporting. Preparing consistent, transparent and high-quality financial statements, following generally accepted accounting principles and with transparent recording of transactions among and between subsidiaries will enhance the credibility of MFIs with clients, investors and funders. In support of this and to protect the institution, its assets and the interests of its clients, MFIs should invest in high-quality annual audits from a reputable firm with microfinance experience. While many organizations view audits as an annual review of the numbers and a rubber stamp on accounting practices, a good auditor and accountant can add significant value to MFIs with appropriate performance measures and tracking systems.

Another Alternative: Guatemala Credit Union Rating Agency

The Guatemala Credit Union movement is working with the World Council of Credit Unions (WOCCU) and the Consultative Group to Assist the Poorest to develop a private organisation to act as a rating or certification agency. This agency will train, qualify and monitor auditors to review participating Credit Unions (who will pay for the service) to ensure that they comply with standards based on the existing PEARLS system (WOCCU's equivalent of the CAMEL system). In addition, the agency will maintain a watch list of Credit unions showing signs of problems and will expect the management of these Credit Unions to prepare and negotiate remedial action plans. Credit Unions who pass certification will be permitted to display the agency's logo of certification (which will be heavily marketed as part of the system). Credit Unions who fail to maintain the standards will have their certification and the right to display the logo withdrawn.

But, in addition to clear ownership and effective governance, there should be at least two other requirements to ensure that clients are fully aware of risk they are facing while seeking to minimise that risk. Firstly the MFI must be required to inform its clients, with clarity and regularity, that their savings are not secured by government guarantee and that the security of their deposits depends on the strength of the institution: its governance, management and the quality of its loan portfolio. These are issues over which, particularly in the case of user-owned and managed organisations, clients have some degree of control. Indeed, in their review of six MFIs of 19th century Europe, Hollis and Sweetman, (1998) argue that "MO [microcredit organisations] with depositors benefited from having interested parties overseeing their operations and withdrawing their deposits when problems began to

---

Yet Another Alternative: Market-Driven Deposit Insurance

Those in quest of a system that does indeed provide deposit insurance for the poor might be attracted by J.D. Von Pishke's proposal (based on a decade of work by Bert Ely). Von Pishke (forthcoming) proposes a system that requires:

1. that all deposits to be insured;
2. that any suitably insured institution be allowed offer deposit services;
3. that the insurer must be a bank doing business in the country concerned;
4. that the insurer have extensive reinsurance; and
5. that some of the reinsurance be off-shore and in hard currency.
6. the role of the state is to define the minimum acceptable insurance contract, to ensure that the parties concerned have the capacity to undertake the obligations, and to ascertain that the parties have appropriate legal standing for enforcement against them.

This market driven insurance scheme is expected to result in a variety of contracts, market-based premiums reflecting insurers' views of risk, and a dispersion of risk. And private insurance would concentrate more on leading indicators (policies, standards and systems) and less on lagging indicators (My God! They're broke. Let's close 'em).

emerge. Depositors provided information on, and monitored, borrowers, and performed administrative tasks in some instances". Secondly, accounting companies need to be trained to audit MFIs and their systems, to review their ownership and governance structures, and to verify the MFIs' compliance with the basic CAMEL requirements. These auditing companies would then be required by law to report on the individual MFIs' compliance with the CAMEL standards to an MFI apex organisation responsible for coordinating and overseeing MFIs' activities. Working together with the member MFIs, this apex authority

---

And Another: A Voluntary Register

Stuart Rutherford has proposed an ingenious scheme for helping the poor better assess the risks they face as they choose to entrust their precious savings to MFIs. The scheme centres round a voluntary register, backed by rule of law. It would work like this:

1. An institution (in Bangladesh the Credit and Development Forum, the MFIs' trade association is proposed) would open a register of MFIs wishing to mobilise deposits. However, the institution would have absolutely no say in whether or not any particular MFI is allowed to register, and absolutely no say whatsoever in what the MFIs chooses to write in its registration document.

2 In the registration document the MFI will give details about itself. Its name, its address, the names of its owners and of its backers, its area of operation, and its resources, its financial products, and so on.

3. It will also have to state on what basis aggrieved parties could make a case against the MFI in the eventuality that it failed to honour deposits that it had accepted. For example, it might give the name and address of some immovable property that it would be willing to be confiscated.

4. The MFI would then be obliged to hand out a copy of its registration document, in easy local language, to every single one of its clients. It would also be obliged to distribute copies of the document to any member of the general public who wanted one. There would also be copies displayed at the local government offices.

5. In this way, clients would be able to compare one MFI with another, and to estimate the balance of risk and benefit represented by 'their' MFI. Unregistered MFIs would, it is hoped, lose business.

As Rutherford notes, to be effective and useful, the voluntary register must be *accurate, up-to-date, simple, clear, and accessible.*

would then publicise MFIs' annual compliance/non-compliance in a very simplified format (perhaps with a system of zero-five star accreditation plaques) – not only at a national level, but also at a local level in the areas where the individual MFIs are working.

This type of system would not be perfect, but nor would any. This type of system would not ensure that no poor people lose their savings, but the system recognises that central banks have neither the capacity nor, as often as not, the will to supervise MFIs. That recognition might just allow the microfinance industry to wake from its dream of finding the perfect system of regulation and supervision, and the resulting inertia. For it is this inertia that is, on balance, more likely to hurt the poor, by depriving them of relatively low-risk savings services and offering only loans that put them into debt. In the long run this inertia will also hurt the MFIs since they lose the opportunity to provide high-quality financial services to their clients and to raise capital by doing so. As Hollis and Sweetman (1998) observe, "depositor-based MOs tend to last longer and serve *many* more borrowers than MOs financed by donations or government loans"

However, it is worth noting that the argument that savings services that are not backed by deposit guarantees and central bank supervision are dangerous for the poor and therefore should be discouraged is akin to arguing that cars are dangerous and therefore should be banned. We are all willing to take risks when we believe that the potential benefits make the risk-taking worthwhile – this is a decision that the poor need to be allowed to make for themselves.

Approaches offering accreditation plaques/certificates or a voluntary register further empower poor people with information on which to make their own decisions – on whether, where and how to save, and with a chance of understanding the associated risk. They are then in a position to evaluate the risks and compare them with those that imperil savings held in the home.

"Savings are important to all of us - more important than loans. Before I used to try to save a few paisa in the house, but we always spent it - a guest came, the children begged for an ice-cream, or something else important came up - the money always went. Then when you <u>really</u> needed the money you had saved it was not there. We need a secure place to put savings - somewhere outside the house, but where we can get access to them quickly when emergency strikes." Morsheda Ahktar, BURO,Tangail member in Bangladesh.

Which ever system, or combination of systems is used, it is clearly time to shake off the paralysis and wake from the dream ... the poor demand that we do.

CONCLUSIONS

Evidence from the remotest of Bangladeshi villages and indeed from all over the world suggests that the poor want to save, and indeed <u>are</u> saving in a wide variety of ways. What had been lacking until very recently among most MFIs was the facilities to allow the poor to save in a way that they could meet current needs and opportunities as well as save for the future. The large MFIs have instead concentrated on providing credit facilities at the lowest sustainable interest rates, and on capturing compulsory savings in order to do so.

There is a clear demand for flexible savings facilities, and it is also apparent that almost all people (including the very poor) want to save, while not all want to borrow all the time. Given these facts, is it not reasonable to suggest that the large MFIs should look at optimising the savings facilities they offer, even if this entails marginally increasing the rate of interest charged on the loans ? Such a policy could allow MFIs to offer services to a larger number of the poor, and encourage the participation of the very poor.

There is a clear preference amongst the poor for voluntary, open-access savings, although compulsory minimum weekly deposits (particularly when they are client-defined) are also often welcomed since they provide savings discipline and an opportunity to safeguard savings from "trivial" spending. These preferences, when met with flexible and responsive savings facilities, can result in large-scale savings mobilisation. Indeed voluntary, open-access savings schemes can generate more net savings per client per year (and thus greater capital for the MFI) than compulsory, locked-in savings schemes ... and provide a useful and well used facility for clients while doing so.

However, caution should be exercised, because in Bangladesh there is extensive experience that:

a. Small MFIs mushrooming to take savings and lend them back to members almost invariably rapidly run into a demand for credit in excess of the deposits they are able to attract. This results in declining confidence in the organisation until either it collapses or it finds donor/soft loan support to capitalise its credit operations and regenerate confidence; and

b. Given the exposure to this catastrophic loss of confidence, fraud and/or incompetence, only those organisations with a track record of delivering effective credit services should be encouraged to move into large-scale savings mobilisation. For we must remember that under credit-based systems, the MFI must "select borrowers who are trusted by the lending institution. In savings mobilization however, it is the customers who trust the institution" (Robinson, 1995).

Effective (but not restrictive) regulatory systems and (ideally) depositor protection schemes should be in place to underpin the introduction of large-scale savings mobilisation schemes[6]. With such safeguards in place, MFIs that believe in serving the poor (and particularly the risk- and credit- averse poor_est_) and in generating indigenous capital funds, should move ahead with the development of voluntary, open-access, savings facilities. For open access to hard-earned savings, is not just a human right, it also makes business sense[7].

---

[6] This is an issue which is (fortunately) very high on the agendas of the Consultative Group to Assist the Poorest, the Microfinance Network and many other organisations.

[7] And, of course, would make more so if donors would deliver less free capital funding in the form of grants !

Appendix 1

(Exerts from *Savings: Flexible Financial Services for the Poor "and not just the Implementing Organisation"*, by Graham Wright, Mosharrof Hossain and Stuart Rutherford.

A Detailed Example with Thanks to BRAC

BRAC had a policy that required members to deposit weekly minimum compulsory savings of Tk. 2 (raised to Tk. 5 in 1994), plus 4% of all loans disbursed, into the Group Trust Fund savings account. Thereafter, limited withdrawals were possible (25% after 5 years, 50% after 10 years and 100% after 20 years or on resigning membership) subject to a maximum of 3-5% of total savings balance for each Area Office. This meant in practice that members probably had to leave the organisation in order to realise their savings.

In 1993, BRAC introduced a savings experiment in ten branches which were instructed to introduce open-access or "current" accounts for the members. However in an attempt to "see different modes of operation and their efficiency" (Zaman et al., 1994) no fixed guidelines were issued from head office as to how the new scheme should be implemented in the field. A variety of schemes were implemented in a variety of branches (aged between 2 and 8 years), and the study concluded that "the average own savings per head was Tk. 17.7 a month compared with Tk. 13.8 in the (matched) control branches." However, as a result of the high level of withdrawals, the study concluded that, "in the first year of operation, savings mobilization was not enough to cover the operating expenses" (Zaman et al., 1994).

But these conclusions require careful consideration. In the branches where the savings scheme was genuinely voluntary and open (i.e. where the BRAC staff were promoting the scheme and were not dissuading or blocking members from making withdrawals) the financial results look markedly superior. In Paba branch for example the monthly end net savings rose ten-fold in the year, (as compared to less than three-fold in the comparison control branch at Mohonpur). Furthermore, a look at the detailed financial data suggests that a year may have been too short a window of opportunity for the members ... members may have been testing the new savings system to see if it would operate as advertised prior to depositing, and not withdrawing, larger sums.

Similarly Grameen Bank

Since its inception, the Grameen Bank system has required a 5% group tax (deducted at source from the loan) plus Tk. 1 (recently raised to Tk. 2) personal savings contribution to the Group Fund. "To ensure that ownership of the Bank remains in the hands of the poor, and to ensure capital for future growth, it is compulsory for each group to buy shares in Grameen Bank. When the savings in a Group Fund have reached Tk. 600, the group concerned is obliged to buy shares in the amount of Tk. 500 (i.e. 5 shares at Tk. 100 each)" (Fuglesang and Chandler, 1993). Savings today ... share capital tomorrow.

Thereafter, interest free loans are made available from the Group Fund at the discretion of the group. Grameen Bank reports list more than 350 uses of these loans including a variety of social and household needs, health and medical expenses, loan repayment, maintenance, repair and addition to capital equipment, raw materials for manufacturing and processing, farming and trading. And with $ 59.2 million Group Fund loans disbursed from Grameen's inception to December 1995, the facilities have been heavily used by the members.

But until 1995 the members were only allowed to withdraw the personal savings component of the Group Fund and then only when they left their group. The substantial Group Fund (as much as Tk. 3,000 or more for members who have been with the Grameen Bank for ten or so years) was retained in the group. Only since 1995, have the members been entitled to a full refund (including interest) of Group Fund savings when they leave their groups. And better, after ten years with the Grameen Bank, the members who remain are now entitled to transfer all of their portion of the savings in their Group Fund (with interest at 8.5%) into their Individual Savings Deposits (see below).

Other savings schemes under Grameen Bank's system include the compulsory Emergency and Children's Welfare Funds, the voluntary Special Savings (or Centre Fund) and Individual Savings Deposits designed to encourage the members "to build their economic strength by keeping extra income in personal savings accounts". These Individual Savings Deposits earn 8.5% interest, and may be withdrawn on request (irrespective of whether the member has a loan outstanding) from the Branch Office.

Chen noted back in 1992 that the total savings mobilised by Grameen Bank was four times larger than the combined savings of the five major commercial banks in Bangladesh (Khandker et al., 1994) . And by the end 1995 Grameen Bank members had generated a cumulative Group Fund savings of $ 105.4 million, or over 70% of the value of all grants received from donor and other institutions, and were meeting a very important part of Grameen Bank's capital requirements.

The Individual Savings Deposits represent the first open access current account savings scheme among the large mainstream MFIs in Bangladesh. And more, it is policy that people who are not Grameen Bank members can also save using these accounts. However, interestingly Grameen Bank's Head Office MIS does not track Individual Savings Deposit accounts, at present they are monitored at Zonal level instead, and are probably subsumed under the Group Fund heading in the Annual Accounts. This may be indicative of a system under development, or the perceived unimportance of these Individual Savings Deposits, (after all, "Grameen Bank has never deviated from its central vision of credit for poverty alleviation"[Hashemi and Schuler, 1996]). It also suggests that Grameen may have an under-recognised instrument and capital reserve in these Individual Savings Deposits at the branch level.

With the Grameen Bank's new policy, the Individual Savings Deposits assume a tremendous importance ... many members who have been with Grameen for more that ten years are transferring their Group Funds to the Individual Savings Deposits, and some non-members are beginning to open accounts.

We examined three sixteen year-old branches[8] in Tangail, with an average of 2,499 members. This limited and rapid survey revealed that an average of 1,451 (58%) of members had Individual Savings Deposits, and on average 110 non-member accounts had been opened in each branch.

Suraz branch, with the highest number of non-member accounts (200), had attracted Tk. 1,858,700 - an average of Tk. 1,170 per account. However, the 1,424 members and 25 non-members in Atia branch had only deposited Tk. 461,160 - an average of Tk. 318 per account. This low average net savings per member seems to be the result of a high level of withdrawals. In June 1996 at the Atia branch, the Tk. 685,153 withdrawals exceeded deposits by 4%, and Grameen suffered a substantial net outflow of funds. The situation was marginally better in Elashin branch where the Tk. 149,834 June 1996 withdrawals were only 65% of the savings deposited in the month.

These withdrawals appear to be large-scale transactions - in Atia the average withdrawal was Tk. 4,030, a figure that may well correspond to the amount transferred in from the group funds. The relatively large number of accounts, together with the high level of turnover suggests than a significant proportion of members are withdrawing substantial percentage of their Group Funds once they are transferred into the Individual Savings Deposits. This analysis was

---

[8] Elashin, Atia and Suraz as of 9, July 1996

confirmed by the Grameen Branch Manager in Atia - almost as soon as the Group Funds are transferred into their Individual Savings Deposits (net of any loans outstanding), the members are withdrawing them.

What is not clear is why these withdrawals are being made. Are the members now using these substantial sums to establish income generating activities without the burden of the annualised weekly interest <u>and</u> capital repayments ? Or are they being used to improve housing, to pay off burdensome loans, or to buy land and other assets ? Or is it to test the new system (which has been introduced after years of member pressure for access to their group fund savings), and with time and confidence, Grameen Bank will see a rise in the level of savings per member ? This requires research - it has important implications for the policies and programmes not just of Grameen, but also for the other large MFIs in Bangladesh.

On the basis of their experience in Tangail, there is a possibility that Grameen Bank, like BRAC, may conclude that open access facilities will result in a massive outflow of savings and thus precious capital. But we should not lose sight of the build-up to the change in policy that allowed members to withdraw from their substantial Group Fund savings: a right won after years of protest and, in Tangail, a strike during which many groups did not meet. At the end of 1995, in the whole of Dhaka District there were around 18,000 general loanees with repayments more than 25 weeks overdue, but in Tangail there were nearly 60,000, and the cumulative un-repaid amount had climbed to over Tk. 82 million or $ 2 million[9]. It may take a while for the members' confidence to be rebuilt. Time will tell.

---

[9]   Unpublished Grameen Bank internal report.

Chapter 4

REPLICATING MICROFINANCE SYSTEMS: ARE BLUE PRINTS ENOUGH ?

The MicroCredit Summit reaffirmed and gave politically-charged impetus to the commitment to reach large numbers of the poor with MicroCredit services as soon as possible. In order to do this, increasing numbers of organisations are "replicating" the programmes of successful Microfinance Institutions (MFIs). This approach allows rapid start-up using a tested model and systems. Unfortunately, these strengths are also weaknesses, since the models being replicated usually require substantial modification to make them appropriate for local conditions. Replication of a scheme designed for densely populated Bangladesh in (for example) sparsely populated mountainous areas is neither feasible nor desirable.

Furthermore, close adherence to "blue-prints" is likely to substitute for careful research into the needs and opportunities for the provision of financial services for the poor - and thus the design of appropriate systems. All institutions seeking to provide appropriate, quality financial services in a new environment need to examine the "financial landscape" in which they will be operating. This will allow the institution to understand the options and to become aware of the competition they will face from existing formal and informal financial service providers.

Replication also risks the suppression of innovative and creative ways of providing still better financial services - particularly when promoted by powerful apex funding organisations as is currently in vogue amongst donor agencies. Apex funding institutions allow donors to support larger numbers of small Microfinance organisations, but risk unintentionally suppressing innovation through their operational norms and reporting requirements.

Perhaps the most dangerous form of "replication" is that driven by consultants, leaders or donors designing and/or recommending systems they only partly understand, and thus giving incomplete and/or blurred blue-prints. With the success of the Microfinance industry, the growing international reputation of the Grameen Bank, and the drive to reach large numbers of the poor, there are many alarming examples of this happening.

Finally, there is a tendency towards using credit as a way of attracting clients to meetings (where they can be required to participate in other activities - such as family planning etc.). This "part-time banking" is dangerous both as a result of the complexity of providing financial services and because the clients come to rely on and expect permanent access to savings and credit facilities, and are likely to suffer when and if the organisation stops or "withdraws".

> *"Ironically it is the success of the "first wave" finance-for-the-poor schemes ... that is the greatest obstacle to future experimentation. Most designers and sponsors of new initiatives have abandoned innovation, and "replication" is leading to a growing uniformity in financial intermediation for the poor." (Hulme, 1995)*

THE GOSPEL

The implementation of MicroCredit schemes in the name of "Grameen replication" has become almost a religion. The MicroCredit Summit was, to a large extent, a convocation of the disciples who pledged to spread the word, and reach 100 million poor by the year 2005. One can easily imagine that quality may be sacrificed on the altar of quantity.

This fear was greatly heightened for those practitioners who attended the MicroCredit Summit Preparatory Committee meetings, which were ably managed and manipulated by the dedicated and extremely professional RESULTS team. During the second of the Preparatory Committee meetings, in Washington in September 1996, practitioners attending attempted to stage a revolution in the interest of best practices. Speaker after speaker noted that the very name of the "MicroCredit

Summit" would send the wrong message, and that with MicroCredit as the rallying cry, the vision couldbe more simply stated as "driving 100 million poor women into debt by the year 2005". Others noted that the astronomical projections for the amount of capital required from donors to fund the effort could be raised, in substantial part, through providing appropriate savings services. Almost all concluded that the name should be changed to "Microfinance Summit" or perhaps "MicroEnterprise Summit" - but not "MicroCredit Summit".

The reaction from the podium was to politely agree that savings might be important, and then to stick firmly to the Summit's original name on the basis that it was somehow easier to explain to the general public that poor people needed loans so that they could develop profitable microenterprises. Besides, the name "MicroCredit Summit" had already gained some substantial recognition and the stationery had been printed. A few light cosmetic changes referring to the importance of savings and financial services were buried deep down in the Summit's Final Declaration, but the credit-driven model had won the day.

In retrospect, what we practitioners had failed to understand was that the Summit was being staged as primarily as a Public Relations exercise to raise public awareness of the potential of "credit for the poor". It had been formulated in this manner (despite the presence of leading Microfinance practitioners - including Nancy Barry of Women's World Banking, Ela Bhatt of SEWA and Michael Chu of ACCION on the Organizing Committee) because the Summit was the brain child of Sam Daley-Harris, (whose RESULTS organisation had long been lobbying in Washington on behalf of Grameen Bank) and Professor Yunus. The Grameen Bank's name and its remarkable success in reaching literally millions of poor women in Bangladesh (which, sadly, still represents a hopeless "basket case" to most Americans) would be a powerful symbol to demonstrate that there was indeed a way of helping the very poor. In a time when people all over the world seem to be less and less willing to contribute to or pay taxes for development programmes, it was (and still is) important to showcase the "success stories". Thus, the inspiration and driving force behind the Summit was the Grameen Bank's internationally renowned and respected credit-driven model. The ultimate aim of the Summit was to publicise MicroCredit's success and potential, and thus raise the funds to "put money into the hands of poor women".

In order to reach the ambitious goals of the Summit, existing institutions will have to expand, and many new MicroCredit organisations must be established. In many respects, the easiest way of establishing new organisations is through the process of "replication", whereby the "replicator" organisation takes the blue-print of an existing successful institution and attempts to implement it. Indeed, this approach is being promoted by many agencies. But it requires careful consideration.

There is a remarkable level of diversity in the implementation methodologies followed by organisations inspired to "replicate" - even amongst those "replicating" the same model. However, this diversity is not usually driven by careful research and design methods to create economically appropriate systems tailored to meet the needs and opportunities of the environment in which the organisation operates. More generally the diversity of systems is driven by the needs of the project or the institution implementing it: their existing groups, non financial service objectives (such as the delivery of family planning commodities or community conscientisation etc.), the donor agencies' disbursement schedule or blue-print implementation models. These systems then often perform poorly and require extensive modification in the light of hard reality (geography, topography, demography, economy, society, culture, communications and infrastructure etc.) in the field.

There is now an increasing recognition that donors' Microfinance "projects" should support the development of sustainable institutions designed to deliver cost-effective quality financial services to their poor clients on a permanent basis. This is a big step forward: previously projects came, delivered loans and then left, often leaving "beneficiaries" in much the same position as they were before. This recognition also makes clear the need to identify and support an institution separate and distinct from the "project" or process of supporting the institution. Implicit in attempts to create sustainable institutions is the need to make the institution, its financial services and the systems to deliver them, appropriate for the local conditions ... and not just to impose a blue-print Microfinance programme developed and designed in a distant land in an alien environment.

BLUE-PRINTS FOR REPLICATION

When an institution is developed (or under the old school a project is implemented) from the beginning as a Microfinance programme, it is common to see the system driven by blue-prints (such as those promulgated by the Grameen Trust/CASHPOR, FINCA or Foundation for Development Co-operation (FDC)) rather than by a careful analysis of the needs and opportunities in the communities in which the institution operates.

Get Ahead Foundation's Revealing Research

Churchill's (1997) description of the rehabilitation of South Africa's largest NGO lending programme by the Calmeadow team - from 50% to 3% loan loss demonstrates how blueprints can often cause profound trouble for those that follow them without reference to client's needs. "Based on the original recommendation of USAID, Get Ahead only issued loans for 12-month terms. After conducting market research in 1993-4, Get Ahead realized that its product was inappropriate for the needs of its clients. Borrowers complained that loan sizes were too small and the loan term too long. ... Get Ahead's decline, and recovery, emphasize the importance of adhering to the two basic tenets of microlending: excellent client service and strict delinquency management."

The blue-print approaches, such as those being promulgated by Grameen Trust/CASHPOR, and more recently ASA, risk attempting to standardise rather than optimise systems and client service, and do it irrespective of the diverse settings in which they are implementing. In many ways, these approaches help in that they offer tested methods and systems, but hinder in that they do not encourage adequate research into local constraints, needs and opportunities. The blue-prints can be seen as, and indeed often are, substitutes for research and analysis. In this respect the emphasis of UNDP's MicroStart on reviewing the "Strategic Environment" and "Market" through secondary data analysis and multiple interviews makes this a more situation-responsive and responsible blue-print. But, despite these significant limitations, there are some notable successes that have arisen as a result of these types of blue-print approaches. The blue-prints can often give a reasonable starting point that can then be modified in the light of experience and client demand ... if the institution learns to listen.

Centre for Agriculture and Rural Development (CARD) Inc.

The Centre for Agriculture and Rural Development (CARD) Inc. in the Philippines defines itself as "A Grameen Bank Replication Project", and has replicated the Grameen methodology faithfully with little deviation except to drop the Grameen Bank's salutes and exercises. As of December 1997, it had 10,868 members who have borrowed nearly $500,000 and maintained a 100% repayment rate. This is particularly remarkable in that the Centre for Agriculture and Rural Development was previously a community development organisation offering balloon-based repayment loans and suffering the consequences in repayment terms - with default rates in excess of 50%. However, in response to the demand of is clients, the Centre for Agriculture and Rural Development has now transformed itself into a rural bank in order to offer savings services - thus demonstrating the flexibility of an experienced, self-confident organisation increasingly committed to providing quality financial services to its clients.

But blind adherence (often enforced through donor implementation methodology and reporting requirements) to these blue-print replication programmes does little or nothing to innovate, to search for improved ways of meeting the needs of the poor for financial services. It is this failing that is in many ways one of the most dangerous, since it not only risks failing to address community- or location-specific needs and opportunities, but also ingrains and institutionalises a limited number of high-profile models with all their increasingly well-acknowledged short-comings. Less well-known, but in many ways more successful, models (often those which have not accessed large amounts of donor funding and therefore have not been subjected to endless evaluation missions, peer reviewed research and profiling in public relations publications) are often overlooked.

Furthermore blue-print programmes usually ignore existing informal sector savings and loan groups and systems from which they could usefully learn and which they could harness to strengthen their programmes. Pal (1997) provides an interesting description of Credit

---

Rutherford's Questions
The Basis for Designing Quality Financial Services

An organisation wishing to get involved in financial services for the poor might ask the following questions during its surveys of its proposed area of operation.

- *How do poor people manage their savings deposits ?* Are there savings banks, or deposit takers, or insurance salesmen, or savings clubs ? Do the poor have access to them ? If not, how do they save, and how convenient do the poor find the available forms of savings?

- *Can poor temporarily realise the value of assets they hold ?* Are there pawnbrokers or are there schemes that allow then to mortgage land or other major assets safely ? If such devices exist, are they exploitative or enabling ?

- *Can poor people get access to the current value of future savings ?* Are there moneylenders willing to advance small loans against future savings ? Are there rotating savings and credit associations (ROSCAs) or managed or commercial chits, or co-operative banks or NGOs that offer loans against small regular repayment instalments ? Do the very poor have access to them ?

- *Can poor people make provision for known life-cycle expenses ?* Can they provide for daughters' marriages, their own old age and funeral, and for their heirs ? Are there clubs that satisfy these needs, or general savings services or insurance companies that will do as well ? Are there government or employer-run schemes ?

- *Can poor people secure themselves against emergencies ?* What happens when the breadwinner is ill, or when a flood or drought occurs ? Does the government have schemes that reach the poor in these circumstances ? If not, what local provision can people make?

- *Can poor entrepreneurs get access to business finance ?* If so, in what amounts and at what cost ?

(Rutherford, 1996b)

with Education, the Freedom From Hunger model, modified to fit the local situation using pre-existing system of "caisses populaires" (credit unions), "caisses villegoises" (smaller village banks) and "tontines" (ROSCAs) in Burkina Faso. This helped the programme overcome not only the challenges of Burkina Faso's social systems, but also those presented by the huge distances between villages. She notes that in this case, "replication ... does not refer to what Hulme termed the "blueprint method" (1993) whereby one approach, in this case the GB" [Grameen Bank] "model, can be universally applied to a variety of situations and contexts" (Pal, 1997).

It is this need to explore the existing informal and formal sector environment (the "financial landscape") that has been largely ignored to date, but the importance of which is increasingly recognised as a prerequisite for designing appropriate quality financial services for the poor (see for example Johnson and Rogaly, 1997). Rutherford has listed the types of questions that a client-responsive Microfinance Institution should ask in designing its system and products (See previous page).

Answering these questions will allow the Microfinance Institution (MFI) to identify opportunities to provide savings and credit facilities or alternative pawn/mortgage facilities, to promote Rotating Savings and Credit Associations (ROSCAs) or Accumulating Savings and Credit Associations (ASCAs), self-help groups or credit unions. The process of asking and eliciting answers to these questions will also give the MFI important information on the magnitude of financial transactions underway within the community, and thus useful information for setting loan sizes etc. In short, the process will give a good overview of "the financial landscape", and what, if anything, the MFI can contribute - as well as an overview of the competition it will face.

MASS-PRODUCTION BLUE-PRINTS

Similar blue-print approaches are coming to the fore with the increasing interest in second tier, apex organisations. These are greatly favoured by donors as a way of financing many relatively small Microfinance organisations without having to worry about them on an individual basis - the responsibility for supervision is given to the apex organisation. Furthermore, some argue that the better apex organisations do not simply wholesale capital funds, but also provide technical training and back-up. There are two fundamental problems with this: firstly it sets up an inherent conflict of interest and secondly it can lead to suffocation of innovation.

The conflict of interest arises from the apex organisation's dual role as financier and technical assistance provider. As a financing institution, the apex will want to lend its capital to its client MFIs as quickly as possible (and therefore may be willing to cut corners in terms of quality irrespective of concerns relating to long-term portfolio quality). The apex will also be keen to demonstrate (both to the MFI and the world at large) the effectiveness of the technical assistance it delivers, and be under significant pressure from the recipient MFI to follow the assistance through with capital funding. In the event of one of the MFIs it funds facing problems that threaten its investment, the apex is likely to deploy its technical assistance capability to protect its capital. In addition, in the words of Gonzalez-Vega (1998), "When large amounts of credit are used to *persuade* the MFO" [Microfinance Organisation] "to accept the technical recommendations of the apex organisation, the MFO may find that it is not really obliged to repay the loans if failure of its own lending activities can be attributed to poor technical advice from its dominant implicit partner" (the apex organisation). Gonzalez-Vega goes on to note, "Furthermore, a *sine qua non* for institution-building to be effective is the willingness of the MFO to accept the advice of the provider of technical assistance. When technical assistance is tied to borrowing, it is hard to tell if the MFO wants the advice."

This leads us to the second fundamental problem posed by apex organisations: that they once again risk the promotion of one specific approach to providing financial services without adequate recognition of all the options open to client organisations. The level of risk depends largely on the philosophy and approach of the apex organisation, but these apex institutional arrangements can result in the suffocation of more creative approaches to the provision of financial services to the poor. This risk needs to be better acknowledged by the donor agencies funding the apex organisations, and mechanisms to support more innovative and client-driven models should be promoted.

PKSF's understandable search for quality partner organisations also has had another, little recognised, but very dangerous result. One of PKSF's requirements is that partner organisations have a track record:

Palli Karma Shahayak Foundation

The Palli Karma Shahayak Foundation (PKSF) has become a successful and often cited, "model", apex wholesaling financial institution. Established by the Government of Bangladesh in 1990, it has an independent, seven-member Governing Board, which is responsible for policy decisions.

PKSF has received grants of nearly $25 million from the Government of Bangladesh, and (in 1996) another $105 million soft loan from the World Bank. These funds are lent out to partner organisations at rates varying between 3.0% and 4.5% pa depending on the size of the partner organisation. This interest is used to cover the costs of delivering the credit and monitoring its use, and of proving some basic technical assistance and training services to around 150 partner organisations. PKSF ostensibly prefers no specific Microfinance model, programme or system, and theoretically encourages innovation and research. However, in practice PKSF insists that is partner organisations charge a "reasonable" rate of interest to customers for their loans, and the interest rates of NGOs financed by PKSF range between 9% and 15%. In the interests of operational efficiency, PKSF has a standard monitoring, MIS and reporting system for small organisations. This effectively forces these partner organisations to follow a PKSF-driven (Grameen Bank-based) model and stifles any significant innovation or departure from it.

However, this may be changing, after long negotiations, PKSF has showed admirable flexibility, compromised and agreed to lend to Proshika without insisting on major changes in Proshika's savings and credit methodology. Whether, this precedent reflects the large amounts being borrowed by Proshika or is indicative of a more flexible policy in the future remains to be seen.

that they have been operating for at least one year, and have a 95% repayment rate. This has meant that many well-intentioned, would-be credit NGOs have set about forming groups, collecting savings and lending them back to their members with the aim of achieving PKSF's track record criteria and accessing capital funds from it. At the beginning of programmes, clients are justifiably sceptical about the capacity of NGOs to deliver on their promises, and almost inevitably the demand for loans far outstrips the capital raised through the (usually compulsory, locked-in) savings programme. If, as is often the case, confidence lapses and repayments falter, the NGO suddenly faces a situation where it cannot meet PKSF's requirement for a 98% repayment rate, and is unable to access additional capital funds to meet its clients' demands for loans. Then the vicious circle is complete, for without funds from which to offer loans, the would-be MFI is unable to meet the demands of its clients who begin to lose confidence in the organisation, and to reduce or withdraw savings deposits, thus further reducing the organisation's ability to lend. Soon the repayment rates falter further, confidence declines yet more and finally the savings of poor clients are lost to loan defaulters or in the costs of administering the programme. One cannot help worrying that the enticing prospect of PKSF funds may have encouraged several of the failed NGOs that litter rural Bangladesh to "take a gamble" on their members' savings.

INCOMPLETE BLUE-PRINTS

But perhaps the most dangerous form of "replication" of all is that promulgated by consultants or leaders in agencies with limited knowledge and experience of the systems they are recommending. The Grameen Bank name has now acquired such an aura, such a mystique, and is so closely associated with successful credit operations that it is invoked as a matter of routine in all matters to do with development credit. In other parts of the world, the FINCA model has acquired a similar mystique.

The Catanduanes Agricultural Support Programme (CatAg) was set up on the basis of the pre-project report of a senior consultant hired by the European Union. Indeed, this consultant was so popular in Brussels that he was hired to make nearly half a dozen pre-project reports in preparation for programmes to be implemented in the Philippines. In each case as an integral (and often central) part of his report, he made almost exactly the same recommendation. His recommendation was a blurred photocopy of the Grameen Bank's system ... with several key pages missing. He recommended the establishment of 5 member "Guarantee Groups" that would federate together into "Savings and Loan Societies" (SLS) and operate their own revolving loan funds - to be injected into the SLSs by the benign donor. Thus each 25-50 member SLS would be capitalised, trained how to manage its revolving loan fund, and live happily ever after.

The Central Cordillera Agriculture Project (CECAP), was faced with the same recommendation in the pre-project report, but a little thought by management and a visit to Catanduanes convinced the project not follow this path. (See the chapter "Central Cordillera Agriculture Programme: System Design Process - In Progress" for a description of what CECAP actually did). Experience has shown us time and again that, without external support, such self-managing groups rarely if ever work. For example, CARE, Bangladesh's Women's Development Project, delivered a broad range of health, skill development, and savings and credit with group formation, under a community development programme in Tangail for three years before withdrawal. Ritchie and Vigoda's (1992) subsequent evaluation found that "over half of the savings and loan groups ... are no longer in existence" 20-44 months after withdrawal. Many community development specialists in Bangladesh would see it as an impressive success that so many groups had survived. BRAC has also given up as impractical trying to create free-standing Village Organisations to look after their own affairs.

This problem is not confined to Bangladesh - the entire Village Banking movement has long-since recognised and responded to the need to provide on-going services to village-based groups. "At the International Village Banking meeting in 1994, the concept of graduation was discussed by managers and proponents of village banking from all over the world. The failure to have banks actually graduate from their programs as a phenomenon witnessed by many programs ... At this meeting, it was decided that the word "graduation" in reference to village banking should be abandoned. Instead, there was an emphasis on establishing ties to as many formal financial institutions as possible" (World Bank, 1997).

These ties are important to help the village-based group manage their funds better: excess savings not lent out amongst the group can be placed on deposit to earn interest, and when there are inadequate funds to meet the group's credit needs, these can be borrowed from the formal financial institution. Furthermore, and in many cases, most importantly, the formal financial institution can provide the security, book-keeping and auditing services necessary to maintain cohesion and trust among the village-based group's members. It is for this reason that most indigenous, self-started village groups such as Revolving Savings and Credit Associations (ROSCAs), Christmas clubs or funeral funds tend to be time-bound and self-liquidating. This built-in natural termination provides the benefits of having an automatic audit as the scheme closes. Either all the money is there and everyone has been paid, or it is not;

Two Strategies and Two Outcomes

Stuart Rutherford differentiates between the two strategies pursued by outside agencies (be they development or private sector) and poor people themselves as they seek to design and deliver financial services. The former tend to use a strategy of "permanence and growth" and look to create sustainable institutions that deliver financial services to an ever-increasing number of clients - MFIs, banks, co-operatives etc. By contrast poor people themselves generally use a strategy of "replication and multiplication" and look to create many small self-contained, often self-liquidating schemes - ROSCAs, Christmas clubs etc.

There is another important difference between these two strategies and the types of schemes they spawn. The permanence and growth institutions tend to encourage the long-term build-up of funds through relatively slow, but steady, saving (and are therefore extremely well suited for addressing longer-term savings needs such as house building, pensions etc.). The latter replication and multiplication schemes tend to encourage the rapid accumulation and disbursement of funds (and are therefore better suited to meeting shorter-term savings needs such as purchasing small assets or financing festivities or rituals etc.).

These differences explain why the poor will often hold accounts in permanence and growth institutions while enthusiastically participating in a variety of replication and multiplication schemes - the different schemes are fulfilling very different needs. Furthermore, it is because of their differing roles that ROSCAs and other shorter-term schemes often attract markedly more savings than secure, interest-bearing accounts with financial service institutions and this is the fundamental basis for the participants' decisions as to whether to participate in the next "round" of the scheme if it is to continue. In addition, regular pay-outs solve the problems that large, accumulating sums of money create in villages - onerous book-keeping, the envy and attention of those outside (and sometimes even inside) the scheme, the need to store and protect the capital and so on.

The model proposed by the consultant and adopted by CatAg made one other fundamental error: that of putting revolving capital funds directly into the village-based group. Capitalising the group directly adds to the need to maintain excellent records and trust amongst its members, and provides a large temptation to "split the money and run". Even at this early stage, it would not be imprudent to suggest that, as soon as the CatAg programme finishes, many of the SLSs will find the

---

Invoking the Name of Grameen

One final example of "replication" in the name of Grameen, can be taken from the Central Cordillera Agricultural Project area in the northern part of Luzon, Philippines. In 1997, the project began to hear of a special pre-election project proposed and driven by the President's office, for the benefit of the poorest Provinces in the Philippines. In the Province of Ifugao alone, the LandBank's National Livelihood Support Fund was lending (at 12% pa) P. 3 million ($ 120,000 when the scheme was devised) to a selected co-operative in each Municipality (populations averaging around 2,500 households) for on-lending (primarily) to Agrarian Reform Communities (ARCs).

These co-operatives were given a list of Agrarian Reform Communities members divided into groups of five thus creating "instant" Grameen groups as lucky recipients of loans. The Department of Agrarian Reform has submitted the lists of Agrarian Reform Communities to the co-operatives involved, and they appear to contain a cross-section of the community, including the elite. These "Grameen groups" will take loans at 20% pa repayable either on a monthly or balloon basis. The co-operatives involved are allowed to retain their own collateral requirements, and simply have to worry about collecting the loans. Thus the scheme uses the Grameen name and then proceeds to break almost every one of the fundamental principles that have made the Grameen system successful.

weekly meetings or book-keeping too onerous, or will lose faith in the Treasurer, and will simply divide up the SLS's fund amongst the members and disband. Indeed, even as CatAg is being implemented, there are already examples of this happening.

To compound the problem and make it even more intractable, because the capital funds have already been handed over to the SLSs to manage, they have no incentive to link to an apex formal financial institution. The SLSs have the capital funds (indeed in most cases the amount of capital held by the SLS exceeds the demand for loans amongst its members), and do not wish to pay for the services of an apex organisation at all. CatAg has now recognised this problem and is scrambling to find a solution - and it is proving to be very difficult. Almost every possible solution requires significant additional investment, and still carries a high risk of failure. There is a very real possibility that this 5 year, $14 million programme may prove to have been an extremely elaborate way of handing a few thousand pesos to each "beneficiary". It would have been more cost effective to have distributed the cash from the outset, and wrapped up the project after a month.

The National Livelihood Support Fund programme is by no means an isolated example - many schemes world-wide claim Grameen inspiration and then ignore the principles that have made the Grameen Bank so successful. Perhaps one of the most important tasks for those involved in the Microfinance "industry" is help clarify and promote some basic principles and best practices - without issuing them as commandments set in stone: a difficult balance to strike. The chapter entitled, "The Principles of Microfinance" makes an attempt to do this.

PART-TIME BANKERS

In addition to poorly designed "blue-print programmes", increasing numbers of the development organisations - both Governmental and Non Governmental - are jumping on the Microfinance bandwagon as a sideline. These organisations tend to get sucked into providing savings and credit services by a combination of two factors. First, their clients demand these services, and they are seen as a way of persuading them to come to meetings (which are then also used to pursue other agendas). Second, the organisations often see savings and credit as a way to make a little money and thus address their donor's demands for "improved sustainability" or "increased self-financing". Neither of these are good reasons for organisations that do not specialise in savings and credit to enter into this complex field. The risks are too high.

Certainly, increasing numbers of NGOs (and indeed Government programmes) are using credit as the lure to encourage the poor to form groups which are then used to deliver other extension services - health and family planning, literacy etc. In Bangladesh, JOICEFP's programmes in Gorashal and Feni, Gashful's in Chittagong, as well as many others, are using credit as the chief motivating force to gather groups which are then given the family planning and health inputs that address the central or real objectives of the programmes. Freedom From Hunger's experience is typical, "Freedom From Hunger [FFH] entered village banking with the underlying aim of reducing malnutrition. In FFH's experience, providing solely nutrition information was not enough to attract regular active participation by poor people. The financial services portion of the program was developed to entice participation and improve poor people's ability to generate income for food" (Holt, 1994).

It is difficult to overstate the dangers of getting into savings and credit as a sideline. Banking is a complex business. The financial accounting, the systems of control, the management of cashflow and client confidence, the management information systems and the staff and client training necessary to implement a savings and credit programme are extremely complex. And more, once an organisation has started to provide savings and credit services to its clients, it is almost obliged to continue to provide them. This obligation arises from two sources. First, recovering loans from clients who know that no further loans/financial services are going to be made available is notoriously difficult ... and if the organisation cannot get its loans back, it probably cannot give its clients' savings back. Second, clients who have had access to financial services use these to better manage their household income and expenditure, and they and their businesses become increasingly dependent on having access to those financial services ... on a long-term basis. Few readers of this book, and no business of any size, could manage without access to a bank account, credit cards and periodic loans. It is therefore imperative that those organisations which get involved in the provision of financial services not only do it on a professional basis, but also do so with a clear commitment to provide permanent, quality services to their clients ... anything less is a recipe for disaster.

CONCLUSIONS

It is perhaps the complexity of delivering financial services and the knowledge that organisations must seek to establish sustainable MFIs, together with the success of Microfinance programmes world-wide, that has given rise to the epidemic of blue-print-driven replication. After all, there is still a huge unmet demand for quality financial services. Despite widespread demand, it is estimated that institutional finance is unavailable to over 80 percent of all households in developing countries (Christen et al., 1996 and Rosenberg, 1994). A conservative estimate of Microfinance demand all over the world is about 2.5 billion people or 500 million households (Robinson, 1997). The MicroCredit Summit's ambitious target of "reaching" 100 million families by the year 2005 would therefore address only 20% of the demand. But blue-print replication will not lead to quality financial services tailored to meet the local needs and opportunities of the community the institution is trying to serve. Indeed, it is likely to result in a system that forces the people using it to manage their way round its inappropriate rules, regulations, systems and services. Introducing a system of financial services without having researched the financial landscape (see "Central Cordillera Agriculture Programme: System Design Process - In Progress" for a description of one way of going about this process) and the needs and opportunities it presents, is similar to assuming that you can drive a city sedan on all roads. What worked in Bangladesh will not necessarily work in Nepal, Burkina Faso or the Cordillera.

The process of replication must include a period of research and reflection, pilot-testing, monitoring and modification, to tailor the "model" system being replicated for local conditions. And the modifications should maintain most, and ideally all, of the basic principles of Microfinance (see the chapter on "The Principles of Microfinance"). In the words of Christen et al. (1996), "... the emerging model for micro-finance appears to be widely applicable, if sensibly adapted to local circumstances." Without this the Microfinance industry , which was born of a willingness to experiment and take risks, will perpetuate in-bred systems in a spate of regressive reproduction instead of researching, learning and tailoring in a process of progressive evolution to optimise services. In the rush for replication we <u>must</u> not sacrifice quality for quantity.

SO WHAT SHOULD WE DO?
IN PRACTICE

SECTION 2

SO WHAT SHOULD WE DO?
IN PRACTICE

Chapter 1

THE PRINCIPLES OF MICROFINANCE

*The past three decades of experience - spear-headed by the Grameen
Bank - has given those involved in developing and implementing
Microfinance programmes a reasonably clear set of principles or
"best practices". These principles underlie almost all successful
Microfinance Institution's (MFI's) systems, and seem to be applicable
world-wide, irrespective of the setting.*

*The principles presented are based largely on the Bangladesh
experience and are not offered as "set in stone", "must follow"
requirements, but as a brief overview of the basic building-blocks of
most successful Microfinance programmes. They are perhaps best seen
not as inviolable rules, but rather as essential elements that should be
incorporated into group-based Microfinance system design whenever
possible.*

*MFIs should take time with the group formation process, and ensure
that the groups have been adequately trained before they get access to
loans. Groups <u>must</u> self-select on the basis of mutual trust and
friendship as they are expected to provide both peer pressure and peer
support as part of the group guarantee mechanism. The importance of
targeting the poor, and particularly poor women, has been
demonstrated time and again.*

*MFIs should seek to establish permanent institutions and sustainable
systems that deliver quality financial services for clients (not
beneficiaries). Optimising financial services and the systems to deliver
them is best done through an investment in pilot-testing. Finally, it
should be noted that government institutions are rarely able to
implement successful savings and loan programmes - credit is too easily*

politicised and NGO workers are generally better motivated to work with the poor.

MFIs should promote saving before they issue loans - it promotes discipline and provides some of the capital necessary to finance the loan portfolio. Open-access savings facilities also provide an important service to the risk-averse poor, and will result in the MFI attracting a larger number of better-satisfied clients.

Loans should be delivered at full-cost, on an individual (not group) basis but using a group guarantee mechanism (while recognising the time-bound limitations of group guarantee). Repayments should be scheduled on a small regular basis - often weekly - this breaks down the loan into small, manageable instalments that can be paid from the regular household budget. Given that money is fungible within households, tying loans to "productive" purposes is largely meaningless, possibly even counter-productive - MFIs would do better to recognise the needs of the poor and provide loans irrespective of purpose. Loans should be given for short time periods -rarely for more than a year, often less - as short term loans generally carry a lower risk. Finally, as with formal sector banking, credit history should give clients access to larger loans over time - this is often an important incentive to repay.

BACKGROUND

Over the last decade there has been substantial and growing interest in "Microfinance" programmes. These programmes are characterised by a very different approach than traditional agricultural credit programmes, and by their markedly superior loan recovery rates. The Grameen Bank is the best known, and in many ways the most influential, of the Microfinance institutions, and it is Grameen's success that has spawned thousands of imitators ... often using the Grameen name with little or no understanding of the principles and practices underlying it. This chapter tries to examine some of the principles underlying successful Grameen-influenced, group-based Microfinance systems, and what are some of the now generally accepted "Best Practices" in Microfinance.

GROUP FORMATION

Like many traditional agricultural credit programmes, groups are often (but by no means always) the basis of many Microfinance systems.

However the process of group formation, and the nature of the resulting groups is markedly different.

Take Time

Organisations implementing Microfinance programmes take time to analyse the need for financial services in the community. Using participatory techniques they review the "financial landscape" in order to develop appropriate systems or "products" (see *Quality Financial Services* below). In the process, they generate interest and awareness among the target group (see *Importance of Targeting the Poor* below) without using the lure of loans to attract beneficiaries. Thereafter, a great deal of time and effort is spent to pilot the activities (see *Pilot-Tested Activities* below) and to train the groups. Usually group members are required to meet regularly (generally weekly) and to save regularly for around 3-6 months before they are able to take the "accreditation" or "recognition" test (which ensures that they know the rules of the Microfinance system). Thereafter, only if they pass the test do the group members become eligible for loans.

Self Selection by Groups

Because of the group guarantee system and the regular meetings (see *Peer Pressure and Peer Support* below) groups must self-select. That is to say that the groups are formed by the members of the community themselves not by an outside agency. The result is small groups

---

Gawat or Reciprocal Exchange Groups

Throughout the Cordillera (and indeed throughout the developing world) groups of households of similar economic status have informal agreements to provide each other with interest-free loans of rice or of cash whenever they have the means. These loans help to smooth out the peaks and troughs of income and expenditure, and to keep some rice in the household granary. The system of reciprocity extends only to small quantities of rice and small amounts of money - enough to ease day-to-day needs and cover small-scale emergencies, but rarely more.

(typically of 5-15 members) of people who <u>trust</u> each other - often based on existing indigenous groups (in the case of the Cordillera, usually "*gawat*" groups - see box above). These groups, because they are drawn from trusted friends and neighbours, are more resilient and willing to help each other out during the inevitable times of stress.

Peer Pressure and Peer Support

Peer pressure and support are the basis of the discipline of the typical Microfinance group. Experience has shown that with a group of 5-15, the group is small enough to effectively enforce group peer pressure and collective responsibility, and large enough to handle the repayment of missed instalments when a member defaults (see *Group Guarantee* below). If the number is greater, it is harder for the group to maintain peer pressure and collective responsibility. Similarly, the compact closeness of a group allows peer support when any one member of the group falls on hard times or faces social or economic difficulties. The Filipino Development and Social Welfare Department's (DSWD's) slogan of "All for one and one for all" is appropriate.

Many Microfinance programmes also have a special "Emergency Fund" jointly owned and managed by the group to help members facing problems with repaying their loans. These Emergency Funds are generally used to advance interest free loans to group members facing legitimate problems repaying their loans, and further reinforce the peer support element of the group dynamics.

Romeo's Emergency

Romeo is a member of the Mahogany Savings and Loan Group in Lagawe. He took a loan for his wood carving business and was repaying it weekly until disaster struck: he cut his hand and the wound turned septic. Suddenly Romeo could no longer work, and worse, was faced with medical bills for his treatment in hospital. Fortunately, the Mahogany group was a cohesive one and had developed a group Emergency Fund. For the first two instalments, the group paid on Romeo's behalf and thereafter they agreed to lend him P. 1,000 from the Emergency Fund - enough to cover the cost of treatment and the loan instalments due until his hand had healed.

It is because of the peer pressure element of the group's responsibility that close relatives are generally barred from being members of the same group by Microfinance institutions. It is also very difficult to enforce group peer pressure effectively when close relatives belong to the same group. For example, if a daughter and her mother were in the same group, it is difficult for the daughter to apply pressure to her mother if the mother was wilfully not repaying her loan. In some settings, however, because of the size of families and the scattered population, it is difficult to implement this principle and (for example) the Central Cordillera Agricultural Programme (CECAP) is experimenting with a policy that no two members of the same household can be in the same group.

Importance of Targeting the Poor

Successful Microfinance institutions make special efforts to target the poor. There are several reasons for this. The first is the desire to address the needs of the more disadvantaged members of the community. The second is that *the poor are better credit risks*. Throughout the world the richer elite of

---

The Cordillera Elite

The small elite of surplus farmers and salaried people at the top of the social and economic ladder (for the Cordillera region's barangays show strongly marked social differentiation) already enjoy access to formal financial services provided by municipal-level banks and Co-operatives. Furthermore, they have also been astute at 'capturing' whatever has in the past been offered by outside agencies, including Central Cordillera Agricultural Programme phase I. They are used to "toughing it out" and refusing to repay the loans until the agency leaves the area or stops trying to collect the loan.

Felipe Balawan, had taken a loan to raise chickens - only half of the loan taken had been invested in the project and the rest had been diverted for other more pressing purposes. He was clearly not very interested in the project and had assigned his small children to look after the poultry, most of which quickly died. Each week, loan officers squeezed past his jeepney and newly acquired truck to hear him explain that he was too poor to repay the loan, and besides he had been told that the Programme was phasing out and forgiving all loans.

communities has become expert in "capturing" credit, particularly any subsidised or low cost credit, offered by agencies and organisations. The elite is more easily accessible, better educated, more articulate and more powerful - and thus easier to lend to and more difficult to recover from. On the other hand the poor are usually in greater need of, and with less access to credit (and indeed financial services as a whole - see *Quality Financial Services* below). The need of the poor for these services (and thus desire to comply with their terms and conditions in the hope of getting further access to them), together with their relative powerlessness, has meant that they have proved to be better credit risk and much more "credit-worthy" than the rich elite.

Importance of Targeting Women

Throughout the world women tend to run the day-to-day household budget, and are primarily responsible for well-being and development of their children. These two factors make them the best focus for Microfinance programmes - they have consistently proved themselves to be better at saving, and at repaying loans on time, and the profits they make on their business activities are invested in their family, and not gambling, drinking, cinemas or cigarettes !

PERMANENT INSTITUTIONS AND SUSTAINABLE SYSTEMS

Successful Microfinance programmes start with a clear objective to set-up permanent institutions or systems designed to provide financial services on a long-term sustainable basis. This objective implies several key things - good quality financial products or services, delivered by an appropriate institution on a profitable basis to satisfied clients who continue to value and use those services.

Quality Financial Services

Quality financial services reflect the needs of the community not the financing institution. The needs of the poor in the community that the Microfinance programme is planning to serve should have been determined during the participatory techniques used review the "financial landscape" (see *Take Time* above). Financial services include not just credit, and indeed often stress savings over loans - particularly for the risk-averse poor (see *The Risk-Averse Poor* below).

A Working Definition of Financial Services for the Poor
With thanks to Stuart Rutherford

Financial services for the poor consist mainly of services that enable poor people to get hold of usefully large sums of cash. They fall into two main types:

1. those that allow the poor to *build up lump sums through giving up the consumption of income*

 - *savings* and *insurance* do this by amassing or buying access to a future lump sum by giving up consumption now

 - loans often do this by providing a lump sum now in return for consumption given up later

2. those that *allow assets to be converted and reconverted into and out of lump sums of cash*

 - the various forms of mortgage and pawn are the main examples

---

For example, in the Cordillera, the Central Cordillera Agricultural Programme's work has shown that the key cash expenditure item for the poor (and the one that drives them to the informal money-lenders and 10% interest per month most often) is education expenses - particularly the expenses at the beginning of the school year, payable in May/June. A savings facility to allow people to put money aside before then would greatly help them manage their household income and expenditure patterns more effectively - and save them a great deal in interest payments, thus increasing net wealth.

For Clients Not Beneficiaries

Microfinance organisations with a commitment to sustainability serve "clients" who pay for the financial services they receive, not for "beneficiaries" receiving subsidised loans. This distinction is tremendously important since it dictates the attitude of the Microfinance organisation's staff to the group members (clients are served, beneficiaries are patronised), and the attitudes of the members toward the organisation (clients are buying services, beneficiaries are expecting hand-outs). These attitudes make the difference between a successful and sustainable, business-like financial services organisation and a failure - handing out loans with little commitment to, or expectation of, recovering them.

Pilot-Tested Activities

In order to optimise the savings and credit system, it is always a worthwhile investment to spend some time pilot-testing the programme. This will allow the implementing organisation an opportunity to "learn by doing", another of the characteristics common to successful Microfinance institutions throughout the world. Pilot-testing provides the organisation an opportunity to explore the optimal implementation methodology and monitoring and evaluation systems in a tightly controlled and supervised area. In addition, the pilot-test sites provide opportunities for on-the-job training for staff.

Institutional Framework

Successful Microfinance programmes have usually been implemented by independent non-government organisations dedicated to serving the poorer parts of the community. The former ensures that they are free from political influence and intrusion (for throughout the world politicians have always used credit - particularly subsidised or practically non-repayable credit - as a tool for political, rather than economic, ends) and thus free to make objective, business-based decisions in the best interests of the institution. The latter ensures that they conscientiously target the poor (see *Importance of Targeting the Poor* above) and can rely on motivated and committed field workers. In addition, it is important that the institution is well governed (at Board of Trustees/Directors level) and managed (on a day-to-day basis), and has well trained staff to implement the system. This latter aspect in particular is common to successful programmes world-wide: all have invested heavily in the development of their field staff and the field manuals they have to work from.

SAVINGS VS. CREDIT

Traditionally the Grameen Bank has placed more emphasis on the credit aspects of its programme. However, this is changing, and Grameen is now following other more progressive Microfinance institutions and moving away from compulsory, locked-in savings (levied as part of the loan and not available for withdrawal) to voluntary, open-access savings (deposited at will by the members and available for withdrawal, usually on demand).

Savings First

Even under the original Grameen system, group members had to save for several months before they were eligible to borrow (see *Take Time* above). This allows the members to develop the discipline of meeting and of putting some small amount of money aside regularly. The requirement to save first also results in an investment in the institution that will then lend to them - thus the loans they receive are financed not just by a faceless outside agency, but also by their own savings and those of their friends and neighbours. This idea is often referred to as *"Hot vs. Cold Money"*. The money provided by outside agencies is "cold", but that provided by oneself and immediate friends and neighbours is "hot". Borrowers are much more likely to be committed and conscientious about repaying "hot" money ... indeed many of the large financial services organisations in India (credit unions etc.) are unwilling to accept outside "cold" money for fear of reducing the discipline within their members.

In addition, appropriate emphasis on savings can reduce the overall level of outside capital needed by the Microfinance Institution - thus allowing precious development funds to be spread further, and permitting the institution more flexibility in its working methods. " ... when they mobilize deposits, lending institutions can develop lending programs and practices more appropriate to the needs and capabilities of local customers rather than relying on targeted program regulations on loan size, term structure, disbursement schedule and repayment plan" (Meyer, 1998).

The Risk-Averse Poor

Savings play another very important role. For the very poor, the prospect of having to find the money to repay a loan according to a specific and fixed schedule is a very risky one indeed. These very poor people often prefer to avoid increasing (or "leveraging") their risk through taking loans, and would much rather develop a lump sum through careful and pains-taking savings. In this way the very poor can, little by little, as the circumstances of their household income and expenditure flows permit, build up a useful sum of money ... without the additional risk and cost of taking a loan.

Jyothi the Deposit Collector
With thanks to Stuart Rutherford

Jyothi is a *'deposit collector'* from Vijayawada in India. She makes money out of poor people's (mostly women's) need to save up for small expenditures like school fees or clothing or house repairs. Such women find it hard to save at home so they give small amounts regularly to Jyothi who calls every day (or every few days). The customers have a card with 220 cells on it. When they have paid a fixed amount (say 10 rupees) for each cell they get back the value of 200 of the cells (2,000 rupees) and the deposit collector keeps the rest (200 rupees) as her fee for the service. This system is common throughout India (and probably elsewhere too) and illustrates that *many poor people are willing to pay for an opportunity to save.*

LOANS

The credit side of the Microfinance institution's activities are its source of income, and therefore of particular importance. As the source of income, and thus the basis of the sustainability of the organisation, particular attention has been focused on ensuring that loans are repaid.

Full-Cost Loans

As noted above, all successful Microfinance institutions are designed from the outset to be sustainable and thus to be financially viable - and as such provide loans on a full-cost basis (usually an effective rate of around 24-36% per year, or 2-3% per month). It has been shown from South America to Asia that what matters to the poor is not a few percentage points of interest, but the regular and secure availability of loans. After all, the competition are the informal sector moneylenders typically charging 10% per month. Subsidised interest rates tend to attract the wrong type of borrower (see *Importance of Targeting the Poor* above), and encourage the wrong type of attitude towards the rationale for offering the loan (see *For Clients not Beneficiaries* and

Institutional Framework above), thus resulting in poor repayment records.

Individual Basis

International experience has shown that loans given on an individual basis are more easily collected. This is for several reasons. First, group operated projects tend to run into one of two problems: either the project is dominated and run ("captured") by one individual within the group or there are disputes within the group on who has what responsibility for the implementation of the project. Second, the group guarantee principle (see *Group Guarantee* below) depends on individuals pressuring one another or supporting one another to repay their individual loans … at the extreme, group loans (particularly in view of their share, "covariant", risk) could encourage group support <u>not</u> to repay. Thirdly, the "covariant" risk of group loans means that the group members' have "all their eggs in the same basket" - if the project is successful, all well and good, if it goes badly, then they are <u>all</u> in trouble. Finally, with individual loans, the lending institution knows exactly who is responsible for the repayment of the loan, and does not get lost in a maze of group members referring to or blaming one another.

Felipe , Trying to Run a Group Enterprise

Felipe, an articulate young man, was working on Co-op papers when we arrived at his fairly substantial timber house. A few years back the USA-based NGO Christian Children's Fund (CCF), lent P. 100,000 to 55 villagers and helped them set up a Co-op that worked a ginger field collectively (at CCF's suggestion). Members made no cash savings but labour hours put in by them counted as 'savings'. However, disputes arose over who had to tend the beds, and when it came time to harvest, prices were poor so the crop was not harvested. The loan from CCF remains unpaid, and disputes among the Co-op members continue, with each blaming the other for the failure of the project.

Group Guarantee

Group guarantee is the mechanism that will enable the Microfinance institution to lend to group members without stringent loan collateral requirements (e.g. real estate and chattel mortgage). A group guarantee means that the group members commit themselves to repay the loan borrowed by any of their member(s) to the lending institution if the said member(s) default. It makes use of both peer pressure and peer support (see *Peer Pressure and Peer Support* above) to bring about strict credit discipline. The joint and several liability implied in the group guarantee means that a loan of one member is, likewise, an obligation of each member of a group. This means that when a member defaults on his or her loan, the Microfinance institution can lien the assets of the group as well as the personal assets of the group's members (including their individual share capital and/or savings deposits) to recover the loan.

This mechanism is further strengthened by the 2:2:1, staggered loan disbursement method. Under this method two members must make all their repayments on time for four weeks before the next two loans are released, and those four must continue to make all their repayments on time before the final loan is released. This is also a mechanism for peer pressure. The other group members who have not received their loans have to ensure that those who already received their loans do not fail to pay their weekly loan amortisation, lest their borrowing privileges are suspended. (However, see the chapter, "Optimising Systems for Clients and the Institution" for a discussion of how effective group guarantee is in the long term, and how continued access to quality financial services may be the key determinant for ensuring continued loan repayment).

Small Regular Repayments

One almost standard feature of successful Microfinance institutions throughout the world is a loan repayment schedule based on small regular (often weekly) repayments. This repayment schedule seems strange to those used to traditional agricultural credit programmes which have balloon repayment schedules under which the loan principle is repayable after the harvest. The regular repayment schedule is designed to break the repayments down into small, manageable instalments that can be saved out of the flow of income and expenditure in the household economy. Thus this repayment schedule recognises that the typical farm household has many and varied sources of income and types of expenditure. Managing these to repay the loan in small instalments is far easier for farmers than having to find large sums of money to finance balloon repayments at a later date. For example, for the borrowers under a Grameen Bank-inspired scheme operating in a small village market in Ifugao this was also the case. Initially they got agreement from the project to meet and repay every two weeks, but after a couple of months returned to the normal weekly repayment schedule because the amount was "twice as big and therefore twice as difficult to find".

In this respect, these loans can be seen as "advances against future savings". Similarly, this is why moneylenders wanting to acquire, or continue to use, land mortgaged to them will often insist on being paid in one lump sum (i.e. on a balloon basis) - they know it will be much harder for the poor borrower to manage this, and so they can continue to use (and possibly even acquire) the mortgaged land.

Conversely traditional agricultural credit gives a loan for a specific activity and expects the loan repayments to come from that specific activity. But as noted above, farmers' household economies are extremely complex, providing a multitude of opportunities (perhaps not supported by the agricultural credit programme, but far more attractive - say for example a parcel of land at a bargain price or rent) and facing a multitude of threats (which require immediate attention, and money - say for example an illness in the family). Furthermore tying loan repayments to harvest means that if the farmer is to find the large balloon repayment sum, he is forced to sell his produce immediately after harvest ... at the very time when the price is the lowest.

The Dilemma of Rice

Many of the loans given in the Cordillera are for rice - these loans are meant to help the subsistence farmers. The lending agencies have tended to fix a balloon-based repayment schedule with the principle payable after harvest. This has presented the farmers with a dilemma: how to manage that big lump sum repayment when it is due. In the Cordillera only 8% of households sell rice, and even if they are forced, by a balloon based loan repayment schedule, to sell immediately after harvest, they get the worst possible price. And yet, if there is any way that increased rice production can help the farm household, it is by reducing the household's expenditure on buying rice ... an expenditure that occurs in small (often weekly) transactions.

Flexible Purpose

The discussion in *Small Regular Repayments* above also touched on another important issue - that of "loan diversion". Credit projects throughout the world have faced loan diversion - borrowers using their loans not for the purpose given on the loan application form or proscribed by the project, but for another more pressing purpose. Often loans are diverted for "providential" or "non-productive" purposes, to meet emergency medical or education expenses (both of which, incidentally, can also be seen, in the long run at least, as "productive"), but loans are also often diverted because the farmer sees another more viable or lucrative opportunity. Given that cash is "fungible" and the complexity of farmer's household economies it is increasingly clear that trying to tie loans to specific uses without addressing other needs and opportunities is naïve at best.

More Cows Than People ?

In Bangladesh, clients regularly use "cow fattening" as their standard "purpose of loan" on the loan application form. The activity is acceptable to MFIs' management, most households have cows, and these can be displayed in the unlikely event that the lending institution's loan officers care or come to check up on the purpose of the loan. But few loan officers are interested, and the (almost entirely fictitious) data is effectively being collected for the benefit of the MFI's Annual Reports (see Todd, 1996). Typically, each year MFIs report around 15-50% of loans being used for cow fattening/milk production. With nearly 10 million borrowers in Bangladesh, many of who have been involved in MFI programmes for more than five years, it is surprising that one can move for cows in the country.

In the Cordillera, given the people's remarkable and commendable commitment to education, it is not surprising that loans ear-marked solely for agriculture are (in part at least) diverted to finance schooling costs. It is for this reason that successful Microfinance institutions world-wide do not tie their loans to specific types of projects, and where their policies insist on providing their general loans only for "productive" purposes, almost invariably have a mechanism to provide credit facilities to meet providential needs, or simply turn a "blind-eye".

Short Loan Duration

Microfinance (and indeed agricultural credit) practitioners across the globe have found that longer-term loans are usually, if not inevitably, associated with poorer repayment. This is particularly the case if the interest accruing on the loan is not collected regularly. The collection of interest (and indeed shorter loan duration) keeps the loan "in front of the borrower" - so that he/she is always aware of the liability and obligation to repay. The alternative approach to reducing lender's risk on longer-term loans is, of course, to insist on physical collateral. This approach has two disadvantages: firstly, it almost automatically excludes the poor from participating in the programme for want of physical collateral; and secondly the collection and disposal of collateral is a difficult proposition for formal sector financial institutions - even more so when they are associated with and committed to development activities.

Increasing Loan Size and Credit History

As noted above, in order to reach the more "credit-worthy" poor, the group guarantee system has been used to do away with the need to demand physical collateral. Another important mechanism has been borrowed by the Microfinance institutions from mainstream bankers: that of increasing loan size on the basis of credit history. As noted above in *Full-Cost Loans* the poor greatly value access to financial services and are willing to pay (and repay) to maintain them. A very important part of the motivation to repay outstanding loans is the knowledge that upon completion of repayment, (usually larger) follow-on loans are available. All businesses, including those of the poor, need regular access to credit in one form or another - it is rarely sufficient to give one or two loans and then expect a business to be adequately capitalised or to manage its own liquidity from its reserves. In addition, for the lending institution the completion of loan repayment is another chapter in the development of an individual's credit history - and her/his creditworthiness.

Chapter 2

BEYOND BASIC CREDIT AND SAVINGS: DEVELOPING NEW FINANCIAL SERVICE PRODUCTS FOR THE POOR

Increasing numbers of Microfinance Institutions (MFIs) are seeking to diversify the financial services they offer to their clients. There is a growing understanding and acceptance of the diverse nature of the credit needs of the poor, and awareness that not all of these are addressed by pushing "productive loans". Thus there is a pressing need to examine the best ways of designing and introducing new financial service products into MFIs.

BURO, Tangail is committed to providing flexible and responsive financial services to its clients and operating in what is perhaps the most competitive market in the world of Microfinance - in a District where almost all the major (and nearly a hundred minor) Bangladeshi MFIs are operating. Having long been a market leader in open access, voluntary savings accounts, BURO, Tangail is currently testing a wide variety of savings and loan products. The methods used to develop these new products broadly followed four key phases of financial service product development:

1. ***Research to identify needs and opportunities***
   This includes a review of the competition and products offered by both the formal and informal sectors, conducting market research as an integral and on-going part of staff's interactions with the clients, and through contacting other market leaders in the Microfinance industry.

2. ***Design and pilot testing***
   This includes the detailed design, costing and pricing of new products, prior to their initial implementation on a pilot-test basis.

3. *Monitoring and evaluation of the pilot test*

   This includes monitoring the financial and organisational consequences of the new product and conducting market research among the clients to review how the product was perceived and used.

4. *Revision and scaled-up implementation*

   Once these analyses have been completed, the MFI can make the necessary amendments to the product, its pricing, delivery, marketing etc. before going for scaled-up implementation.

These apparently straight forward steps are, in fact, relatively complicated to implement. The BURO, Tangail methodology is examined with additional material and insights from a recent series of studies of successful innovative and poor-responsive banks financed by GTZ as part of the work of the CGAP's "Financial Instruments (Savings Mobilization) Working Group", and Marguerite Robinson's work on Bank Raykat Indonesia (BRI).

The chapter offers a generalised methodology for those committed to going beyond basic credit and savings by developing new financial service products for their clients.

> *"A sustainable program is far from static. Keeping up with client needs is a constant challenge"*
>
> *(Edgcomb and Crawley, 1994)*

BACKGROUND

As the Microfinance revolution continues, increasing numbers of Microfinance Institutions (MFIs) are seeking to diversify the financial services they offer to their clients. In particular, there is a growing awareness that improved client-friendly savings facilities can provide not only an important financial service to the poor, but also that such facilities will actually provide more capital funds for the MFI than the compulsory savings systems that have been so prevalent (Robinson, 1995 and Wright et al., 1997). Indeed there is a wide-spread belief that voluntary and accessible savings facilities may result in the inclusion of the poorest 10-15% of the population, who are averse to risk (and thus to taking credit), and are therefore not being served by most MFIs.

Furthermore, there is a growing understanding and acceptance of the diverse nature of the credit needs of the poor, and an awareness that not all of these are addressed by pushing "productive loans".

In the words of Hulme and Mosley (1997), "Our main finding is the need for the designers of financial services for poor people to recognise that "the poor" are not a homogeneous group with broadly similar needs. ... Recognising the heterogeneity of the poor clearly complicates matters for scheme designers ..." But it is clearly extremely important. Thus there is a pressing need to examine the best ways of designing and introducing new financial service products into MFIs.

This chapter is again written on the basis of the experience of BURO, Tangail which is committed to providing flexible and responsive financial services to its clients and operating in what is perhaps the most competitive market in the world of Microfinance. Tangail District is located two hours drive north of Dhaka, and offers a pleasant day trip from the capital for busy donor representatives and visiting consultants. Almost all the major indigenous Bangladeshi MFIs have branches in Tangail: Grameen Bank, ASA, BRAC and Proshika are all well represented, as are perhaps as many as a hundred smaller (often single village based) MFIs. The competition between MFIs is therefore growing, and in some villages, intense, and clients have opportunities to "shop around" for their financial services. As a result, there is widespread multiple membership of MFIs (some "guestimates" suggest that as many as 40% of clients have two or more accounts). Tangail is therefore the perfect proving ground for new and improved financial services: indeed the clientele demands it (Abdullah et al., 1995).

Having long been a market leader in open access, voluntary savings accounts, BURO, Tangail is currently testing a wide variety of savings and loan products (for details see the Section entitled: Operations Research Programme at the end of the chapter, "BURO Tangail System and Services Under Development"). The methods used to develop these broadly followed four key phases of financial service product development:

1. research to identify needs and opportunities,
2. design and pilot testing,

3.   monitoring and evaluation of the pilot test, and finally

4.   revision and scaled-up implementation.

These are examined (necessarily in a somewhat general manner) below.

Additional material has been taken from a recent series of studies of successful innovative and poor-responsive banks financed by GTZ as part of the work of the CGAP's "Financial Instruments (Savings Mobilization) Working Group", and Marguerite Robinson's work on Bank Raykat Indonesia (BRI).

REVIEW EXISTING SYSTEMS

The MFI should review and catalogue what financial services are being offered by both the informal and formal sectors in and around the geographical area where it works. This review should, of course, include a review of the MFI's own financial services, and its clients' responses to them. It should ask: why have these services grown up or been developed ? how well are the services meeting the needs of the poor ? is the pricing of the financial services reasonable ?

> *Under the discussion of "lessons learned in the design and handling of demand-oriented savings products and technologies", top of the list of success factors for the Rural Bank of Panabo was "Adaptation of "classical" savings products to the needs of small depositors." In addition, the paper notes "Replication of other success factors in a competitive environment." A financial institution that is competing with other banks for customers' deposits can replicate promotional measures such as the execution of raffle contests or the payment of a higher savings interest rate" (GTZ, 1997c)*

The informal sector in particular will often provide important indicators of the types of financial services and products that the poor need, as well as some options for providing these: after all the informal sector is there because there is a market for it. For a fascinating description of 58 varieties of financial service systems for the poor see Rutherford's "A Critical Typology of Financial Services for the Poor" (1996a). Both the informal and formal sectors will be the competition when the MFI introduces the new financial service products, so it is important to pay careful attention to their pricing, delivery and marketing strategies.

CONDUCT MARKET RESEARCH

Market research should be conducted informally on an on-going basis through poor-friendly sensitive staff paying careful attention to issues facing the poor - both clients and non-clients - and listening to them articulating their needs.

> *The field-research conducted as part of the preparation for Rural Finance component of the EU-funded Central Cordillera Agriculture Programme, revealed that the most important financial services-related issue facing the poor in the Cordillera was how to manage school expenses. As a result of a remarkable commitment to educating their children, every year, in June, households all over the Cordillera had to find substantial sums of money to meet the costs of buying uniforms, books etc. In the absence of savings facilities, households were taking loans (at 10% interest per month) from moneylenders in order to finance these school expenses. There was a clear need and demand for secure savings products to help meet education costs without going into debt.*

Encouraging field-based staff in particular to be aware of the organisation's interest in developing financial service products to help the poor more effectively manage their household economies may in itself lead to the description and reporting of needs and possibly ideas to meet them. This process can be facilitated and improved through a series of workshops with staff focusing on the needs of the clients in the areas in which they work.

> *"BRI found that the key of market research was to learn from clients what they wanted and then incorporate this information in both the product and its advertising. Studies on savings motives and preferences of rural people throughout Indonesia identified four major characteristics a savings facility must combine:*
>
> - *Safety/security*
> - *Convenience*
> - *Liquidity*
> - *Positive return" (GTZ, 1997 b).*

Another way of obtaining insights is for the MFI to ensure that the search for needs and opportunities is built into the terms of reference of visiting evaluation teams - particularly if they are going to be using qualitative and case-study oriented techniques. All donor agencies should be interested in improved product development, not least of all since it will lead to better, more appropriate and user-friendly services being provided to the poor and possibly even allow inclusion of the poorest.

Market research can also be conducted in a more formal manner through needs surveys, which are often difficult to do effectively. Surveys imply quantitative driven instruments, which limit the opportunity/ motivation for follow-up and probing, discovering what is really important - particularly for poorer households. At best, needs surveys will usually rely on the further development of issues and ideas by the review of indigenous informal systems and/or the informal market research mechanisms outlined above through focus group discussions or similar techniques.

> *"BCS [Banco Caja Social] relies on market studies before introducing new savings products to the wider public. In general, desk-work market studies are combined with empirical tests with a limited random sample. In addition BCS closely watches market research carried out by competing financial institutions" (GTZ, 1997a).*

REVIEW THE LITERATURE AND CONTACT MARKET LEADERS

There is an increasing amount of experience with a diversified series of financial services products for the poor, and with it an increasing body of literature documenting and discussing that experience. Any organisation preparing to design a new product should examine any relevant literature that it can find and try to contact those with experience in implementing such products ... there are likely to be important lessons which need not be learnt the hard way ! As the Microfinance net-working and e-mail and Internet services grow, this experience exchange will become more easy.

DESIGN, COST-OUT AND PRICE NEW PRODUCTS

On the basis of the results of identification of needs and opportunities activities outlined above, the organisation should be in a position to design new products. The key is to introduce new products on an incremental basis - one, or a very few, at a time-so that the organisation's staff and clients can manage, monitor and understand them properly. Careful attention must be given to the interactions between different financial service products being offered by the MFI - from both organisational and financial perspectives.

> *"The common denominator underlying savings programs of Bank Dagang Bali, BRI's local banking system, and BancoSol is that the programs were designed specifically to meet local demand for security, convenience of location, and a choice of savings instruments offering different mixes of liquidity and returns. These programs were all designed with extensive knowledge of local markets; moreover BRI learned from BDB, while BancoSol learned from both. Financial institutions from developing countries all over the world are now learning from all three" (Robinson, 1995).*

A Small Selection of International Net-working Addresses
(there are many more)

ACCION International, 120 Beracon Street, Sommerville, MA 02143, USA or 733 15th Street NW, Suite 700, Washington DC 20005, USA.   Tel. 1 617 492 4930 or 1 202 393 5113
Fax.1 202 393 5115 or 1 617 876 9509 Email. acciondc@hers.com

Agricultural Cooperative Development International, 50 F Street, NW, Suite 900, Washington DC 20001, USA. Tel. 1 202 879 0224
Fax. 1 202 626 8726 Email. gcarter@acdivoca.org

Association pour leDroit a l'Initiative Economique (AIDE), 111 Rue Saint Maur, 75011 Paris, France. Tel. 33 1 4355 9894
Fax. 33 1 4355 9883

Centre International de Developpement et de Recherche (CIDR), B.P. 1, 60350 Autreches, France. Tel. 33 44 42 1106/1112
Fax. 33 44 42 9452   Email. cidr@compuserve.com

contd.

continued from: A Small Selection of International

Calmeadow, 120 Dunvegan Road, Toronto, ON M4V 2R3, Canada. Tel. 1 416 467 1097   Fax. 1 416 467 4690
Email. international@calmeadow.com

CASHPOR, 4/1 Jalan Permata 4, Taman Permata, 70200 Seremban, Negeri Sembilan, Malaysia. Tel. 606 764 5116 Fax.606 764ˈ2307
Email: gibbson@pc.jaring.my

Consultative Group to Assist the Poorest 1818 H Street, NW, Room G4-115, Washington DC 20043, USA.   Tel. 1 202 473 9594 Fax.1 202 522 3744   Email cproject@worldbank.org

Development Finance Network, The Ohio State University, Dept. of Agricultural Economics, 2120 Fyffe Road, Columbus OH 43210 1099, USA.   Fax. 1 614 292 7362
Email. listserv@lists.acs.ohio-state.edu

Foundation for International Community Assistance (FINCA), 1101 14th Street NW, 11th Floor, Washington DC 20005, USA. Tel. 1 202 682 1510   Fax. 1 202 682 1535
Email. finca@villagebanking.org

Foundation for Development Cooperation, PO Box 10445, 232 Adelaide Street, Brisbane, Queensland 4000, Australia.   Tel. 61 7 3236 4633   Fax. 61 7 236 4696   Email. fdc@ozemail.com.au

Freedom From Hunger, 1644 Da Vinci Ct., Davis, California 95617, USA. Tel. 1 916 758 6200   Fax. 1 916 758 6241

Grameen Trust, Grameen Bank Bhaban, Mirpur 2, Dhaka 1216, Bangladesh   Tel. 880 2 9005348   Fax. 880-2-806319 Email. gtrust@citechco.net

Microfinance Network 733 15th Street NW, Suite 700, Washington DC 20005, USA. Tel. 1 202 347 2953   Fax. 1 202 347 2959/393 5115 Email. craig_churchill@msn.com

Opportunity International, 1111 North 19th Street, Suite 501, Arlington, VA, USA. Tel. 1 703 522 8155   Fax. 1 703 522 8049

SEEP Network c/o PACT, 777 United Nations Plaza, New York, NY 10017, USA. Tel. 1 212 808 0084   Fax 1 212 682 2949 or 1 212 692 9748 Email. seepny@undp.org

contd.

continued from: A Small Selection of International

Women's World Banking/International Coalition of Women and Credit, 8 West 40th Street, 10th Floor, New York, New York, NY 10018, USA.   Tel. 1 212 768 8513   Fax. 1 212 768 8519

Email. wwb@igc.apc.org

World Council of Credit Unions (WOCCU), 5710 Mineral Point Road, Madison, Wisconsin 53705, USA or 805 15th Street, NW, Suite 900, Washington DC 20001, USA.   Tel. 1 608 231 7130 or 1 202 879 0224   Fax. 1 608 238 8020 or 1 202 626 8726

Email. mail@woccu.org

The design of the new products should reflect, as closely as is feasible, the needs expressed by the clients and the opportunities offered by the market while still ensuring that they also meet the MFI's organisational and financial requirements. Thus, for example, if there is a demand for contractual savings agreement (CSA) facilities[1], the periods on offer (both for regularity of savings deposits and the time period of the CSA) should be driven by a combination of:

1.   *the clients' needs*: what are the most convenient regular deposit periods (weekly, bi-weekly or monthly) ? what are the typical uses for the facility (education, marriage ceremonies etc.) and thus the best terms/duration of the CSA ?

2.   *the MFI's needs*: how often can staff collect and account for these regular deposits ? how will these interface with the staff's existing duties and routines ? what is the organisation's need for capital ? does it have the management information systems and fund/liquidity management systems to manage the resultant fund flows effectively ?; and

---

1   Contractual Savings Agreements (CSA), commit clients to save a specified amount, every specified period, for a specified number of periods in return for a pre-determined pay out on successful completion of the CSA. Thus for example a woman with a 14 year old daughter that she expects to marry off at 19 years of age might undertake a CSA to save 10 rupees a week for five years in return for a lump sum of 3,500 rupees on successful completion of the CSA.

3.   *the market in which the MFI is operating*: the market will not only provide the competition, but also dictate the level of product recognition: if the new product is a better priced or delivered version of an existing facility already known and accepted in the community, it will probably be easier to "sell" than a brand new product which has to be explained at length to potential clients.

These latter, organisational issues, together with <u>cost analysis</u> will be the basis on which the product must be initially priced before comparing that price to the market. The cost of delivering and administering the product must be carefully analysed, for later comparison with the earnings that are expected to be derived from the product. Thus, for example, if a new 3 month providential loan product (repayable in weekly amounts) is under consideration, the MFI would examine how staff would collect and account for these regular repayments ? how will these interface with the staff's existing duties and routines, and thus what would be the marginal or incremental costs ? what additional book-keeping and portfolio tracking systems would be required ? what would be the expected level of take up of the new product, and thus what are the implications for the above issues and the organisation's liquidity and capital funds ? what level of risk is involved, and therefore what level of bad debts are expected ?

Given the commitment of most MFIs to institutional sustainability, the above cost analysis will provide an indication of the minimum <u>price</u> at which the new product can realistically be delivered. Similarly, unless the MFI is delivering an entirely new or significantly improved product, the competition will give an indication of the maximum price that clients are willing to pay for a similar service. Between the two is where the MFI should price its financial service product ... at least for the pilot-testing phase.

IMPLEMENT THE NEW PRODUCTS ON A PILOT BASIS

It is important to implement the new products in a limited number of easily accessible and representative[2] branches so that the results and

---

2   In terms of client mix, characteristics, socio-cultural and economic variables etc. and in terms of the staff and systems of the MFI.

issues can be monitored easily and any necessary corrective action be taken promptly. If several products are to be pilot tested, they should be initially introduced in <u>separate</u> branches so that the marginal effects on operations and financial results can be monitored.

> *"It is difficult to estimate accurately for each instrument - in advance of the savings mobilization effort - what the labour costs will be, what the demand will be, and what interest rates will serve to make the instrument attractive and profitable. Therefore, pilot projects are needed to set appropriate interest rates for savings instruments, and to establish suitable spread" (Robinson, 1995).*

When introducing the new products, the MFI will have to amend bookkeeping systems to ensure that the financial flows and receivables/payables arising from the product can be properly and promptly tracked and controlled. Thereafter the MFI must conduct the training necessary to ensure that outreach staff can promote the product and record the transactions that go with it, and that the branch level staff can effectively account for it using the new systems. Finally, when these steps have been completed the MFI and its staff can then undertake the marketing exercises to promote the product.

Senior staff of the MFI should regularly visit the branches where the new services are being delivered to review how the services are being sold and implemented in the field, how the services are being received by the clients, and the effect of the new services on the organisational and financial management systems. These visits will allow for rapid corrective action where necessary, and provide first hand knowledge of the issues that will prove invaluable when it comes to evaluating the results of the pilot test.

> *BURO, Tangail's piloting of Contractual Savings Agreements was pilot tested in only two branches: the two experimental branches were given a target of opening only 12 CSA accounts each per month. This demonstrates the conservative, limited scope and care taken by BURO, Tangail to pilot test and constantly review the dynamics of the new scheme's implementation. The actual performance is given below (taken from Rutherford and Hossain, 1997).*
>
> *contd*

continued from page 155

Contractual Savings Agreement Scheme size	Pathorail branch		Selimpur branch	
	7 months to Dec. '96	11 months to April '97	7 months to Dec. '96	11 months to April '97
Taka 5	11	11	7	- [3]
Taka 10	42	43	43	-
Taka 15	2	2	40	-
Taka 20	72	73	0	-
Taka 25	0	2	0	-
Taka 50	0	2	2	-
Branch Total	**127**	**133**	**92**	**100**
Total Taka (Taka 40: 1US$)		**67,586**		**47,130**

MONITOR FINANCIAL AND ORGANISATIONAL CONSEQUENCES

The MFI should pay careful attention to both the financial and organisational results of introducing the new product, both on a short and medium term basis. Regular visits to the branches should examine the effects on the number and nature of clients, on the workload of staff at all levels of the organisation, and on costs, liquidity, capital funds and ultimately profitability. Clearly, these will change over time and the "short and medium term" will vary according to the speed of marketing outreach and resulting client take-up of the new products, as well as the timeframe of the products on offer. It is often easier to understand the dynamics of products with a shorter maturity than those that require longer-term commitments from the MFI and its clients. Nonetheless, as soon as possible, the MFI should attempt to project the long-term financial and organisational implications of the new financial service product being pilot tested.

CONDUCT MORE MARKET RESEARCH

As part of the pilot testing process, the MFI should also conduct periodic evaluations through its staff (and, where necessary or desirable, consultants) to examine the clients' perceptions and use of the

---

3   Analysis not carried out by the review team

new product. These surveys can be conducted through both informal discussions and more formal qualitative techniques (focus group discussions etc.) in an attempt to examine the reactions of clients to the product (both positive and negative), and in particular how could the product and its delivery be improved to better meet their needs.

BURO, Tangail are starting to use "Customers' Consultative Groups" which are formed of elected kendra leaders and hold regular consultations with the Branch staff, occasionally with Head Office staff in attendance. These Customers' Consultative Groups were formed to "develop an increasingly co-operative form of participatory management" and "allow the BURO, Tangail staff a better understanding of the needs, grievances, problems, opportunities and constraints (economic and social) of the members; and give the members a clear understanding of their organisation, its opportunities and constraints (financial and operational), and its policies" (BURO, Tangail, 1996).

Particular attention should be given to the risk of over-extending the clients' household economic flows from which savings deposits or loan repayments must ultimately come. Many MFIs (and indeed formal sector financial organisations) have experienced problems when the loans issued exceeded their clients' capacity to repay, and contractual savings agreements present similar risks.

MAKE NECESSARY AMENDMENTS

As a result of the monitoring and evaluation steps outlined above, the MFI will be in a position to amend the product design, pricing and marketing, or implementation systems (book-keeping, training etc.) in order to optimise it. These amendments will involve revising not only the design, delivery, marketing and accounting systems wherever necessary, but also reviewing the cost-analysis and thus the pricing of the product in the light of the experience and data gathered during the pilot testing. By this stage, the MFI should be in a much better position to prepare these analyses and to finalise the pricing and marketing of the product.

"The design of <u>trade marks</u> for savings products at BCS, BAAC and BRI has proven to attract depositors. These three institutions promote savings products that have self-explanatory names (BAAC's "Save to Increase your Chances", BCS's "Grow Every Day" and "Savings of the Rural Community" accounts) and showy trademarks. While special product labels make it easier for customers to understand the particular design of each savings product, they also help to distinguish the products from those offered by competing financial institutions.

Except for RBP, market studies have been relied upon as important tools to develop and introduce new savings products. Analysis of market potential, field pilot testing of new savings products and re-testing of the revised products on a larger scale are common practices. BRI and BAAC have undertaken extensive field testing, taking between one and two years, before launching each of their new savings products nationally. BCS and RBP constantly observe the savings conditions and marketing strategies of their competitors" (GTZ, 1997d).

SCALED-UP IMPLEMENTATION

Once the process of reviewing the pilot testing experience and data, and making the necessary amendments has been completed, the MFI is almost ready to implement the new product throughout the organisation. Before doing so, the MFI should ensure that the accounting systems for the new product are fully integrated into the organisation's management information system, while also being available for separate analysis and tracking. The scaled-up implementation of the new product will require extensive training and distribution of revised bookkeeping and marketing systems, and may therefore best be done in a phased manner if the MFI is a large and widespread organisation.

AND BEYOND ...

"When the instruments, pricing, logistics, information systems, and staff training are completed, the program is ready to be gradually expanded throughout the branches of the institution.

contd

continued from page 158

When the institution has successfully expanded its instruments and services to all branches, and such new branches as may be opened, the emphasis should switch from the logistics of expansion to the techniques of market penetration. The former is a necessary, but not sufficient, condition for massive deposit mobilisation. When well run institutions offer appropriate deposit facilities and services, they can quickly gain the accounts of people living or working nearby the bank offices; this is known as the "easy money". Market penetration of the wider service area, however, requires other methods. These include: development of a systematic approach to identification of potential depositors; implementation of a staff incentive system based on performance (so that the staff will seek out the potential depositors, rather than waiting for them to come to the bank); development of effective methods for intra-bank communication; more extensive market research; a major overhaul of public relations; and massive staff training" (Robinson, 1995).

Introducing a range of high quality financial services will respond to Wood's (1997) concerns, "It seems important to have a more disaggregated understanding of the poor, and to recognise the diversity of their capacities, social position, family circumstances and livelihood options. They are not a homogeneous, undifferentiated mass, to be offered an undifferentiated, single, universal package of financial services." Furthermore, as Berenbach and Guzman (1994) remind us, "Market responsiveness is another element of success. Programs that want to attract and maintain a large client base must adopt a package of services and a means for service delivery that satisfy client preferences."

The development of the variety, flexibility and quality of financial services to meet the wide diversity of needs of the poor is the challenge for forward thinking and successful Microfinance Institutions.

HOW HAS IT BEEN DONE? CASE STUDIES

Chapter 1

CENTRAL CORDILLERA AGRICULTURAL PROGRAMME: SYSTEM DESIGN PROCESS — IN PROGRESS

Designing a system to deliver quality financial services, appropriate for the local situation, its needs and opportunities, is a difficult process. It first requires research into the "financial landscape" in which the system is to operate. Then action or operations research is required to test and refine the proposed system and services. This chapter is a case study in the process that was used to design the Central Cordillera Agriculture Programme II (CECAP II) "Rural Finance System" which comprised Self-Help Groups linked to Co-operatives.

The European Union started CECAP in conjunction with the new democratic government of Corazon Aquino in 1989 primarily in order to placate the people of this mountainous region. The programme was driven by political concerns and distribution of funds was primarily achieved through grants rather than loans, with predictable development results. In 1996 the second phase, CECAP II, was redesigned as an integrated programme that included a rural financial services system component. The designers of this component sought to create a truly responsive, practical and sustainable system.

Research on the successes and failures of CECAP I was undertaken to uncover approaches which might be applicable in this market, without wholesale replication. They researched the CECAP area by means of an extensive primary data gathering exercise focussing on lengthy interviews with CECAP I staff and the potential clients of the Rural Finance System. By investigating the "who, what, where, when and why" of the financial landscape, and using experiences and ideas from their research, the designers developed the background needed to conduct a problem analysis. By doing so, they determined whether the proposed interventions were likely to meet demand and address the critical issues identified by the data gathering exercise. Finally, having done all of the research, describing and analysing the unique aspects of the financial landscape, determining the potential difficulties, and the solutions, the team was fairly well satisfied that a client responsive, structurally sound and financially feasible programme had been designed.

The initial system was pilot tested and monitored in five zones, all offering different challenges, and involved nearly 1,000 clients. An external consultant with extensive international experience was contracted to review and evaluate the research and design work completed, the initial system design and the results of the pilot testing. The staff of the programme played a central role in the on-going research and pilot testing process which was based on Participatory Rural Appraisal and Focus Group Discussion techniques. A programme of quarterly workshops was initiated to get feedback and make recommendations and adjustments for on-going improvement of the system

After nearly nine months of pilot testing and consultations with stakeholders (from clients to the co-operatives that are the semi-formal sector "backbone" of the system), the system had been refined and modified, and detailed system design and implementation procedures had been finalised. In addition, the major issues and challenges facing the CECAP II Rural Finance System had been identified, corrected when necessary and documented.

The initial investment paid-off as the system received widespread praise and acceptance by its clients. By the end of June 1998, ten months after the start of pilot testing, the system had attracted 1,864 clients who had saved P.835,889 ($21,000) in their own village-based "Savings and Loan Group Funds", disbursed P. 1,239,204 loans from these Funds, and taken additional loans of P. 332,000 from the co-operatives to which they had been linked.

However well received the programme is, it is not expected to <u>ever</u> be "finalised" action research is an on-going process, further modifications are expected as the system matures and the environment in which it operates changes with time.

THE SETTING

The Cordillera is the mountainous region in the north of Luzon, the largest island in the Philippine archipelago. The mountains are home to the "Igorot" people responsible for carving some truly remarkable rice terraces out of the hillsides. These thousand year-old terraces, covering hundreds of square miles, are often called, (particularly by the Philippine Tourist Authority), "the Eighth Wonder of the World". The description is appropriate - the terraces, and the landscape from which they have been sculpted, are indeed stunningly beautiful. The indigenous people of the Cordillera maintain and are proud of their traditions - the only exception being the traditions of revenge-killing and head-hunting, which are slowly dying out.

The infrastructure in the Cordillera is extremely limited - many villages are several hours from the nearest road, roads are often blocked by landslides, and many Municipalities and towns are cut off for the six months of rainy season each year. In addition, the remote and scattered nature of the small villages and towns means that the population density is extremely low. In many ways the Cordillera is the antithesis of Bangladesh.

THE PROGRAMME

The Central Cordillera Agricultural Programme, or CECAP, was first established in 1989 as part of the European Union's attempt to support the new democratic regime of Corazon Aquino in the Philippines. The Cordillera had long been a hot-bed of the National People's Army's insurgency activities, and CECAP was an attempt on the part of the new Government to demonstrate its concern for the indigenous people of these remarkable mountains. As a consequence, CECAP was primarily driven by political considerations and was largely a grant-giving programme. However, towards the end of CECAP's seven-year duration, a credit-based component was started to finance some of the "micro-projects" proposed by its "beneficiaries".

After the evaluation of CECAP I, a follow-on programme (imaginatively named "CECAP II") was designed by consultants sent by the European Union. Important differences were instituted in the design of CECAP II. Primarily, the programme was to be largely market driven and credit-financed–hand-outs (excluding the large infrastructure development projects envisaged) were replaced with loans and an emphasis on "enterprise development". Much of this was, in theory, to be financed through a sustainable "Rural Finance System". The Rural Finance component charged with establishing this sustainable financial services system for the people of the Cordillera. Other components in the CECAP II programme included:

- Agriculture (improve agricultural practices, and where possible promote new, higher value crops),
- Natural Resource Management (to mitigate or reverse the environmental degradation in the mountains),
- Marketing and Enterprise Development (to market the produce and assist the artisans),
- Infrastructure (to rehabilitate roads and irrigation systems, and to build bridges and footpaths to improve access to the more remote communities), and
- Institutional Development (to promote and develop sustainable community-based institutions in support of all the other components).

Seven international consultants were hired to implement CECAP II, which started in July 1996. Graham Wright was hired from Bangladesh on the basis that the CECAP II Rural Finance component was essentially to be a Grameen replication programme, and therefore (in the spirit of eternal optimism) that his lengthy experience in Bangladesh would be useful.

According to the European Union's Memorandum of Agreement with the Government of the Philippines, the overall objective of CECAP II is the promotion of "self-sustaining improvement in living conditions for rural communities in the Central Cordillera", emphasising "a community-based participatory approach" consistent with "the socio-economic practices of the indigenous cultural communities". The specific objectives of the programme are to "increase income and strengthen resource management capabilities". These objectives are to be achieved through a flexible programme emphasising the "provision of technical support, advice and training, and the strengthening of the capital base of the rural communities, both through the strengthening of savings generation and the injection of additional complementary funds; and through investment in small-scale infrastructure or environmental protection actions, aimed at improving the physical basis for sustainable increases in production, incomes and savings".

THE RURAL FINANCE COMPONENT

It is important to note that in the CECAP II programme the Rural Finance component's objective is not "the development of a MicroFinance Institution (MFI)", but the development of a sustainable rural finance system. This recognised that CECAP II is a relatively short-term outside programme destined to withdraw after seven years, and that the creation of a sustainable MFI in such difficult conditions would be almost impossible. Besides, after a little initial research, it was clear that much of the Cordillera had a good network of financial service providers in the form of co-operatives. Thus the programme has the following objectives.

General Objective

1. To develop a viable rural financial system consisting of a sustainable network of savings and credit groups and co-operatives that is able to provide a range of financial services to its members/clients.

Specific Objectives

1. To identify and strengthen small-scale or informal savings and loan groups;

2. To identify and strengthen larger co-operatives and formal savings and credit organisations;

3. To establish a credit extension scheme to encourage the larger co-operatives and formal savings and credit organisations to complement the capital available in the small-scale or informal savings and loan groups;

4. To promote appropriate and sustainable linkages between the small-scale or informal savings and loan groups, the larger co-operatives and formal savings and credit organisations, and the formal financial sector.

INITIAL RESEARCH AND SYSTEM DESIGN

The CECAP II Rural Finance System Design Process

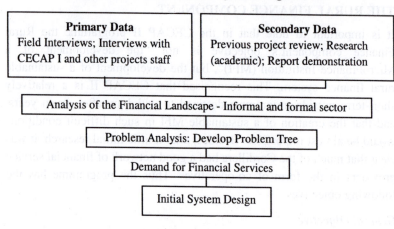

Financial Landscape

In order to design a system to meet these objectives, the designers started by examining the complete "financial landscape" of the Cordillera - rather than taking the narrow view and looking only at the formal sector services on offer, the designers also examined at the informal, financial services systems. Designers generally overlook informal financial services systems - at their (and the community's) peril. Traditional systems exist because they are useful to their clients. They are thus important guides as well as the competition for those of us seeking to establish financial systems to serve those communities in which they operate.

In order to conduct an initial exploration of the "financial landscape" of the Cordillera, secondary data from the CECAP I work,[1] and some limited research studies[2] were combined with primary data gathered through interviews with CECAP I staff[3] and the people of the Cordillera.

---

[1] special thanks to Brenda Saquing, Rodney Must, William McKone and Jocelyn Badiola for their contributions

[2] special thanks to Susan Lund

[3] special thanks to Ruben Wacas, Alexander Dulinayo, Peter Pawid, Moses Duphany, Eremita Berame and Flora Molintas

This examination of the financial landscape in a remote, relatively under-monetised area revealed a rich and diverse tapestry of financial and semi-financial systems and organisations being operated by the people of the Cordillera. The initial reports noted the existence of informal in-kind and cash credit, savings, savings and credit systems as well as informal and formal financial co-operatives and formal sector banks.

INFORMAL SAVINGS AND CREDIT MECHANISMS

Credit

In-kind credit is mostly given among neighbours (*"gawat"* groups) and very often without any interest charges. It is common that when a household is short of rice, neighbours willingly share their surpluses - the borrower being obliged to return the same volume of rice after harvest. Labour is also often accepted as payment for an in-kind loan.

Susan Lund's Study of *"Gawat"* Groups

study was conducted in four Igorot villages near Banaue in 1996, and was concerned with informal lending between villagers. She found that most loans are taken for consumption and are from family friends and neighbours on a reciprocating basis (that is, both sides understand that the borrower is obliged to offer a loan back to the lender at some unspecified future date, but not of any fixed amount). Loans are typically given at no or very low interest, and the terms/length are varied and loose. Lund found little use of guarantors or collateral, and rare inter-linking of credit with other factors. Borrowers and lenders know each other and each other's affairs well: they exchanged loans and gifts in the past and will do so again

These arrangements are "Not so much a market as a network of relationships," and Lund surmises that they provide insurance and thus smooth consumption. Loans are "state-contingent" - loans flow to those in need after income shocks most of which are not covariant[4] in these villages. Almost every household is involved: only 3 out of 206

contd.

---

[4] Covariant shocks are those that occur together affecting many households simultaneously– for example a drought that affects the crops of an entire village.

Continued from: Susan Lund's Study

---

households had not done it during the study's 9-months period, and
nearly half of such loans are between first-degree relatives. Repayment
is rapid - mostly 2 or 3 months, at borrower's convenience. Repayment
is very good (only 1 in the 1,142 studied by Lund were in default),
enforced by threat (or fear) of exclusion from future deals. The average
value of 'Lund' loans was 1,170 pesos.

Cash credit is used for providential and business investment
purposes. Providential purposes include education, health, food, and
housing repair and construction. This kind of credit is usually received
from neighbours (typically very small amounts, but often interest free),
co-operatives (at 1-3% per month interest over a maximum of 3-5
months) and moneylenders (at 10-20% per month interest). The amounts
borrowed typically range from P. 200 to P. 5,000.

Business and larger longer term loans are usually popular in
relatively better-off households in accessible *barangays* (villages).
These loans are given by co-operatives and moneylenders. Co-
operatives lend on the basis of typically 2-3 times the members' share
capital/deposits, and require repayment over one year. Moneylenders on
the other hand, lend an unlimited amount but select their borrowers
based on previous repayment performance. The moneylenders are also
flexible in terms of loan duration providing interest instalments are paid
on time. The usual amount for business and long term loans range from
P.5,000 to P.30,000. Co-operatives generally treat loans of less than
P.5,000 as providential, requiring repayment within 3-5 months.

Moneylenders have been active in the Philippine for centuries and
until comparatively recent times represented the only real source of
credit. Condemned by the church, outlawed by the state and frowned on
by society, the moneylenders kept their financial dealings secret and
kept no accounts open to scrutiny. Traditionally, moneylenders were
rich landowners. Today, landlords, traders, schoolteachers, and
shopkeepers may engage in these activities.

In the Central Cordillera markets, the so called "five - six"
arrangement, whereby the borrower receives P. 5 in the morning and
repays P. 6 to the lender in the evening, is common. The interest rate of
20% per day may seem usurious but the moneylender does not engage in
such transactions every day of the year and the annualisation of such

rates of interest is not meaningful. Moreover, the borrower does not generally consider the interest rate to be excessive as he may well be able to make a profit with the use of the borrowed money, usually from trading activities, sufficient to give him an attractive return after repayment of the loan. More typical moneylender rates in the *barangays* are 10-20% a month.

Other systems involve the mortgaging of land, which is then effectively owned by the lender until the loanee repays. In these cases, the lender is then free either to cultivate the land himself (and take all the harvest proceeds) or to share-crop the land (often with the loanee). The effective rate of interest under such systems is probably even higher than the 10-20% per month for cash denominated loans outlined above.

As with all traditional moneylender systems, the ability to get a loan at all is more important than the interest rate charged. Equally important is the lack of procedural red tape involved, the fact that collateral is not normally required and the speed of issuance of the loan. As the lender and borrower are usually well known to each other, the lender has a good understanding of the borrower's loan project, which he may well be able to monitor in the normal course of *barangay* life. No high degree of literacy is necessary on the part of the borrower nor are any time-consuming trips to the nearest town.

There are however, potential disadvantages and risks in these sources of credit. Most moneylenders are only prepared to give short-term loans and then, usually for traditional rather than innovative activities. Where trade credit is extended, there may be an obligation to sell produce to the lender at low prices. Borrowers may become excessively obligated to moneylenders in ways which have nothing to do with their loans, such as to be obliged to lend political or other support, to perform services or refrain from actions of which the lender may not approve. Personal conflicts, real or imagined, may prevent deserving borrowers from being able to get loans at all. These disadvantages may become severe, the more unequal in power or status the relationship between the borrower and lender becomes.

Savings

Non-perishable farm produce, (rice, corn, root crops etc.) is usually stored to guarantee food availability until the next harvest season. Any extra cash from sale of produce and from wages is usually invested in livestock (especially pigs and caribou) which in turn can be sold in the event of emergency needs for cash. If the household has a substantial amount of cash surplus, it is used to buy rice fields or to build a house. Small amounts of cash that remain unused are kept and secreted in the household for emergency purposes.

The emphasis on saving "in-kind" in the Cordillera probably reflects i) the additional prestige associated with owning livestock and particularly land, ii) the view that cash declines in value (hardly surprising in view of the very low real rates of interest offered by co-operatives in the area), and iii) the limited needs for cash in what remains a relatively poorly monetised region of the Philippines. This apparent antipathy towards saving in cash, and a similar unwillingness to make regular small savings, were considered likely to be important and difficult challenges for the CECAP II Rural Finance System.

Rural households in the CECAP area seldom save money in banks because of the distances to these institutions. Some also feel "intimidated" dealing with these institutions because of their perception that banks are for the rich, and a dislike of the (known or unknown) intricacies of the process of dealing with the banks.

Savings and Credit

In the CECAP area there are also a variety of examples of participatory group schemes designed to intermediate small amounts of cash (or kind) savings into larger sums - indeed one pre-project mission's survey estimated that 60% of the respondents belonged to one or more *"paluwagan"* or informal savings and loan group. Discussions with CECAP I project staff indicated that this estimate is over-optimistic even when the widespread traditional labour-pooling groups are included. Other systems of non-cash savings and credit that may have been included in the mission's survey: such as the regular setting aside of rice in the household *"isang dakut"*, and the use of rice bundles saved and lent out to households who in turn repay both the principal and interest in rice.

Nonetheless, it appears that the use of pooled-labour sharing systems as a form of saving is declining as increasingly labourers require cash for their services. This may reflect both the increasing monetisation of the *barangays* and the increasing levels of landlessness in the

Agawa Og-og-fu or ROSCA

The "Og-og-fu" system is popular in Mountain Province as a form of pooling labour. However, a modified, monetised version of "Og-og-fu" is being practised by one women's group in Agawa in the Municipality of Besao. The group has nine members who are neighbours. Initially, each one contributed an amount of P. 500, and thus started the "Og-og-fu" or ROSCA. Then the group members identified their individual projects which needed funding, and together evaluated each project on its merit and the urgency for its implementation. The group then made a consensus decision on the priority order of project funding, and gave the pooled funds to the members in the order agreed upon.

After that, each member was obliged to continue saving and come up with the P.500 for every two months and each member received the fund on the basis of the pre-agreed arrangement. Members found the cash from labour derived from farming activities, from household salaried members, and from the sale of vegetable produce. The projects supported out of the fund were not solely for income generation. Some members utilised the fund for housing repair and children's college education but the majority invested in swine fattening.

Cordillera. These factors may also account for the fact that some of the traditional "in-kind" labour-pooling and commodity-saving systems are being adapted to run cash-based savings systems that intermediate small amounts of regular cash savings into larger capital sums. Included in this category are the rotating savings and credit associations (ROSCAs) in which each member makes small regular savings and in turn (agreed by mutual consent, lottery or bidding) receives the lump sum generated.

ROSCAs run for a finite period of time whereupon the books are closed. The ROSCAs then usually reform with the same or slightly modified membership. The finite time-span is seen by many commentators as an important strength of such schemes as it maintains transparency. It is indeed possible that co-operatives in the CECAP area (which often seem to suffer from lack of confidence in the book-keeping of the management) could also conduct a "public audit" and book-closing annually.

There are, of course, many other forms of informal savings and credit group. Field visits revealed several accumulating credit associations (ACAs) in which each member makes a one-off savings deposit into a collective fund from which members may borrow at interest (usually 3-5% per month), thus increasing the fund over time.

The Maggok Accumulating Credit Association

In one *sitio* (para) of this remote *barangay*, 13 friends set up a "loan scheme" back in 1986. The idea was taken from one of the village elders, and each of the friends put P. 12.50 into the fund. Since 1986, they have always kept the fund lent out charging interest at the rate of 5% per month, and it has already grown to over P. 30,000. Repayments are usually monthly or balloon, and terms are usually for about 6 months. Receipts are not used, and there is only one set of books.

The *paluwagan* is not simply that of a disciplined approach to savings and credit, it is a system based on principles of collective action which have evolved over the centuries from ancient customs such as community labour and rice sharing. It is based on strong peer pressure and group solidarity which lead to low risk of default. It is highly flexible, tailored to the needs of the members, disciplines people to save and has negligible transaction costs.

Membership is not confined to the lower income groups. Members come from all walks of life. They borrow mostly to invest in a productive activity, build a house, purchase durables, or pay school or medical fees.

Jolowon Accumulating Credit Association

In May 1995 Magdelena and eight of her trusted friends and immediate neighbours started a small scheme to help them save to meet the emergencies and opportunities that arise so regularly in their day-to-day life - and in particular to help them deal with education costs for their children. Initially, they each deposited P. 100 in the fund, and a month or so later they deposited another P. 100, bringing

contd

Continued from : Jolowon Accumulating Credit Association

the capital of the fund to P. 1,800. The rules the friends agreed for the fund were as follows: members could borrow funds for a maximum of three months at the rate of 10% per calendar month, and all the profits would be retained in the fund until the group agreed to wrap-up the fund.

The members used their loans to meet emergency education and health needs and to finance trading opportunities, and (even at 10% per calendar month) found the credit facility tremendously useful as a way of smoothing their uneven cashflows. Later they agreed that non-members could also borrow from the fund if a member acted as guarantor and was liable to make up any shortfall not repaid by the loanee. By October 1995, they had accumulated around P. 9,000, and for the first time since they had started the scheme, not all the fund was out on loan. By June 1996, the fund had grown to more than P. 13,000, and the group had a surplus of P. 5,000 funds not out on loan, stored in an account at the co-operative in Lamut. The group is now considering reducing the interest rate on loans to stimulate demand.

In addition, there are various types of *barangay*-based, informal groups and associations organised on the basis of an activity being pursued by the group (e.g. health, sanitation, commodity production, civic works etc.) or to meet a common need. The usual membership ranges from 5 to 30 individuals from different households in the *barangay*, and often, the most successful organisations of this type are those formed by women.

Banguitan Women's Association

One example of a successful *barangay*-level group is the Banguitan Women's Association in the municipality of Besao. The group is composed of 20 mothers who shared a common need of establishing a store in their *barangay* to sell quality consumer goods. Each member contributed P. 200, and the pooled money was used as the Association's initial capital. This capital was then augmented by a loan from CECAP I. One member offered a small space in her house to use as a stock room and selling area. Purchasing and selling was done on a rotation

Contd..

Continued from : Banguitan Women's Association

---

basis, each member ran the store for a week without pay. Every evening the members gathered together in the store to undertake group auditing of the day's transactions. After two years of operations, the members' initial capital of P. 4,000 plus the CECAP loan of P. 30,000 had increased to over P. 80,000. Part of the proceeds was used to purchase a residential house which now serves as the store and shop.

The group members have not yet taken any profit out of the business but they are now planning to use some of the proceeds for lending among themselves.

Finally, there are several informal co-operatives in the CECAP area. The informal co-operatives are following co-operative principles but are not registered with the Co-operative Development Authority. They however have the potential (and often intention) of graduating into a formal type co-operative. They were often organised as an offshoot of intensive campaigns from government agencies and NGOs, who are strong believers in co-operative as a strategy for grassroots development.

These informal co-operatives are usually *barangay*-based and so the degree of cohesiveness is expected to be strong. The members belong to a socio-economically homogenous group and share similar problems and aspirations. The natural intrinsic relationships among members are expected to provide the backbone for the success of these organisations. Usually, lending or trading in consumer goods is chosen as the first business activity.

However, in many cases these co-operatives are weak which may be a result of the hurried or poor organising done to initiate them. Often, after a group received a co-operative orientation course, the group members were presumed to be ready to organise and run a co-operative. Groups would then select officers and collect share capital from members, and even start business operations without having formulated operating policies or record keeping systems. In situations such as this, problems inevitably crop up over time and distrust grows between officers and members. In addition, some co-operatives were organised to gain access to government soft loans and so the organisation disappeared as soon as the loans were sanctioned and disbursed.

Pangol Multi-Purpose Co-operative

One example of a successful informal co-operative Tanudan is the Pangol Multi-Purpose Co-operative which was assisted by CECAP I. The 30 original members belong to a distinct tribe in Kalinga. Essentially, the basic strategy they employed in raising their group fund required each member to contribute a minimum of P. 500 each by saving at least P. 50 a month given to the group's treasurer. The fund grew fast as each member saved enthusiastically. The co-operative members businesses are likewise doing well not least of all because of the continued patronage of the co-operative's members. The co-operative has set aside 30% of its capital to lend to co-operative members for providential purposes. After two years of successful operations, the Pangol Multi-Purpose Co-operative registered with the Co-operative Development Authority.

The existence of these informal financial institutions demonstrates the high propensity among Cordillera people, rich and poor, to save and exercise fiscal discipline. However, for the most part, in isolated rural communities the potential savings of the people are uncollected, and their credit needs unfulfilled.

FORMAL SECTOR FINANCIAL INSTITUTIONS

The difficult terrain, poor communications and unpredictable climate of the Central Cordillera coupled with the apparent perception that the rural population is un-bankable, has limited the penetration of formal financial institutions to the urban centres, particularly in the lowlands, where access is easiest and trade is most developed.

Banks

Few banks are present in the rural areas of the Central Cordillera. They are largely based in the larger towns in the lowlands and appear to be patronised by large farmers. One exception is the Land Bank of the Philippines (LBP), which is a leading provider of financial services to the rural communities through its branches and field offices, of which a handful are in the CECAP area. Its priority lending programmes are described as loans to individual farmers, primary co-operatives and rural financial institutions. Even so, because of the need for collateral, few small farmers are able to access LBP loans.

In recent times, the LBP has used some accredited savings and loan co-operatives as conduits providing funds at 14% to 18% interest for on lending at 16% to 25%. The interest spread looks to be unattractive by comparison to the spreads available on members' savings. The Depatment of Trade and Industry (DTI) also implements a programme to channel funds to non-government organisations at 7% per annum for re-lending to registered co-operatives at prevailing commercial rates of around 18%.

Co-operatives

There are around 470 registered Multi-Purpose/Savings and Loan Co-operatives in the region, many of which were established to access subsidised, low interest loans from now defunct government schemes.

Co-operative Grameen

The Agricultural Credit Policy Council is the official regulatory body for the rural finance sector. As well as operating credit guarantee schemes, it is in favour of innovative approaches to address the credit needs of the poor and has been supporting 30 Grameen Bank replication schemes in the Philippines. One of these is operated by the Banaue Savings and Credit Co-operative, however it has not been a success and in December 1995, the last month from which data is available, their repayments were only 67%.

The reasons for the lack of success of this programme revolve around several issues. First, the system was a Grameen Bank replication that was particularly unsuited to the CECAP area because of the uneven cashflow in the barangay households. Uneven cashflows obviously limit the ability to make regular savings and to find the money for the weekly loan repayments required. Furthermore, when groups have no obvious reason to meet regularly (because they cannot make regular savings) and their members live some distance apart, peer pressure and group unity are compromised; this was the case here. Finally, the programme suffered as a result of the poor motivation and performance of the extension worker hired by Banaue Savings ad Credit Co-operative to work with the groups.

Lagawe Multi-Purpose Co-operative

An example of a very successful co-operative in the CECAP area is the Lagawe Multi-Purpose Co-operative. It was established in 1985 and currently has assets of P.19 million and some 1,600 members, 40% of which come from the town and the rest from throughout Ifugao Province. The normal share holding is P.500 which can be accumulated in ten instalments of P.50. A savings account can be opened with a minimum amount of P.25 but will not attract interest until P.500 has been saved.

Loans are based on a multiple of share holding - either two or three times the loanee's share capital at the co-operative. The maximum loan limit is P.100,000. Interest rates vary from 12% upwards depending on the type of loan, most of which are for trading purposes. In accordance with co-operative norms in the Cordillera, interest is deducted at source. Loans are approved by the Loans Committee, which meets twice a month. Borrowers must have approved collateral, usually real estate.

Many are thought to be dormant if not actually bankrupt. Most Multi-Purpose Co-operatives in fact only provide savings and loan facilities to their members.

The most successful co-operatives are found in the towns, important municipalities or near main highways. Coverage is limited in rural areas. They are usually self contained in the sense that they are capable of generating their own loan funds from internal savings mobilisation. Some are able to access funds from the LBP, the Department of Labour and Employment (appropriately enough - DOLE), the DTI or other Government agencies.

Co-operatives are at a disadvantage as compared to banks as they can only mobilise savings from their members rather than the public at large. The better-managed co-operatives can take advantage of their local orientation and self-selected member orientation. They complement rather than compete with other financial institutions.

The interest rates paid on deposits by Savings and Loan Co-operatives are relatively modest at between 5% and 6.5% per annum, which is significantly below the current rate of inflation of about 9%. Interest charged on loans is between 15% and 20% (deducted at source) depending on the length, purpose etc. giving an effective spread of around 20% to 30%, depending on the repayment schedule. Annual dividends paid out to shareholders are in the range of 4% to 6%. [5]

Problem Analysis

After thoroughly examining the "Financial Landscape", the researchers were able to analyse the problems faced by the poor in getting access to financial services. Looking at the root problem and the branches that followed from there, the researchers developed a "Problem Tree" to create the framework and recognise the challenges for the CECAP II Rural Finance Programme. The problems facing the poor range from location to perception of creditworthiness.

POOR ACCESS TO FORMAL SECTOR INSTITUTIONS

As discussed, the Central Cordillera area is characterised by rugged terrain, an unpredictable climate and poor communications. Banks and the larger co-operatives are generally found only in the main urban centres. Therefore, CECAP works in the barangays which are frequently isolated, far from commercial centres and difficult to reach by road.

The issue is not only one of proximity or access to rural institutions on the part of their potential customers. The terrain, climate and communication difficulties within the CECAP area create barriers to the timely delivery of production inputs and the effective marketing of produce surpluses. These factors make small-scale agriculture and other income generating enterprises inherently more risk-prone, and therefore less interesting to prospective lenders.

STRINGENT LENDING CONDITIONS OF FORMAL SECTOR INSTITUTIONS

The formal financial sector is characterised by top-down administrative procedures, form filling, delays and red tape. These procedures are time-consuming, invariably lack flexibility and impose conditions, in particular the need for collateral, which the poor are often unable to meet. These problems are exacerbated by illiteracy, possible prejudice

---

[5] This information on the "financial landscape" was taken from the initial Rural Finance Strategy document written by Graham A.N. Wright and Ruben Wacas, which in turn was developed on the basis of documents prepared by Brenda Saquing, Rodney Must, William McKone and Jocelyn Badiola, supplemented and substantiated by extensive field-based research.

against women and, the perception by banks that there are high risks associated with lending to small farmers.

Prospective borrowers of small loans may find the formal institutions unwilling to accommodate their needs because of the relatively high transaction costs involved in processing small sums. Borrowers, on the other hand, tend to resent the intrusive (as they see it) questioning into their financial status which they contrast with the mutual trust basis of borrowing from the informal sector which satisfies their needs for self respect rather than damages their pride.

PERCEIVED CREDITWORTHINESS OF THE POOR

Lending from the formal banking system is, in general, only available to those able to offer collateral. Small farmers, landless labourers and the poor do not have the option to save and thus the cash money or the physical assets required to guarantee the loan.

This lack of assets is further compounded in the CECAP area by the lack of a fully implemented land policy which would give small farmers rights to land. As a result, prospective borrowers are forced to rely for working capital on the informal sector where security arrangements are more flexible.

Even where the poor do use formal sector financial service institutions, these funds are unlikely to recycle back into the rural communities. Not only do the poor have less collateral and savings, the smaller loan sizes needed in the rural area carry a higher loan transaction cost than the formal financial institutions desire. Ironically then, the savings of the poor are more likely to be lent to the comparatively wealthy, urban borrower who can both meet the lender's conditions, and to whom the lender is attracted because of greater profitability resulting from lower transaction costs.

HIGH INTEREST RATES IN THE INFORMAL SECTOR

Interest rates prevailing in the informal sector are influenced by the nature and extent of personal relations between the parties, the degree of risk in the project, the availability of funds in the community, the length of the maturity period of the loan and the extent of competition from the formal financial market.

Precise information on interest rates is under-researched in the Programme area but in one study (SETA, August 1995) interest rates were found to range between 18% and 900% per annum. Formal sector

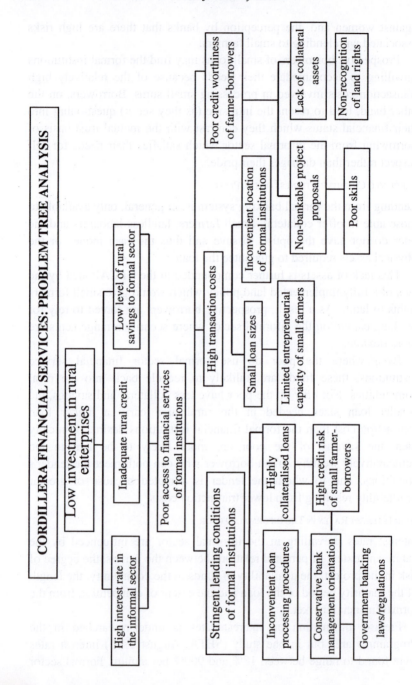

CORDILLERA FINANCIAL SERVICES: PROBLEM TREE ANALYSIS

Low investment in rural enterprises

High interest rate in the informal sector

Inadequate rural credit

Low level of rural savings to formal sector

Poor access to financial services of formal institutions

Stringent lending conditions of formal institutions

High transaction costs

Poor credit worthiness of farmer-borrowers

Inconvenient loan processing procedures

Highly collateralised loans

Inconvenient location of formal institutions

Lack of collateral assets

Conservative bank management orientation

High credit risk of small farmer-borrowers

Small loan sizes

Non-recognition of land rights

Government banking laws/regulations

Limited entrepreneurial capacity of small farmers

Non-bankable project proposals

Poor skills

interest rates at that time were 14-16% per annum. Clearly there is a huge potential niche market somewhere between the two.

Trader credit is commonly practised in the Central Cordillera. Determining the actual rate of interest in the case of credit advanced to farmers by traders for production   as an advance payment for the purchase of the crop after harvest is not at all transparent.   This is oftentimes to the disadvantage of the borrower since the final payment for the produce will be discounted.

POOR RATES OF RETURN ON SAVINGS OFFERED BY FORMAL SECTOR

Although a relatively minor issue for the poor, the rates of return on savings do matter to the better off who are able to access the formal sector services. Currently, formal sector institutions such as banks offer interest on current accounts at around 4-7% per annum. Even the larger, more established co-operatives only offer 5% and 6.5% per annum, plus annual dividends paid out to shareholders in the range of 4% to 6%. With the current rate of inflation in the Philippines at about 9%, these give (at best) very marginally positive, and often negative, real interest rates - and thus offer poor incentives to save through the formal sector.

Demand for Financial Services

Once the Problem Analysis and Problem Tree has been completed, the next step is to analyse the "financial landscape" to review and analyse the potential demand, and thus to develop mechanisms to respond to this demand[6]

ECONOMIC BACKGROUND

The demand for financial services within the CECAP area varies substantially according to the accessibility of, and economic activity in the *barangay*; and then within the *barangay* itself according to the level and nature of individual households' cash income and expenditure. Overall the CECAP area suffers from lower than average cash penetration by comparison to the rest of the Philippines, and many particularly remote *barangays* are still dominated by exchange/barter based economic activity. Within the area, typical average household monthly cash income ranges from between P. 500 and P. 2,500, but this

---

[6]   This problem analysis is taken almost directly from a series of documents authored by Ruben Wacas, Brenda Saquing, Rodney Must, William McKone and Jocelyn Badiola.

hides often extremely lumpy, seasonal cashflows, particularly in the more remote *barangays*.

There are several key sources of cash in the rural barangay/ municipalities in the CECAP area:

Irregular

- Most cash crops (coffee, corn, fruit, vegetables etc.)
- Sale of livestock (poultry, chicken, pigs etc.)
- Migration Labour
- Remittances from overseas contract workers
- Seasonal projects implemented by Government (e.g. road maintenance, building water supply systems, schools etc.)

Regular

- Wage (Day) Labour
- Trading
- Handicrafts
- Some cash crops (banana etc.)
- Salaries from Government/Projects etc.
- Pensions

However, those households with regular sources of income are relatively limited in number. The analysis indicated that most of CECAP II's target households may have difficulty in making regular cash savings, but could greatly benefit from facilities that will allow them to deposit lump sums.

A detailed study[7] in the Lamut area indicated that 41% of the poor households, and 48% of the medium-income households participated in a *paluwagan* contributing/depositing an average of P.500 and P.700 per month. Although this data looks somewhat questionable (the figures are considered extremely optimistic by CECAP I staff, and poor households ostensibly contributed an average of 24% of their declared income) and is drawn from a relatively accessible and economically active area, it provides some indication that there is both a desire and propensity to save among households in the CECAP area. It is also interesting and important to note that the discipline of regular compulsory savings was particularly valued by the members.

---

[7]   As part of the initial CECAP II project design process conducted in 1995.

The success of initiating savings and loan co-operatives, together with the proliferation of informal savings and credit schemes, also suggests a strong demand for savings facilities. The lumpy nature of cashflows in the *barangays* currently necessitates the "storage" of savings in non-cash assets: livestock, land etc., which can sometimes result in a net loss on liquidation.

In addition, international experience has shown time and time again that there is a strong desire and capability among the poor to save. A comparable programme (initiated by Action Aid) in the remote mountains of northern Vietnam (where the tribal people are, if anything, poorer) showed a significant propensity to save, and generated substantial savings.

DEMAND FOR CREDIT FACILITIES

Clearly not all households will seek to borrow at the same time. Furthermore, it is important to differentiate between the demand for short-term "providential" credit (to meet emergency needs - education expenses, health care, food in the lean season, schooling, social and other costs) and investment credit for income generation activities.

The demand for **providential credit** is likely to vary substantially from household to household, and according to the time of year, but typically as much as 25-50% of all households are likely to need a providential loan at any one time. Historically commentators have tended to overlook the importance of providential loans, while seeking to emphasise productive investment forgetting the important role of income, asset and human capital protection and development played by such loans.

The demand for **investment credit** is also likely to vary substantially from *barangay* to *barangay* (according to the level of access and monetised economic activity). Furthermore the demand for investment credit will also vary from household to household: some have adequate funds for their limited activities, many are risk-averse and not interested in further expanding or diversifying their activities, and for others, the timing is not yet right. It is estimated that typically, only around 40-50% of the households will need investment credit in any one year.

INITIAL SYSTEM DESIGN AND IMPLEMENTATION METHODOLOGY

> *"The key to developing a viable financial system is to encourage the most simple organizations to emerge at the lowest level, and to provide increased linkages and co-ordination between institutions and between the formal and informal sector so that the limitations of the simple organizations can be overcome." (Meyer, 1988)*

Looking at the existing financial services providers, the problems facing the poor in accessing financial services and the demand among the population for financial services, a tentative conclusion was reached as to initial system design and implementation methodology. Putting this into practice allowed the researchers to undertake action research to validate the research results outlined above, gather additional information, and test the system being proposed.

Implementation Issues

There are limited opportunities for income generation in the Programme area as a result of poor communications, poor access and marketing bottlenecks. Viable credit projects are therefore limited and savings were stressed as a key, central component of the Rural Finance System.

Because CECAP I was largely grant-based, the recovery of loans issued at the tail end of the programme proved difficult, and around $200,000 loans remained outstanding – a problematic legacy. Overcoming the "grant" image of CECAP I posed a special challenge to CECAP II. Changing the image required special attention changing the mind-set of all stakeholders - staff, external agencies (LGUs, NGOs, Co-operatives etc.) and the community.

The uneven (and often extremely limited) cash-flows, and remoteness of some *barangays* presented special challenges: indeed there are likely to be many *barangays* for which a Rural Finance System is neither feasible nor appropriate.

CECAP II used a phased approach (starting with the less remote *barangays*) to allow the Programme to develop experience and learn lessons in places it can easily monitor and move quickly to sort out problems and repair any damage. Rather than launch the programme on a large scale, the phased in approach allowed more effective on-the-job training for new staff (and for CECAP I staff learning a new way of operating), facilitated the involvement of co-operatives, and provided demonstration Savings and Loan Groups for sceptical target group members in more remote *barangays*.

It was clear from the remoteness of the communities, the sparse population density in the Cordillera and the review of the financial landscape that there was no sense in trying to replicate the Grameen Bank as had been recommended in the initial programme design and documentation of CECAP II. With the rich tradition of informal self-help groups and the high quality of co-operatives in the Cordillera, an alternative approach was not only feasible, but also desirable. Accordingly, the initial system proposed using small, self-selecting "Savings and Loan Groups" (SLGs), meeting together in one place at one time (referred to as "Savings and Loan Societies") in order to reduce the cost of providing outreach services to the SLGs. In order to develop the culture of saving and to build up funds that could be accessed and used at short notice within the community, the SLGs meet and save together weekly. From these SLG members were to take small-scale emergency loans, repayable on terms and conditions decided upon by the group members themselves.

Thus the small SLGs follow the traditional lending/savings arrangements of trusted friends and neighbours. CECAP II conducts community meetings to discuss the proposed system and encourages friends and neighbours, (often existing *"gawat"* groups), to form SLGs. Once this was completed, CECAP II then trained the SLGs in a basic book-keeping system designed specifically for them, and encouraged SLGs to conduct their own small-scale financial services: regular limited access savings and small scale intra-group loans from their own SLG Funds.

Once the SLGs members wanted access to more extensive savings and credit facilities, they were required to federate (a minimum of 4-5 SLGs or 20-25 members) into Savings and Loan Societies (SLS). SLGs were designed to meet weekly initially at their SLS[8]. Upon maturing, SLSs met bi-weekly in order to link and transact with Key Co-operatives

---

[8]   It is important to note that the SLS is simply a time and place where SLGs come together to conduct their business and interact with the CECAP II and/or Key Cooperative staff.

(KCs). Once the introduction to KCs was made, the SLG members started to save regularly at the KC. *See Appendix 1 for the SLG Organising Progress.*

In view of the plan to link the self-help SLGs to KCs, the programme conducted three CECAP-Co-operative Consultative Forums to discuss the proposed policies and procedures with the KCs. These provided extremely useful insights into the co-operatives' views of lending to the poor. The KCs had, under government pressure, previously attempted Grameen-influenced lending which had not been successful. The effort left them confused about group lending and sceptical about how to involve the poor. The Forums also allowed CECAP to build interest in and support for the proposed Rural Finance System among the KCs as they recognised a feasible and potentially financially lucrative system. The KCs showed great interest in the system, for two reasons. Firstly, they were aware that their membership was largely drawn from the more wealthy in the community and they were keen to extend and deepen their membership. Secondly, the co-operatives in the Cordillera needed an alternative system to improve loan recovery – collateralised land was proving hard to realise in the event of default[9] and portfolio at risk was mounting – and were therefore interested in looking at group guarantee-based system. The KCs were given training on the CECAP II system (and where necessary on some basic institutional development and management issues), as well as capital funds (initially on a loan basis-with the prospect of conversion to grant basis for good performance) to on-lend to members of SLGs.

The linkage with the KCs and formal sector institutions did not begin in the initial implementation/pilot stage. In the later part of the Programme CECAP II planned to develop links between the KCs and formal sector co-operative banks or banks

---

Thus the initial system design could be summarised as follows:

Savings and Loan Groups federating into
Savings and Loan Societies linking to
Municipal Key Co-operatives linking to
Formal Sector Banks

---

9   This is a problem that is very common in community-based and managed organisations – it is very difficult to appropriate and sell the land of friends, family and other community members.

It was this system that was taken into the field for pilot testing in five zones. Each of the zones were markedly different in terms of the conditions the system would face: varying access to markets and the lowlands, differing indigenous and groups population density (or better said "sparsity"), and some with viable KCs, others with none. The pilot testing of the system was combined with a programme of action research to learn still more about the financial landscape and how it varies amongst the many different indigenous groups and between the valleys in the mountains.

PILOT-TESTING AND ACTION RESEARCH

The CECAP II Rural Finance System Design Process

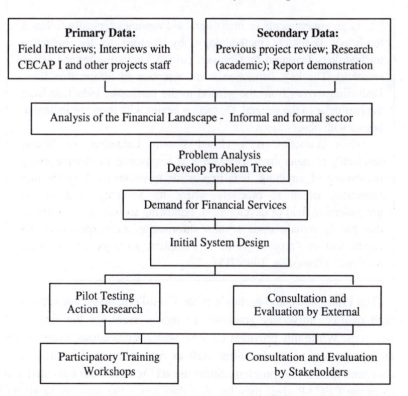

The initial research and design phase took about three months. At the end of that time, the system designers felt confident that the situation was 'workable" and hired a small number of field staff, called "Rural Finance Officers" (RFOs), to pilot test the system and conduct action research in the field. The pilot testing was to review the system "in action in the field" and the action research was designed to further develop the staff and management's understanding of the "financial landscape" and socio-economic situation within which the system would be implemented. Given the diversity of settings within the project area, there were a remarkable range of issues, opportunities and threats uncovered by the on-going action research – this proved to be an important education for the staff.

Action Research

" ... large governments or multilateral aid agencies typically follow a top-heavy deductive methodology, by contrast to the inductive methodology favoured by Grameen (which Yunus has termed action research). The key distinction is the direction of information flow: Deduction moves from the general to the particular, induction from the particular to the general. Deduction begins with theories; induction begins with observations.

While deduction is a closed system, induction, or "action research", remains open: Because it is impossible to observe every occurrence of anything, it is impossible to prove anything through induction, which is precisely where its advantage lies in the unpredictable field of development. Following an inductive approach, one has to remain open to new information and experiences: an experiment or "project" is never complete, an argument is never resolved" (*Bornstein*, 1996:215).

The Philippines, and particularly the Cordillera, boasted a number of high quality, university graduates to recruit from for the field staff positions. While this provided CECAP with a tremendous resource and the opportunity to use front-line staff as researchers and facilitators, it also presented a real problem. Since the RFOs were both educated and from the CECAP area, they felt that they knew the answers to all the questions before they had asked them. They were convinced that there was no significant or substantive "social stratification" within the

Cordillera - "we are all poor rice farmers". They were quite sure that the poorer households would not be able to save, and particularly not on a weekly basis. Finally, most had worked on traditional agricultural credit programmes, and required complete reorientation away from project-tied credit for "beneficiaries" to the provision of financial services to discerning "clients".

Staff had to be trained in Participatory Rural Appraisal (PRA) and Focus Group Discussion techniques. By requiring them to conduct the action research and validation of the system design, they were able to overcome their prejudices, unlearn "traditional agricultural credit think", and at the same time provide useful inputs into the process of forming and training SLGs and refining the system. The RFOs were trained to use the following PRA tools:

1. Wealth Ranking
2. Seasonality Analysis of Income, Expenditure, Savings and Credit;
3. Seasonality Analysis of Wage Labour Availability (and where it is available);
4. Venn Diagrams Analysis of organisations/individuals providing financial services;
5. Mobility Mapping of the flows of cash - where it is earned and spent

The results obtained from the use of these PRA techniques were then used to probe more deeply into issues related to the availability of cash and financial services in the villages, as an integral part of the process of preparing to form SLGs in each village. The RFOs were required to submit a detailed report on each area where they initiated work following a carefully defined format – see Appendix 2 for the PRA, FGD Summary Report.

After gathering this information, primarily through participatory rural appraisal, the recommendations and conclusions of the RFOs was sought.

REGULAR PARTICIPATORY TRAINING WORKSHOPS

Every two/three months throughout the pilot testing and action research phase, week-long training workshops were held to discuss what had been learnt in the field. These workshops not only assisted the process of making important improvements to the system and implementation methodology, but allowed the designers to see the perceptions and prejudices of the RFOs changing. By the second workshop they returned amazed by the desire and ability of the poor to save and save weekly. Their previous feelings about the lack of social stratification, as well as their beliefs that wage labour was only very seasonal were likewise shattered as they continued to hold focus group discussions and perform participatory rural appraisals. By the third workshop, the RFOs were convinced not only of the high level of social stratification in the villages, but also of the relatively high availability of wage labour - particularly if the labourer was willing to travel outside his/her village.

In addition, a full day of each of these training workshops was dedicated to the discussion of problems, issues and successes from the field. These sessions allowed the RFOs to propose changes to the implementation methodology, seek guidance, resolve (often simply organisational) issues and share experiences so that they could further improve the way they sold the idea and system in the field.

Clients' Consultative Groups

In retrospect, the design and pilot testing process should have included the establishment of "Clients' Consultative Groups" in each of the pilot test areas to provide additional guidance for the design of the system and the financial services offered. These groups are usually formed of the clients elected into leadership positions within the implementing organisation's groups. The leaders are chosen on the basis of their ability to look at and consider the "big picture" of the MFI's objectives, constraints and options, as well as the needs and opportunities facing their colleagues and peers, the MFI's clientele. This would have helped resolve key issue of whether the resistance to the proposed weekly repayment schedule arose from co-operative norms in the Cordillera, or from a genuine need.

The pilot testing process moved ahead with relatively few problems – clients were keen to form SLGs and save, they borrowed and generally repaid their loans with few problems. There were only two serious issues: firstly, the clients objected to meeting weekly during the day time, since they felt that was a time when they could have been working in the fields. However, for the purposes of training and monitoring by CECAP staff who only worked during the week days, this was considered necessary and important. Secondly, many of the SLGs chose to allow lump sum repayment of the loans taken from their SLG fund. Since the use of the SLG funds was meant to be a practice/rehearsal for borrowing larger amounts (repayable on a weekly instalment basis) from the KCs, this was considered to be undesirable by the project staff. These issues were the two most discussed amongst CECAP staff and the system's clients ... and remained so throughout the pilot testing phase.

The former was resolved through the "accreditation process". SLGs were reviewed after three months of operation and if they had correctly maintained their books of account, met regularly, taken and repaid loans on time and shown cohesion and discipline, they were "accredited". Accredited SLGs were recommended to the KCs as "credit-worthy" groups and were permitted to meet with CECAP/KC staff monthly (although their regular weekly SLG meetings continued at times chosen by the members).

EXTERNAL REVIEW OF THE INITIAL RESEARCH AND DESIGN

In addition to this pilot testing and action research process, CECAP II management felt it was important to get a "second opinion" from an outsider, and contracted Stuart Rutherford to critically examine the initial system design and implementation methodology, and to review the pilot test.

Terms of Reference

Examination and Evaluation of Key Issues

Overall Objective of Consultancy

To take a fresh look at the existing financial services in the *barangays* of the Cordillera and to help the Rural Finance component of the Programme to incorporate the findings into their plans to set up a rural finance system.

---

contd·

Continued from: Terms of Reference
_____

The Results

The consultant began his work in the *barangays* with a review of sources and volumes of income, and patterns of expenditure. Apart from providing a general overview of the economy of the different areas or "zones" where the CECAP Rural Finance System was to be implemented (including the degree of monetisation), this exercise probed social and economic status within the *sitios* and *barangays*. In particular, he examined how the household economies of rich, middle and lower income people differed and the differing roles of men and women in the households. Understanding these dynamics of *barangay* life has a direct bearing on whether the proposed Rural Finance programme should target certain groups within the community, and on what kind of services would be most appropriate for that group or groups.

Next the consultant turned to the question of how the different groups manage their money. Since financial services for poor people is largely a question of helping them turn their savings to good use, he concentrated on how, why, and when people save. He looked for, and found, some indigenous group-based savings clubs. Much time was spent looking into the intensive borrowing and lending that goes on between *barangay* residents and between them and outsiders. In some *barangays* there are semi-formal services such as savings and loan Co-operatives, and because the Rural Finance team planned to use Co-operatives in their proposed system he investigated many of them at both *barangay* and municipal level, and looked into how their members used the Co-operative services. The consultancy made the programme acutely aware of the role of outside agencies, such as the Land Bank, the Department of Agriculture, the Department of Social Welfare and Development, and of CECAP I, all of whom have made credit available for Co-operatives and for *barangay* residents.

The consultant's final report focused on some important issues that the initial design had missed or under valued:

1. The need to recognise social stratification and pay even more attention to carefully targeting the poor;

2. The importance of education expenses as perhaps the most important recurring cash expenditure for almost all the households of the Cordillera (and one that could be well managed through savings facilities);

3. The need to pay close attention to gender issues;

4. The problems posed by the conservative collateral-demanding credit policies of the co-operatives in the Cordillera, and how these may have arisen and how to overcome them; and above all

5. The need for savings facilities amongst the poor.

The report went on to review the options for the CECAP Rural Financial System, noting the importance of maintaining discipline (which, for Rutherford, encapsulates frequency - giving volume, regularity - building institutionalisation, and transparency - creating confidence). The consultant endorsed the system and implementation methodology created by the CECAP II staff. The value of having an external consultant of Rutherford's capability review, critique and endorse the plans was a tremendous asset to the management team and the RFOs.

SIX MONTH REVIEW

The pilot testing had been in operation for six months when the first major review was undertaken. The results were as follows:

Zone	# of SLGs	# of SLGs Accredited	#of SLG Members	Total SLG Fund Savings (P.)	SLG Fund Loans Issued (P.)	SLG Fund Loans Repaid (P.)
2	40	19	259	116,520	228,080	141,535
3	30	22	202	75,628	78,000	39,075
4	20	0	122	39,215	19,350	14,859
5	36	18	241	75,383	22,785	19,640
6	17	3	102	32,745	21,058	9,386
Total	**143**	**62**	**926**	**P. 339,491**	**P.369,273**	**P.224,495**

The next months were dedicated to exploring the "accreditation" process of SLGs (i.e. certifying them as credible, cohesive self-help groups ready to take, and group guarantee, loans from the KCs in the programme), examining the process of linking SLGs to KCs, and monitoring the release and repayment of loans.

THE RESULTS OF THE PILOT TESTING AND ACTION RESEARCH PHASE

By the end of the pilot testing and action research process which took around a year in total, the programme had a clear view of the "financial landscape" in the Cordillera, and a clear proposal for a system and implementation methodology (see "SLG Organising Process" below). The RFOs were deeply involved in the process of pilot testing and action research - this had given them a clearer understanding of the issues that would face them as they implemented the system in the field and largely eradicated their prejudices. The process had also proved to be an excellent "on-the-job training" for the RFOs, who in turn were able to provide important inputs into the process of finalising the extensive field manuals.

The involvement of field staff in the design and piloting of a financial services system has two additional benefits. Firstly, they tend to have a greater "ownership" of and commitment to the system they helped develop. Secondly, they are encouraged (and in the case of CECAP, expected) to continue to provide feed-back from the field, and make recommendations on how to further improve the system, as part of an on-going process. This depth of commitment to and understanding of the system also made the first batch of RFOs able to act as "mentors" for the "on-the-job training" of the second group of RFOs recruited to expand the system into new areas.

While the researchers had been sensitising the public in the pilot areas to the CECAP II approach and been active in assisting the formation of SLGs (all of which are self-chosen groups) and SLSs, as well as speaking with KCs as to their future roles, the continual feedback up to this point allowed the researchers to finalise the guidelines for organising SLGs and nurturing them to a state where they were linked to, and served by, Key Co-operatives.

The lengthy pilot testing and action research process had lead to the Detailed System Design and Implementation Methodology as well as a clearly documented discussion of the key issues and challenges facing the Rural Finance System.

DETAILED SYSTEM DESIGN AND IMPLEMENTATION METHODOLOGY

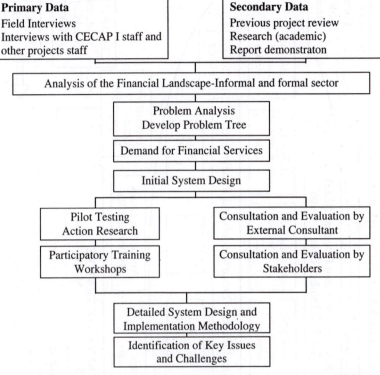

By the end of the pilot testing and action research phase the CECAP II staff and management had a reasonably clear view of how to establish a Rural Finance System in the Cordillera. This is not to suggest that they had solved all the problems (as a quick look at the long list of "Key Issues and Challenges" outlined below will confirm). Nor is it to suggest that the process of "learning by doing" had ended (or should ever end). Nonetheless, the detailed system design and implementation methodology had been completed, and the Rural Finance component was ready to aim for the rapid expansion of the system to bring it to as many barangays as possible. This is now underway using the system outlined below.

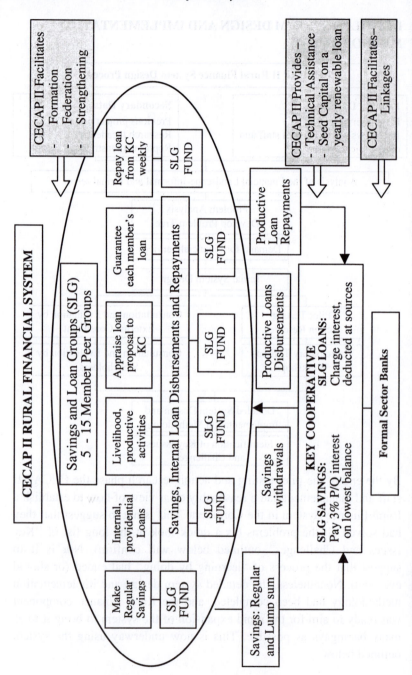

SUMMARY OF POLICIES AND PROCEDURES FOR THE IMPLEMENTATION OF THE CECAP II RURAL FINANCE SYSTEM

Draft Version: October 1997

Thanks to all those who participated in the CECAP-Co-operatives forum (August 28 and September 16, 1997) to revise this document.

Introduction

> *Maria had always struggled with the school expenses for her three children, by the time they were all in high school, she was borrowing about P. 5,000 every June. On this loan she had to pay interest of 10% a month. Maria used to repay the loan by saving a little each month, and it generally took her six months to clear the debt ... and so she was paying a total of around P. 7,000 each year. When asked why she did not save the money before June (and possibly make a little interest on it), Maria look surprised, "But I am too poor to save".*

The development of a healthy and sustainable Rural Financial System (RFS) in the Central Cordillera is a key component of the CECAP II Programme. An effective, trusted RFS will 1) allow the poor of the Cordillera to save money in and take small providential loans from their own self help groups (called Savings and Loan Groups - SLGs), and 2) link these SLGs to a net work of strong Co-operatives giving them access to more flexible savings and insurance facilities as well as larger loans for productive purposes. Thus the Rural Finance System will create a network of groups linked into municipal level Co-operatives which in turn will be linked into the formal sector.

The specific objective of CECAP II is to increase the income and strengthen resource management capabilities of rural communities through a flexible set of strategies including: 1) provision of technical support, advice and training; 2) strengthening of the capital base through savings generation and injection of additional complementary funds; and 3) investment in small-scale infrastructure or environmental protection measures in order to promote sustainable increases in production, incomes and savings. Thus the Rural Financial System has a critical role to play in ensuring the Programme's success.

> *The Rural Finance Component will strive to create a sustainable RFS to serve the people of the Cordillera ... to "take banking services into the barangays". The RFS is designed to help clients save (and when necessary to take loans) in order to manage their income and expenditure patterns more effectively and efficiently, to build up (or access) lump-sums for investment, and to help clients diversify and protect their sources of income.*

Policies to Implement the RFS

CORE INSTITUTIONS AND GENERAL FUNCTIONS

Savings and Loan Groups (SLGs)

1. The SLGs will comprise trusted friends and neighbours. Each SLG will have around 10 members (typically ranging from 5 - 15), and will be based on the existing reciprocal lending groups so common in the Cordillera. These traditional groups undertake small-scale reciprocal interest-free lending of rice and small sums of money to assist friends and neighbours in times of need. In order to maximise the outreach of the RFS and to guard against "capture" of SLGs by large and/or influential families, family members living in the same household are not allowed in the same SLG. The SLGs will form the self-help and guarantee groups that will be the foundation stones of the programme.

2. Saving will be the main emphasis of the programme. Members will be required to build-up an SLG Fund through regular weekly and periodic lump sum deposits. This SLG Fund will be used to extend small providential and productive loans to members.

3. The SLG members will have to undergo 10 training sessions to be scheduled by the SLG and the CECAP II. The components of the training sessions are further discussed in the section on training below. On completion of the 10 SLG training sessions, SLGs who demonstrate an understanding and mastery of the contents will receive SLG Accreditation, which denotes that they are competent and capable SLGs, that have met and save regularly, and have taken and repaid loans from their SLG Fund. Completion of SLG Accreditation will trigger a reduction of the RFO/KCOW's monitoring visits to the SLG from weekly to monthly, thus allowing

the SLG to meet according to their own schedule. The monthly meeting will be a barangay SLG assembly.

4. The SLG is required to meet every week in order to:

   a. Deposit weekly compulsory (regular) savings and in the case of any cash windfall, voluntary (lump-sum) savings into the SLG Fund or the KC (see below);

   b. Withdraw savings from the SLG Fund;

   c. Lend small SLG Fund loans to members;

   d. Collect SLG Fund loan repayments;

   e. Withdraw savings from the KC (subject to the provisions discussed below);

   f. Review, discuss and approve loan applications to be submitted to the KC (see below);

   g. Discuss any current loan borrowed from the KC (for which the SLG members are jointly and severally liable through the group guarantee system) and the project involved;

   h. Make KC loan repayments; and

   i. Attend to other matters concerning the operations of SLG.

5. Each SLG will elect a Chairperson to ensure that all members attend meetings, and to chair the meetings of the group. The Chairperson will get the last chance to borrow from the KC. Each SLG will also elect a Treasurer/Secretary to keep records and monitor the use of and transactions of the SLG Fund, to keep records of the meetings and to deputise when the Chairperson is absent.

6. After a period of a few months, it is expected that the SLG members will want access to more extensive financial services: a broader range of savings instruments (time deposits etc.), insurance schemes (mortuary aid scheme etc.) and larger loans. To access these, it will be necessary to link the SLGs to Co-operatives. CECAP II will therefore negotiate with one trusted and stable Co-operative in each municipality (designated to become the Key Co-operative or KC) to develop a special scheme to link the SLGs into the KC.

7. Prior to linking with the KC, in order to demonstrate the discipline and commitment of the group, all the members of the SLG must

have saved regularly in the SLG Fund and (with exceptional cases - widows etc. exempted) taken and repaid loans from the SLG Fund. Furthermore, members must ideally be able to read and understand their individual SLG Fund passbooks.

8. SLGs who want to have access to the more extensive savings and credit facilities of the KC must join with other SLGs to meet at the same time and place on the same day every week or two weeks in order to bring together a cost effective "critical mass" of clients to transact business with the KC's Outreach Worker (KCOW). The KCOW will provide the regular link between SLGs and the KC, thus "bringing the bank to the barangay" and providing some limited technical assistance with the SLGs' book-keeping etc.

9. The SLG members must then pay the KC's normal membership fees and commit to start purchasing share capital in the KC through their KC savings account, or withdrawals from their SLG Fund, or a combination of these. The SLGs should meet regularly with the KCOW, at least once a month.

10. SLG members must comply with the normal membership policies of the KC. There shall be no dual membership of two KCs or two SLGs. In cases were an existing regular member of the KC is interested to become a member of the SLG, he/she is given the option to choose where to belong. However, if the member's SLG joins the KC, the member must become an SLG member of the KC (his/her share capital would of course, satisfy the requirements for SLG members to purchase share capital - see above) and follow the rules, terms and conditions provided for under the SLG system.

11. When linking to the KC, the SLG members will have to undergo another series of training sessions to be scheduled by the participating SLGs, the CECAP II RFO and the KCOW. The components of the training sessions are further discussed in the section on training below.

12. Before the first KC loans can be released, upon completion of the training sessions the SLG must pass the SLG Accreditation and demonstrate a full understanding of the rules of the RFS and demonstrate that they are ready and competent to be linked to the KC.

13. Once linked to the KC, all the SLG members will guarantee loans taken by fellow SLG members from the KC. The guarantee mechanism will work as follows: once the first two SLG members are granted a loan by the KC, the next two members will be allowed to borrow only if the first two members have made at least four weekly loan repayments, and next two members will only be allowed to borrow from the KC if all their fellow SLG members' repayments are up-to-date. Thus peer pressure and mutual accountability are expected to form the basis for the group guarantee.

14. All subsequent loans from the KC depend on members depositing minimum share capital and savings in accordance with the KC loans rules and regulations outlined below. Members with fully paid up share capital in the KC will receive dividends and patronage refunds in accordance with the KC's rules and regulations.

Key Co-operatives (KCs)

1. The one KC selected to serve each municipality must distinguish SLG activities from its other functions by opening it as a separate window or facility, and accounting for it separately. Similarly, dividends and patronage refunds will be calculated separately for the SLG activities.

2. Existing apex organisations such as NORLU and CAVALCO as well as strong primary co-operatives will be tapped to assist CECAP II in strengthening and developing the KCs.

3. The Key Co-operative Outreach Worker (KCOW) will also be trained as a permanent staff of the KC. The KCOW will work full-time in delivering financial services, both credit and savings at the SLG level. The KCOW will, likewise, be subjected to fidelity or real estate bonding in the amount of P. 20,000 per annum to protect the KCs and the SLG members against theft or loss of collections.

Savings Mobilisation and Capital Build-Up

1. Initially, the members will be required to build-up a fund (the SLG Fund) by agreeing on and making minimum regular weekly deposits (say P10 - 20) in order to develop the habit of regular

periodic saving. Members will of course, be encouraged to deposit more than the group determined minimum whenever possible. The size of the SLG Fund will be further enhanced by members' occasional lump sum deposits (for example after harvest or the sale of livestock etc.) In addition, fines collected due to tardiness or absences during meetings, delay in repayment or non-repayment of loans, as well as the interest charged on loans taken from the SLG Fund, will be added into the SLG Fund. Once it is large enough the SLG Fund will be used to extend small providential (including emergency) and productive loans to members.

2. The SLG Fund will be accounted for through a simple book-keeping system (maintained by the Chairperson and Treasurer/Secretary and held by the Chairperson) and passbooks (held by all members). Official receipts are optional at the discretion of the SLG. Excess funds (not out on loan) will be held by the Treasurer/Secretary possibly (at the discretion of the SLG) in a safe-box with two padlocks (with keys held by the Chairperson and Treasurer/Secretary) or deposited at a financial institution (bank or co-operative) of the SLG's choice.

3. After linking to the KC, SLG members must pay the KC's normal membership fees and commit to start purchasing share capital in the KC through either their savings accounts or withdrawals from their SLG Fund, or a combination of these two.

4. Members will be encouraged to save at the KC and KCs will offer their standard interest rate on savings. Ideally a minimum interest rate of 6% per annum computed on an Average Daily Balance (ADB) and posted quarterly will be paid by the KC on the lowest savings balance held during the quarter (for accounts with a minimum balance of P. 100). Interest earnings will be credited to the member's savings account at the KC.

5. For members with any outstanding KC loan, withdrawal from their savings deposit will be allowed, subject to maintaining an amount (total share capital plus savings) adequate to secure the members' outstanding loan balance. Thus for example, if a member has P. 2,000 loan balance outstanding and has P. 1,000 in share capital and

P. 1,500 in savings, he/she can withdraw P. 500 at will, but must leave P. 1,000 in his/her savings account. [Thus leaving P. 1,000 share capital plus P. 1,000 savings deposit equal to the outstanding loan balance of P. 2,000]. When the member has no loan outstanding with the KC the total amount of his/her savings will be available for withdrawals, subject to the KC's minimum balance requirements.

6. A minimum reserve requirement of 20% of the net savings (gross savings less withdrawals) and Emergency Trust Fund balances held by SLG members should be maintained by the KC at all times. The reserves should be placed in an account that will be able to meet the members' need to withdraw their money at any time. This minimum 20% reserve requirement may be reduced if seen as excessive subject to discussion with and authorisation from CECAP II.

Terms and Conditions of Key Co-operative Loans

Qualification of Borrowers

1. SLG members can avail of KC loans only if the following conditions are met:

a. Have saved on a regular basis for three months or more (including saving with the SLG Fund);

b. Have fully paid their membership fee and (in the case of KC loans only) share capital to the KC;

c. Have accumulated a substantial level of savings with the KC of at least P. 250;

d. Have demonstrated a commitment to and attendance of regular SLG meetings;

e. Have a thorough understanding of the Programme's rules;

f. Have the written endorsement and guarantee of the other members of the SLG (included on the loan application form);

g. The SLG as a whole has passed the SLG Accreditation test jointly administered by CECAP II's senior Rural Finance component staff and (where possible) the KC Outreach Worker; and

h. Have attended the KC's normal Pre-Loan Screening/Seminar procedures.

2. SLG members who have existing past due loans from CECAP I or from other co-operatives, banks and other government-sponsored savings and credit projects will not be eligible to borrow from the KC.

Types and Uses of Loans

1. Loans will be provided to members who meet the conditions outlined above in <u>Qualification of Borrowers</u>.

2. For KC loans, only loans for financing productive activities (agricultural or non-agricultural) particularly those that will generate additional income for the borrowers will be considered. No more than half the members of an SLG can use their KC loans for the same activity. Group loans will invalidate the group guarantee system that is replacing the KC's usual requirements for physical collateral, and are therefore initially at least prohibited. After the SLG members have taken several individual loans however, the KC will review this policy and have the option (at the discretion of the KC) to issue group loans.

3. On request by the members, CECAP II Area Teams will provide limited technical assistance and will help the members to review the technical and financial performance of the their first, second and if necessary, subsequent loans. CECAP II will not however take responsibility for these loans, and the final decisions relating to their sanctioning or otherwise lies with the SLG (who must guarantee them) and the KC (which must disburse and collect them).

Loans Request and Appraisal

1. For KC loans, the SLG member should first inform the other SLG members through the group Chairperson about his/her desire for a loan from the KC. All the other SLG members should discuss the proposal. If the members agree to it then they should endorse it and commit to guarantee the loan by stipulating so on the application form. This will be included in the legal agreement between the KC and the SLG. The loan application form should then be forwarded to the KC for approval.

2. The KC will process and approve (or disapprove) the loan application within one or two weeks (according to the meeting schedule of the KC's Credit Committee), so that the loan can be disbursed to the SLG member (or he/she can be told why the loan application has been disapproved) as soon as possible- ideally at the following week's SLG meeting.

3. Loans will be disbursed to SLGs with 5 members on a "2:2:1" monthly staggered basis (or the equivalent scaled up for larger SLGs - thus for a 8 member SLG, the loans will be released on a 3:3:2 basis). Thus for SLGs with 5 members, once the first two SLG members are granted a loan by the KC, the next two members will be allowed to borrow only if the first two members have made at least four weekly loan repayments on time and according to schedule. Similarly the following loans will also only be issued if all the loanees within the SLG are up-to-date with their loan repayments.

Loan Size

1. The first loan of an SLG member from the KC will be used both to finance an income generation activity and to develop her/his share capital at the KC, and will be known as a "capital build-up" loan. Capital build-up loans will be given up to a maximum of P. 4,000, and the amount to be repaid weekly will consist of two items: (i) the principal amount of the loan; and (ii) her share capital in the KC, which should not be less than 50% of the loan principal payments. Thus, for a P. 1,000 loan with a term of 50 weeks, the weekly payments of the SLG member, should consist of the P. 20 weekly payment for the loan principal and the P.10 weekly share capital contribution, or a total weekly payment of P. 30. After 50 weeks, not only has the SLG member fully repaid her loan but she would also have, by then, P. 500 in share capital at the KC. For subsequent loans, the 2:1 loan-savings ratio will be applied but the weekly capital build up contributions will not be compulsory. Thus for her second loan, the SLG member can again borrow a loan of P. 1,000 under the 2:1 loan-savings rule, but her capital build up contributions will be made voluntary.

2. The size of subsequent KC loans will be closely linked to the members' previous saving activities. In particular, the maximum amount of loan available to a borrower will be calculated as:

> **2 times the member's share capital**
> *plus*   **2 times the members' savings deposited at the KC**

As an example:

    If the member's share capital = P. 1,000 and
    the member's savings deposit = P. 2,000
    Then the maximum loan size available to the member will = **P. 6,000**
    Computation: [2x 1,000 + 2x 2,000]
    Subject to the following ceilings:

First loan	P. 4,000
Second loan	P. 6,000
Third loan	P. 9,000
Fourth loan	P. 12,000
Fifth loan	P. 15,000

  and

for the first three KC loans, up to a total maximum of P. 10,000 per household when loans from the CECAP II Revolving Credit Fund and all other credit sources are also included. (Thus if Mr. Dawig has a loan of P. 5,000 from the CECAP II Revolving Credit Fund, Mrs. Dawig his wife or Mr. Dawig his son {if he lives in the same household} can only take a maximum loan of P. 5,000 from the CECAP II Rural Finance System). For fourth and fifth and subsequent loans the total maximum loans per household will be P. 12,000 and P. 15,000 respectively in line with the RFS policies described above.

Interest, Penalties and Fines

1. Interest and service charge will be computed and managed in line with co-operative norms in the Philippines. Interest charged at the nominal rate of 0.75% per month, and a service charge/Loan Redemption Fund of 3.5% will deducted at source on disbursement of the loan.

2. KC loans will bear the RFS standard interest rate charged at the nominal rate of 0.75% per month, and a service charge/Loan Redemption Fund (LRF) contribution of 3.5% deducted at source on disbursement of the loan. An additional 2.5% of the loan will be deducted at source and credited to the SLG's Emergency Trust Fund (ETF) - see below. Thus if a client requests a KC loan of

P. 1,000, the KC will disburse P. 850 in cash to him/her (P. 1,000 less P. 90 interest, P. 35 service charge/LRF and P. 25 ETF contribution), and he/she will repay a minimum of P. 20 principal per week.

3. Penalties for past due/delinquent borrowers will also be collected. The computation of the amount of penalty will be in accordance with the KC's normal policies and procedures.

Emergency Trust Fund

1. A mandatory deduction of 2.5% from every KC loan taken by SLG members will go to a "Emergency Trust Fund" (ETF) held at the KC in the name of the member's SLG. The ETF will be group-owned and managed by the SLG and no individual member will have any claim on the it The ETF may be used to provide immediate supplementary loans to members having difficulty in repaying their loans due to legitimate reasons (e.g. force majeure). These supplementary loans will be issued on reasonable terms and conditions agreed upon by the members with endorsement from the KC.

2. If any loans made to members of the SLG are more than three months overdue, the KC is empowered to take repayments for those overdue loans from the ETF.

3. Individual members leaving the SLG will not be allowed to withdraw their share of the ETF, it will remain the property of the SLG. In the event of the dissolution of the SLG, the ETF will automatically be credited to the CECAP II capital fund account.

Maturity and Repayment of Loan

1. All KC loans should be repaid in 50 or 25 equal instalments (depending on the SLG's meeting schedule - weekly or every two weeks) over 50 weeks (a year with one week's holiday for Easter and another week's holiday Christmas).

2. However, loanees have the option to pay off loans in advance of this schedule in order to receive an interest rebate and to have greater access to larger follow-on loans.

Collateral Requirement

1. A borrower's share capital plus savings deposit at the KC will serve as collateral for loans taken out. Weekly instalments more than two

weeks past due will be automatically deducted from the borrower's savings account at the KC.

2. Group-collateral among SLG members will also be applied. As with the Grameen Bank approach, should one member of the SLG default on a loan repayment, all members of that group are liable to meet the short-fall. If they fail to do so, and the member defaults, the other members in that group will cease to be eligible for further loans.

3. If a loan is past due for longer than three months, the KC is entitled (but not bound) to use the Emergency Trust Fund, then savings deposits and then (if necessary) share capital to pay off the past due loans of all the members in that SLG, since the savings and share capital were used as collateral for loans taken by the SLG members.

Loan Collection and Restructuring

1. The KC will be responsible for the collection of all loans, and is empowered to use all methods that it sees fit to do so. The KC is therefore encouraged to use its normal loan collection procedures.

2. Loans should be restructured or rescheduled only under exceptional circumstances once all other options (including the full use of the Emergency Trust Fund) have been exhausted.

IDENTIFICATION OF KEY ISSUES FOR THE FUTURE

The pilot testing process had also highlighted several key issues that faced the programme and had to be addressed if it was to succeed, and in the main, the pilot testing process had also suggested what appeared to be feasible solutions to these problems. These were as follows (extract from the report on 1997 activities reproduced in full in Appendix number 3):

Time Delay

Challenge: The significant time period it takes for clients to raise enough funds to pay the full share capital for membership at the KCs has caused unexpected delays.

Solution: Provide "capital build-up loans" to fast-track membership in KCs. A 50% premium added to the weekly repayment instalments to cover cost of share capital.

Scheduling of the Assistance/Monitoring Visits to SLGs

Challenge: Co-ordinating RFO visits with the labour schedules of the SLG members who generally work in the their fields or as wage labourers during the day. Furthermore, the distance between barangays (or even between sitios within barangays) places a time-constraint on the RFOs in reaching all clients.

Solution: RFOs do schedule meetings for evenings or Sundays as an interim measure. However, the longer term solution is grouping several SLGs to allow one meeting to cover several SLGs and the accreditation of SLGs such that meetings are less frequent.

Note: The initial idea of calling the groups of SLGs "Savings and Loan Societies" had produced confusion among residents (and even some staff) who construed SLSs as additional institutions. The groups were thus not "named" anything, rather several SLGs come together for an "Assembly" to meet the RFO and/or Key Co-operative Outreach Worker (KCOW).

Challenge: When the SLGs are linked to KCs, the KCOW would face the same challenge.

Solution: Accrediting the SLGs to reduce the monitoring visits by the KCOW.

Having borrowers make payments when going to the (usually) weekly market.

Side Benefit 1: KCOW's risk reduced in carrying large amounts of cash to/from distant points.

Side Benefit 2: "Mainstreaming" CECAP clients allowing them to build a relationship with the whole co-operative and its staff.

Income Generation

Challenge: As clients focus on savings and providential/small scale productive uses of their SLG Funds (internal borrowing), they delay consideration or pursuit of longer term, potentially sustainable income generation activities.

Solution: An additional module has been added to the initial SLG training to promote IGA activities at an earlier stage in the SLG development process.

Repayment Schedules

Challenge: Selling the idea of weekly repayment when KCs and others have traditionally offered monthly (for salaried workers) or balloon (for specific time-bound projects) basis repayment schedules.

Solution: Seek innovative "marketing" of the weekly savings concept (or repayment) as a means of effectively managing limited cash resources.

Key Co-operatives

Challenge: Overcoming the poor image of many co-operatives which has led many SLG members to distrust and/or fear linking their SLGs, which they are quite happy with, to the KCs.

Solution: Work with KCs and members to overcome distrust and build on positive images over time. Continue to promote the opportunities provided by the more flexible financial services offered by the KCs.

Challenge: Finding sufficient number of qualified KCs in each operational area.

Solution: Create programs to develop existing, weaker, co-operatives into KCs.

Demand Issues

Challenge: Slow up-take of credit as a result of fear of the repayment schedule and the lack of income generation ideas and opportunities in some of the more remote barangays.

Solution: Clarify messages. The Rural Finance System expects to be addressing the following credit needs of the people of the Cordillera: providential (through the SLG Fund) and business and livestock (through the KC loans, and in many cases, also through the SLG Funds).

Challenge: Pollution of the financial service environment in the Cordillera by well-funded, "well-intentioned" donors and others possibly less well intentioned (politically motivated lending).

Sub-Challenge: Not losing CECAP II formed and trained SLGs to these other large capital funds.

Sub-Challenge: Maintaining integrity and good credit culture among CECAP II members in the midst of these developments.

Solution: Largely beyond the control of CECAPII which can only lobby, hope and pray - time will tell what happens.

These issues (like the entire system design and implementation methodology) are still under research – a feature that characterises all high quality microfinance programmes.

RESULTS TO DATE

(December 1998 - 17 months after starting the pilot test)

Zone	# of SLG	# of SLGs Accredited	# of SLG Members	Total SLG Fund Savings	SLG Fund Loans (P.)		KC Loans (P.)	
					Issued	Repaid	Issued	Repaid
2	126	74	870	527,619	1,410,225	1,033,153	519,000	179,773
3	150	77	1,076	477,562	548,762	329,529	522,000	145,703
4	102	45	758	397,542	360,677	190,504	44,000	8,780
5	142	31	1,144	457,290	659,965	279,318	32,000	6,280
6	47	-	408	155,446	175,580	116,188	-	-
Total	**601**	**227**	**4,256**	**P. 2,015,459**	**P.3,155,209**	**P.1,948,692**	**P.1,117,000**	**P. 340,536**

CONCLUSIONS

Conclusions at this point are limited by the age of the programme and its constant evolution. However, the results after 17 months indicate a positive situation, as do the continued focus group discussions and general perception of the programme. There are, of course, problems and short-comings – as there are with all programmes, but the fundamentals seem to be in place: stakeholders have bought-in, manuals have been developed, staff have been trained and clients are joining and using the services at an impressive rate.

Clearly, what is in many ways the most difficult element of the programme, the linkage to co-operatives, remains very much in its initial experimentation phase, but there are hopeful signs that the idea will work, and the systems for action research to develop and improve this mechanism are in place. Achieving "sustainability" in this type of remote setting is a serious challenge and it is reasonable to assume that the system will have to continue to evolve and develop with time – indeed it must.

Appendix 1

SLG ORGANISING PROCESS

Stage 1. AREA SURVEY (Municipal level)

The area survey will be done by the RFO primarily to determine the <u>number of potential RFS clients</u> in CECAP's target barangays and to prioritise the communities where SLGs will be promoted.

The basis for selection of priority communities are as follows:

a. CECAP policy of working in clusters of barangay where programme implementation will begin in the inner circle barangays gradually radiating, thereafter to the outer circle barangays

b. Density of poor households (compact community with at least 3 SLGs or 15 potential clients per sitio)

c. No or limited other GB-type credit programmes in the area (e.g. Development & Social Welfare Department's SEA-K scheme)

d. Credit demand in the area as manifested, among others, by the presence of enterprising women

e. Cost-effectiveness of implementing the RFS in the area (distance to RFO station/KC office; travel time vs. potential number of clients)

f. Attitude of the people to credit as indicated by history of credit programmes in the area (Experiences of existing co-operatives, banks, NGOs, other government agencies, Local Government Units)

The output of the area survey will be an Area Plan which would consist of a sketch map of the municipality indicating the sitios/barangays with their respective household population, road network, distance and travel time to and from the town centre and RFO station, and the number of potential SLGs and clients in each sitio/barangay. The Area Plan will show the total number of potential SLGs and clients that can be targeted in the municipality which could be used for estimating the potential volume of business that can be generated by the KC.

Stage 2. SITE VALIDATION

The Area Plan will be approved by the Zone and the RFS Component after a validation survey that will be conducted jointly by the Zone Planning Officer and the PMO-RFS Staff.

Stage 3. COMMUNITY SURVEY (Sitio/Barangay level)

PRA, FGD and wealth ranking will be done to generate information on the savings capacities and credit needs of households at the sitio or barangay level, and which households should be targeted. When entering a municipality for the first time, all PRA techniques (Mobility Mapping, Venn Diagram, Seasonality of Cash Analysis) should be undertaken. As work progresses, these can be done on a limited sample basis when entering a potentially different barangay. Wealth ranking and FGD, however, must <u>always</u> be conducted as part of the SLG organising process.

During these meetings, the RFO also explains the programme - its objectives, principles, and operating procedures to generate awareness and interest among potential clients. These discussions are also meant to clarify misconceptions, issues, practices, obligations, benefits, and other matters concerning the programme. It is possible, at this stage, that indications of interest on the formation of SLGs will be generated among the participants of these meetings.

Stage 4. COMMUNITY ORIENTATION MEETING

This is a public meeting conducted by the RFO and attended by the local leaders and the potential clients. The purpose of the meeting is to officially launch the RFS in the community. The objectives and components of CECAP and of the RFS, including its rules and procedures, are elaborated during this meeting. This meeting, however, <u>may not be necessary</u> if, during Stage 3 (Community Survey), barangay officials and a sufficient number of potential clients have already been adequately informed about the programme. This could happen when the PRA/FGD is attended by a large group of people virtually transforming, in the process, the activity into a community orientation meeting.

Stage 5. FORMATION OF GROUPS

A potential member must form a group with a minimum of 5, and maximum of 15, members composed of her closest and most trusted friends or neighbours in the sitio or barangay. In forming a group, the following criteria are followed:

a. They must live near each other within the area
b. Only one member from a household is allowed
c. They must enjoy mutual trust and confidence
d. Households with annual incomes of less than P.25,000 will be given priority.

Stage 6. SLG TRAINING

This is a 10-module training course conducted by the RFO for the members of newly-formed SLGs. The training focuses on the philosophy, and the policies and operating procedures of the RFS. In this training, the RFO discusses in further detail the topics and issues taken up earlier during the community survey/ mobilisation campaign and community orientation meetings. The group is required to start its weekly saving during the training. The election of SLG officers and the formulation of SLG policies are done, as well, during the training.

Stage 7. START OF SLG OPERATION

Regular weekly meetings and saving start immediately after the SLG training. Lending from the SLG Fund is started at the SLG's own discretion. The RFO attends the SLG weekly meetings to ensure that the rules and procedures of the RFS are followed by the SLG. (Eventually, however, when the number of SLGs supervised by the RFO will have increased such that it would not be possible for him or her to visit the SLGs on a weekly basis, the frequency of the RFO's SLG visits will be reduced.)

Stage 8. SLG ACCREDITATION

This activity is undertaken, after the SLG had conducted at least 10 weekly meetings, by the senior Rural Finance component staff. The accreditation review is to determine if the SLG members are ready to accept their responsibilities as members of SLG as taught to them during the SLG Training, and if they are prepared to abide by the rules and procedures of the RFS. The SLG accreditation procedure involves a practical test on simple bookkeeping and an oral examination on RFS rules and procedures. Accredited SLGs will be allowed to schedule their weekly meetings at their most convenient day and time and will be recommended for linkage with the KC.

Stage 9. ORGANIZATION OF SLG CLUSTERS/ASSEMBLY

Prior to linkage with the KC, accredited SLGs will be encouraged to form informal clusters or "Assemblies", at the barangay level, to facilitate the provision of services by the KC. SLGs belonging to a cluster or Assembly will be required to hold their weekly meetings together to facilitate the collection of weekly repayments and the disbursement of new loans by the KC in the barangay.

Stage 10. LINKAGE WITH KEY CO-OPERATIVES

The accredited SLGs will be encouraged to open savings accounts, buy shares in the KCs, as well as negotiate for loans with the KCs for their income generating projects. During this stage, the supervision of the SLGs will be gradually turned-over by the RFOs to the Key Co-operative Outreach Workers (KCOWs) who, likewise, will be trained by the Programme on the rules and procedures of the RFS. The RFOs will continue, however, to monitor the progress of the SLGs and to supervise the work of the KCOWs. Training on KC policies and on appropriate income generating projects will also be given to SLG members at this stage.

PRA & FGD SUMMARY REPORT

A. BACKGROUND INFORMATION

State the number of sitios or barangays your team had covered, the inclusive dates you conducted the PRA & FGD, and the types of outputs or information you have generated (such as seasonality of income, cash mobility mapping, Venn diagram, etc.)

B. FINDINGS

[Note: Use the questions below as guides in presenting your findings. Since this will be a summary report, only present or discuss your team's general observations and conclusions. However, use your sitio- or barangay-specific data or information as cases or examples to support your general statements. Only state what you can support with FGD/PRA results. Attach the data from PRA and wealth ranking as Annexes and make cross-references to them every time you present facts or figures.

1. *On Social Stratification (Wealth Ranking & FGD)*

   1.1. Who are the richest people in the community (that is, what type of work do they do/what is their main source of income)? Why are they considered the richest?

   1.2. Who are the poorest households in the community (that is, what type of work do they do/what is their main source of income)? Why are they considered the poorest?

   1.3. In terms of wealth, are the households more or less equal in status (example: most are landowners) or are there wide differences (example: a few are landowners, some are share tenants, while many are landless who depend only on wage labour for income)?

   1.4. Aside from land, what other assets are also considered to be symbols of wealth (or status symbols) in the community (house made of durable materials, employment in government service, cattle, hand-tractor, etc.)? What percentage of the households own these types of assets?

   1.5. On the other hand, what are the symbols of poverty or the distinct characteristics of poorer households?

   1.6. What percentage of the people are "rich", "middle" and "poor"?

2. *On Availability of Cash (Seasonality Analysis & FGD)*

    2.1 What is the people's main source of income? Is income from this source available year round or only at certain periods or months of the year? What do people do/where do they get additional income in between crop harvests?

    2.2 What expenditures do people usually need to borrow money for? At what period or months of the year are these expenditures usually incurred? From whom they do usually borrow money from?

    2.3 Where do people keep their excess cash? Are there any existing formal and informal schemes in the community where people regularly pool their money together for on-lending to members in need (example: paluwagan or ROSCAs, "Gawat [reciprocal lending] groups", funeral societies, co-operatives)

    2.4 Are cash transactions among households in the community frequent or infrequent? How often do they go to the market either to buy or sell goods?

    2.5 What percentage of people are engaged in non-farm enterprises that generate daily or weekly incomes such as sari-sari stores, food vendors, fish/meat vendors, dressmakers, tricycle or jeepney drivers or operators?

    2.6 Is barter still being widely practiced? Is the access road a problem during the rainy season preventing people from selling their produce and purchasing other goods in the market? If so, how long and what months is the access roads closed to all types of motor vehicles?

3. *On Availability of Wage Labour (Seasonality Analysis, Wealth Ranking & FGD)*

    3.1 How important is wage labour to the people as source of income? Is it a major or only a minor income source? How many households in the community are not farming/do not cultivate any land - who depend solely on wage labour for living?

    3.2 Is opportunity for wage labour, inside or outside the community, available year-round or only in certain period or months of the year?

    3.3 What type of work is available in the community? How much are the people paid for their labour? What month(s) do people easily find employment within the community? During these months, how many days in a week do they usually find employment?

    3.4 What type of work is available outside the community? How much are the people paid for their labour? What month(s) do people easily find employment outside the community? During these months, how many days in a week do they usually find employment?

3.5 What month(s), if any, do people have difficulty finding work inside or outside the community?

4. *On Role of Women (FGD & Mobility Mapping)*

4.1 Are women expected to generate additional incomes for their family? What income generating activities are they usually engaged in, if any? Do they also work for wages inside or outside the community?

4.2 If women also work for wages, what type of work do they usually do and how much are they paid? What month(s) do women easily find employment? During these months, how many days in a week do they usually find employment?

4.3 Who keeps and manages/budgets the cash resources of the family - the husband or the wife?

4.4 Do women also migrate to look for work outside the community? Is the nature of this migration temporary or permanent? How long are women usually away from their homes when they migrate temporarily to other places? What percentage of the households has their women members away for more than one month?

5. *On Alternative Types of Financial Services (PRA & FGD)*

5.1 Do people think they can or cannot save? What are their reasons?

5.2 What present expenditures (personal, household, farm) do you think could be easily reduced by the people as additional source of savings? How much can they save weekly or monthly if they are able to reduce these expenditures?

5.3 What are the various ways by which people presently keep or invest their savings? What are the advantages and disadvantages of each of these practices?

5.4 What are their preferences in so far as savings facilities are concerned?

5.5 Did the people have any bad experience with group savings schemes in the community before? What are their concerns or fears in case a new group savings scheme is introduced?

5.6 For what purpose(s) do people borrow? How much are they usually borrowing? Where do they get their loans? What is the term and interest of the loan?

6.   *KC Selection (FGD, Venn Diagram & Mobility Mapping)*

6.1   Where do people usually go to market their farm produce? How often do they visit the place? If the market is not located in the *poblacion* (the main town of the Municipality), how often do they visit the latter (i.e., *poblacion*)?

6.2   Among the various organisations listed by the people, what organisation seems to be the most credible or respected? What could have been the reason(s)?

6.3   Is there any co-operative or financial organisation that appears to be have gained the trust of the people in the community? If none, why could this be so?

6.4   Is this co-operative or financial organisation actually being patronised by the people? (Look at your diagram of the Mobility Mapping. Do people frequently visit this co-operative or financial organisation or not?). If not, what could have been the reason(s) for this discrepancy (that is, they like the co-operative but are not patronising it)?

C. CONCLUSIONS & RECOMMENDATIONS

1.   *On the feasibility of a weekly group savings scheme*

1.1   Given the findings discussed above, is a weekly group savings program feasible in the community? For what purpose? How can it help the people in the community? What is your strongest argument for claiming that a weekly group savings scheme will be or will not be feasible?

1.2   What are the constraints to a successful introduction of a group savings scheme in the community (example: weekly meetings,)? How can we overcome these constraints?

2.   *On the feasibility of a weekly loan repayment scheme*

2.1   Will a group lending program, involving a weekly loan repayment scheme, be feasible in the community? What will be the most likely purpose(s) of the loans, as well as the size(s) of loans that will be needed by the people?

2.2   Based on their present incomes, how much do you think could households allocate for their weekly loan repayment? What percentage of the households, for example, could afford to pay P.100 every week to repay a loan of P.5,000 repayable in 50 equal weekly instalments? How many households could afford to pay P.200 every week to repay a loan of P.10,000 repayable in 50 equal weekly instalments?

3.   *On prospective KC(s)*

3.1   What co-operative(s) would you recommend as KC, if any?

Appendix 3

ISSUES AND CHALLENGES FACING CECAP II'S RURAL FINANCE SYSTEM

DELAYS IN LINKING SLGS TO KCS

The policy requirement that the SLG members pay their full share capital at the KC prior to being eligible to take a loan has meant that the SLG members, who are drawn from the poorest households, are taking a long time to save the necessary funds to meet this requirement. Thus the process of linking SLGs to the KCs is likely to take longer than anticipated. The component is examining ways of "fast-tracking" linkage through special "capital build-up loans" (with repayment instalments increased to include an element that was taken to buy share capital in the KC) for members.

Partly as a function of the above, clients are taking time to come up with income generation activities (IGAs) to be funded by KC loans. Perhaps as a result of the emphasis on savings in the initial training, they have focused primarily on savings and providential/small scale productive uses of their SLG Funds. Only now are the more mature groups (those formed during the pilot activities in Banaue in June 1997) beginning to consider potential IGAs. In order to try to speed up this process an additional module has been added to the initial SLG training to encourage discussion of potential IGAs at an earlier stage in the development of SLGs.

In addition, there is marked concern among the SLG members over the proposed weekly loan repayment schedule. The widespread nature of the co-operative movement in the Cordillera has made the people used to loan repayment schedules that are either monthly (for salaried people) or balloon basis (for some specific time-bound projects). In addition, some households do not have well diversified sources of cash income (indeed in many of the more remote Municipalities barter remains the most the most common form of economic transaction), and thus do not have regular sources of cash to meet the weekly repayment schedule. These households will have to increase their participation in wage (day) labour markets, to use the savings facilities offered by the Rural Finance System as a way of more effectively managing, and the liquidation of livestock assets to increase, their limited cash resources. The component will have to pay special attention to finding ways of "selling" the weekly repayment system to members, and helping them manage their resources to deal with it.

Finally, at this stage at least, and partly as a result of the limited ideas on IGAs and the fear of the weekly repayment system, many SLGs do not want to be linked to a KC. In view of the problems faced by co-operatives in the Cordillera, and the bankruptcy of many (with the attendant loss of members' savings), there is widespread distrust of co-operatives - particularly among the poorer households. The poor seem extremely happy with the SLGs as a mechanism to save, stabilise their financial situation and escape the clutches of the money lenders, but often unwilling to link to or join a KC. This will mean that the CECAP II Rural Finance System will have to work in collaboration with the KCs to promote linkage, and the value of the more flexible financial services offered by the KCs.

SCHEDULING OF THE ASSISTANCE/MONITORING VISITS TO SLGS

In the Cordillera, both men and women labour in their fields and/or wage [day] labour, and thus it is not uncommon to find the barangays almost deserted during the days. Furthermore, because of the distances between the houses and the fields, attending a meeting back in the barangay can cause substantial loss of productive time. Accordingly, SLG members often have difficulty scheduling their meetings during the day on a weekday, and thus the RFOs are under constant pressure to accept meeting schedules on Sundays or during the night.

Furthermore, the large distances between barangays (and even within barangays between sitios) means that the RFOs spend a large amount of their time moving between SLGs- thus reducing the number which they can assist and monitor. In order to address this problem, SLGs are being grouped together so that they can be served simultaneously, and systems of accreditation are being introduced that will trigger the reduction of the regularity of assistance and monitoring visits by the RFOs, thus allowing them to move on and initiate and train new SLGs.

Similarly, once linked to the KC, the amount of time that the Key Co-operative Outreach Worker (KCOW) can devote to each SLG will be limited. Accordingly, the component is working on redefining the role and job description of the KCOW to allow him/her to reduce the regularity of monitoring visits to SLGs depending on an accreditation system that tracks the quality, status and loan repayment record of the SLG. This will also allow the revision of the CECAP II Rural Finance System to address the security issues that have been repeated raised by local staff, co-operative and government officials. Their concern has been that if the KCOWs must collect savings and loan repayments, they will be walking with large amounts of cash and may be the targets of armed attack. It is clear from the component's Participatory Rural Appraisal work that most SLG members go to the Municipal poblacion at least once a week (generally for marketing), and therefore could visit the KC in person in order to make deposits and repayments. This would also have the benefit of meeting the co-operatives' strongly expressed preference for the SLG members to "mainstream" their dealings with the KCs and thus physically visit and build a relationship with the co-operative and its staff.

RESULTANT CHANGES TO THE FRAMEWORK OF THE RURAL FINANCE SYSTEM

The formal grouping of SLGs into Savings and Loan Societies initially proposed was modified - giving a name to the SLSs created confusion and the misunderstanding that it was another institution. In the "inner circle" barangays close to the Municipal poblacion where the KCs will generally be located, the SLGs will simply be grouped without any formal federation. The SLGs will simply meet at the same place at the same time (in an "Assembly") in order to transact business and receive assistance/monitoring from the RFOs and KCOWs.

DEMAND FOR CECAP II CAPITAL FUNDS

With the large capital funds being channelled by other (particularly Government) agencies, the demand for CECAP II's funds may also be reduced, indeed in many cases, the other agencies are likely to seek to use CECAP II formed and trained SLGs to channel their funds.

In addition, (as noted above) as a result of the limited ideas on IGAs and the fear of the weekly repayment system, there may be a slow take-up of credit. The result of the Rural Household Survey (RHS) conducted by CECAP II suggest that only 25.6% of households have "taken any loan during the past 2 years to invest in an economic activity", and conclude that "many farmers cannot improve their farming systems because of insufficient capital". This, however, seems to be at odds with the responses on what households have used loans for (agriculture only accounts for 24.6% of loans taken), and where households would invest the extra money (agriculture was only cited by 16.2% of respondents). People in the Cordillera seem much more interested in investing in "business" (usually trading, but also handicrafts etc.) and "livestock", which together comprise 69.4% of the activities in which they would invest extra money. Excluded from the above analysis, by virtue of the emphasis on <u>activities</u> is investment in land purchase (or, it appears, construction), which, on the basis of the Rural Finance component's initial research, seem to be an important use of credit.

In addition, the emphasis on "economic activities" has meant that the demand for credit has been understated throughout the Cordillera, there is a clear widespread demand for providential credit particularly to finance education, medical and food purchase costs. Indeed the component's work suggests that almost all households have borrowed in the last year. The Rural Finance System expects to be addressing the following credit needs of the people of the Cordillera: providential (through the SLG Fund) and business and livestock (through the KC loans, and in many cases, also through the SLG Funds).

THREATS FROM OTHER AGENCIES' CREDIT PROGRAMMES

Perhaps one of the biggest problems facing the CECAP II Rural Finance System is the risk of being under-cut by other agencies' programmes which are often poorly designed and implemented, and usually credit-driven. The CECAP II's Provinces remain in the "Club of 20" poorest in the Philippines and thus attract large number of Government and Non Government programmes - many of them more intent on disbursing credit than on doing the necessary careful preparation and design to do so effectively, or recovering it. The Rural Finance component's initial research found many examples of co-operatives destroyed by large scale infusions of funds which they were simply unable to manage. Furthermore, the research also revealed many examples of uncollected loans apparently forgotten by the agencies that had issued them - a sure invitation to lax credit discipline which is likely to affect CECAP II's borrowers as well.

The LandBank's National Livelihood Support Scheme's Grameen "replication" amongst the Agrarian Reform Communities" (discussed in detail in the chapter "Replication: Regressive Reproduction or Progressive Evolution ?") "is a good example of the type of politically-motivated loan scheme that threatens the CECAP Rural Finance System. On the face of it, it is probable that these relatively cheap loans will be "captured" by the elite (who are the ones best able to provide the collateral likely to be required by the co-operative), and that there will be the usual poor repayment discipline. However, these massive infusion of funds does present two issues to the CECAP II Rural Finance System: firstly the demonstration effect of another round of unpaid loans, and secondly, it is possible that the co-operatives may seek to use the CECAP II trained SLGs to channel some of these funds. Time will tell.

AVAILABILITY OF KCS

The availability of potential KCs varies substantially from Province to Province. In Ifugao, the co-operative movement has taken strong hold, and there are potential KCs in almost every Municipality. Conversely in Kalinga and Abra, for example, the situation varies from Municipalities where there are no potential KCs to those where there are several weak co-operatives that might be developed into a KC.

Chapter 2

BURO, TANGAIL : SYSTEMS AND SERVICES UNDER DEVELOPMENT

The history of Bangladesh Unemployed Rehabilitation Organisation (BURO) is a sorry tale. An organisation inspired by the principles of "shawnirvar" or self-reliance, BURO set out to mobilise its capital funds from the savings of villagers and eschew donor funds. The villagers did indeed show a tremendous ability to save, but BURO's management and systems were not equal to the complex task of running a savings and credit organisation. Indeed, in addition to failing to distinguish "cash in" from "income", the system's interest and remuneration rates meant that each loan transaction would, inevitably, make a loss.

BURO tried two systems, the Village Resource Development Programme (1985-89) and the Small Savings Scheme (1989-90) in order to mobilise savings from the entire community. In addition to fundamental management and book-keeping short-comings, BURO also faced another problem commonly experienced by Microfinance organisations starting up in Bangladesh. Initially at least (when the organisation is new) the demand for credit exceeds the savings that can be mobilised in the villages. And where the organisation is unable to provide loans, the members' confidence declines, and they entrust even fewer savings deposits to it. To overcome this problem, BURO resorted to playing "shell-games" moving quicker and quicker into new areas in order to mobilise savings to meet the demand for loans and savings withdrawals in areas where they were already operating. The pressure for loans and savings withdrawals grew, and as management became more desperate to meet these growing demands, so the promises and schemes to attract new members and savings became more outlandish.

In 1989, two consultants were funded to train and strengthen the management of BURO. After their initial review and an organisation-wide audit, they concluded that BURO had been operating in 38 districts, with around 350 branches, and had made (at a conservative estimate) losses of around $500,000. The consultants recommended immediate suspension of all BURO's activities so that they could work on re-engineering the organisation and its systems. This recommendation was rejected by BURO's management. Nonetheless, a new model system was developed and pilot-tested in five branches in Tangail district. As a result of the pilot testing, BURO made several amendments to refine the policies and procedures, which generally brought the system closer to poor-targeted savings and credit schemes being run by Grameen Bank and BRAC. BURO retained one key difference: it maintained voluntary, open-access savings as a central part of the financial services being offered to its clients.

Meanwhile, the internal politics of the organisation reached a critical point and the Executive Director, in the hope of securing some funds allegedly available in Pakistan, made a deal to work together with an Islamic political organisation. It was at this stage that BURO, Tangail was launched as an independent Microfinance organisation.

In Tangail, work to test and refine the model, and the extensive efforts to rebuild members' confidence in the organisation continued, and the system started to yield profits. Successive evaluation reviews made positive recommendations, and donors started to show interest in BURO, Tangail's commitment to creating a sustainable Microfinance Institution and developing quality financial services to meet the needs of its clients. Shortly thereafter, BURO, Tangail secured the funding necessary to continue and build on its work and the organisation has now become one of the more innovative and influential NGOs operating in Bangladesh.

"Viability must be an important goal for financial development. In developing countries a viable rural financial institution is one that is self-sustaining, that covers its costs, that provides services valued by rural households and businesses, that serves an ever increasing number of rural customers, that is dynamic in providing new financial products and services, and that actively searches for ways to improve efficiency reflected in reduced transaction costs for itself and/or its customers" (Meyer, 1988).

INTRODUCTION

Sitting inside the cramped corrugated-iron hut, with the sun burning down on the roof, and sweat trickling down my back, I could not believe my eyes. The year was 1990, and I had been sent to review the accounts of Barecha, which I was assured was one of "the more profitable" Bangladesh Unemployed Rehabilitation Organisation (BURO) branch offices. Having overcome the shock that there were almost no records to speak of, I had set about reconstructing the books for a month. The Branch Manager was most interested in what I was doing ... clearly all these financial calculations were new to him.

After extracting all that I could from the dog-eared cashbook, I was left with an analysis broadly as follows:

Cash-In (Tk.)		Cash-Out (Tk.)	
Savings Deposits	27,000	Loans Disbursed	10,000
Loan Repayments/Interest	3,500	Salaries	9,000
Sale of Forms	230	Office Rental	2,000
		Stationery	1,400
		Transportation	1,330
Total	**30,730**	**Total**	**23,730**

"There," said the Manager, with a great deal of satisfaction, "another Tk. 7,000 profit last month. I knew this was one of the most successful branches". I was not sure whether to laugh or cry.

On visits to other branches, tears were clearly the most appropriate response. And I was not the only one shedding them. I met members unable get access to the precious savings they had entrusted to BURO, Branch Managers barricaded into offices under siege by enraged depositors, and Village Development Workers (BURO's front-line field workers) forced to sell their wedding jewellery to try to refund savings that had been lost.

I have spent years wondering, and never completely concluding, whether BURO was a huge, appalling fraud (similar to the Social Economic Development Organisation - SEDO, which collected millions of Taka in poor people's savings, and then made off with them all) or simply a disaster driven by incompetent, untrained management. Certainly, talking to the Executive Director, Major (Retired) Wahidul

Hossain, one could only be struck by his commitment to the vision of involving <u>all</u> members (rich and poor) of the village community in the development process ... and by his almost complete lack of understanding of the damage that BURO was actually doing.

The laxity of Bangladesh's regulatory and supervisory framework (which will be discussed more in the chapter "Savings: Services for the Client or Capital for the Institution?") provided the environment for the tragedy to unfold. The only two members of BURO's National Executive Committee that I ever met were a TV journalist and a lawyer/MP serving as part of President Ershad's regime. During the two years I struggled to help extricate BURO (or more particularly its members) from the disaster enveloping them, the National Executive Committee rarely ever met, and certainly had no real idea of what was happening to the organisation and the members whose interests they were to serve and protect. And, of course, the books of account had never been audited. Until 1989 (despite constant searching) BURO never received any foreign funding, and it appears that as a result of this, it slipped through whatever flimsy regulatory net existed.

The irony of this is that in many ways it is the independent local initiatives that require the most supervision. As we saw in the chapter on "Replication" there are hundreds of (often unregistered, let alone monitored or supervised) local organisations being set up by well-intentioned, but ill-equipped individuals, collecting savings from their poor members, and then sliding into slow agonising failure and loss. Indeed a well-respected Government and World Bank-funded organisation may be inadvertently promoting this epidemic of tragedy throughout the villages of Bangladesh.

THE ANATOMY OF A TRAGEDY

Village Resource Development Programme (VRDP) 1985-89

Major Wahidul left Shawnirvar, Bangladesh to establish the Bangladesh Unemployed Rehabilitation Organisation (BURO) in 1985. BURO initiated its activities in eleven districts in the same year using the Village Resource Development Programme as the system for local resource mobilisation. Continuing from the Shawnirvar movement from which BURO evolved, the organisation tried to incorporate representatives from all classes and categories of people in the villages, and to draw them into working together for the development process rather than focusing on class differences. This approach was markedly different to the tried and tested "target group" method of Grameen Bank and all other NGOs operating in Bangladesh.

The merit of this approach was that only through mobilising the resources of the more affluent members of society for on-lending to the poor could the organisation fund itself. The Rural Finance Experimental Project (RFEP)'s Terminal Evaluation Report of 1982 provided the rationale for attaching importance to the non-target group savers. "Analysis of savings performance in the RFEP shows that the target group cannot of themselves provide the funds needed for lending. It is only by tapping non-target group deposits that such funds can be raised."

Under the Village Resource Development Programme, members were required to invest an admission fee of Tk. 10 and Tk. 200 in shares in the organisation. Interest of 10% was paid on members' savings deposited with the organisation, and interest of 20% on principle was charged on loans. Village Resource Development Committees (VRDCs) were to be formed to lead the community development process, to sanction loans and to ensure their full repayment. However, very few Village Resource Development Committees ever reached this ideal.

The Village Development Workers (VDWs) reported directly to the district office, and were paid 7.5% on all the savings collected from members. The Union Organisers (also reporting directly to the district office), received an additional 2.5% on savings deposited. An additional 10% of savings collected were to be remitted to the district/head offices to meet administrative and salary expenses. Subsequent analysis showed these remittances to be inadequate. Thus the cost of the organisation's capital was 10%, and its additional operational costs were at least 20%, before provision for bad debts.

During this stage of its operation, BURO was extremely decentralised and without any real accounting system. District Organisers were appointed by the Executive Director, and dispatched to commence operations in the districts with almost no training at all. As a result, the organisation expanded rapidly, and ran into large-scale problems. Almost none of the staff had adequate training or experience, the Village Resource Development Committees were rarely formed, there were almost no financial records and where loans were issued, they were often given to relatively affluent and influential members of village society.

In addition, BURO commenced a rural insurance scheme without the actuarial or administrative skills to do so, choosing to offer a scheme whereby if a member died, his family would get a sum of Taka equal to the number of BURO members in the union. This scheme was only implemented in a few districts.

The lack of a clear business plan, compounded by inadequate accounting records and misappropriation by BURO staff, resulted in an extremely high bad debt rate. Inevitably, the organisation made ever-increasing losses. Very soon, the organisation was engaged in a strategy of cashflow manipulation, a "shell-game", wherein they had to continue to mobilise savings to meet members' demands for repayment of savings and share deposits. Without accounting records, the losses that the organisation was sustaining could be ignored and hidden as long as the cash was available to meet immediate requirements. More and more district offices were opened in order to find the cash to try to run the organisation, and the promises made to members and potential members became more and more far-fetched. For example, district officers were instructed to inform the members that once they had deposited the Tk. 200 share capital, they would receive a loan of Tk. 1,000 within three months. Without external capitalisation on a massive scale, these loans could never have materialised. And indeed, they did not.

As a result, members became increasingly disenchanted with the organisation and the pressure for repayment of savings and share deposits increased dramatically, forcing the closure of operations in many districts. In the words of Clarence Maloney (1990), "In many places BURO collected shares and savings, but was unable to finance projects of more than 5 or 10% of members. This caused the members who did not get loans to become discouraged, and has been a major cause of set-back to the work in a number of districts. BURO officials repeatedly state that when members pay their shares and savings, they expect some loan or other assistance, and if it is too long in coming, they withdraw, and the reputation of BURO suffers".

BURO started operations in ten districts in 1985, and the following year initiated activities in ten more districts. An additional eighteen districts were added in 1987, giving the total of thirty-eight districts with around 350 branches. However, by the beginning of 1989, fifteen districts had terminated operations with huge losses to the members and local staff of the organisation. The inferno was catching, the tragedy was unfolding at a terrifying rate.

Small Savings Scheme (SSS) 1989-90

In an attempt to improve the flow of cash, and thus to preserve its operations, BURO started the Small Savings Scheme (SSS) in 1989. The Small Savings Scheme retained most of the characteristics of Village Resource Development Programme, but added union level branches that operated as "mini-banks" and encouraged members to save regularly. A fixed deposit scheme promising, what was for BURO, an uneconomical rate of return (circa 18% pa over 5 years) was initiated in some districts. Village Development Workers continued to tour the village households collecting savings deposits, and in some districts, a thana level supervisory office was added. Security deposits were collected from branch and district office staff, and were then channelled into loans.

Under the Small Savings Scheme, the system remained loss making both in theory and in practice and additional schemes were commenced to try to make up these losses. These schemes were as follows:

1. *Delta Life Insurance*: As a follow-up to the attempts to initiate rural life insurance activities, BURO began working with Delta Life Insurance. A village life insurance scheme that provided for benefits upon the death of the insured was offered. Premiums were collected by the Village Development Workers for a 10% commission, and (when the Village Development Workers did not withhold them against their unpaid salary/commission) were re-invested in the local BURO organisation at a 20% interest rate, thus further raising BURO cashflow and cost of capital. However, this arrangement was terminated as BURO ran into increasing problems and was unable to submit premiums to Delta Life Insurance in accordance with agreed policy.

2. *Local Business Schemes*: These were designed to provide additional income to the offices, and included fish farms, chicken hatcheries, small garments workshops, nurseries etc. The businesses were usually run by the BURO district office staff. Since the staff responsible for these projects rarely had the technical competence to do so, the schemes often made

additional losses, and diverted the staff's attention away from responding to the financial inferno raging around them.

Like the district offices, most union branch offices kept only cashbooks, and thus had no control over savings, loan repayments or no idea of profit and loss. Furthermore, this lack of control facilitated, if not encouraged, dishonesty, and misappropriation by BURO staff was not uncommon. In 1990 when I first analysed the BURO activities in the Barecha branch, the estimated loss rate was over 50%. (See analysis above). This was a surprise to BURO management who felt that the Small Savings Scheme should allow the organisation to be self-financing, and had been unable to differentiate between cashflow and profit.

The sheer magnitude of the problem was highlighted by M. A. Quader Kabir & Co.'s special investigation report of June 1990, which found that the organisation had probably made a loss in excess of $500,000, or (50% of members' savings deposited) before:

1.   Provision for bad debts
2.   Provision for depreciation
3.   Full provision for interest payable on savings accounts
4.   Full provision for commission or salary payable to staff.

INTERVENTION

At this stage the USAID-funded PACT/PRIP project hired Tony Drexler, an experienced American development consultant, and Graham Wright, a British Chartered Accountant as Technical Advisors to try to reorient, train and stabilise BURO. PACT/PRIP also gave BURO some funds to hire some experienced staff and better equip the head office. The Technical Advisors helped recruit an accountant, Mosharrof Hossain, an ex-Grameen Bank Area Manager, Shiv Prashad Saha, and an outstanding training expert, Mukidul Islam. With these three, and several of BURO head office and Tangail District staff, including Zakir Hossain, they started to re-engineer BURO.

After the initial audit of all the districts in which the organisation was functioning, it was clear that the only responsible course of action was to close operations in almost all districts. The longer branches stayed open, the more savings they attracted, and the more losses they made. In a country with more developed business and regulatory frameworks, BURO would have been placed in receivership while attempts were made to salvage whatever possible. The Technical Advisors proposed that BURO suspend operations and issue bonds or certificates of obligation to its members while the training proceeded, the system was redesigned, and capital funds were raised. The District Organisers, fearing the angry scenes that would inevitably follow, fiercely opposed to such a move and were backed by the Executive Director. The Technical Advisors' pleas for responsibility to the poor members, for consideration of the long-term issues and for understanding that staying open for business would only make matters worse, fell on deaf ears.

Worse, the Technical Advisors even found instances where Major Wahid sanctioned the opening of additional new offices, and was interviewing and hiring managers for them. All this was done without the knowledge of the finance and training departments (which were headed by the newly recruited Mosharrof Hossain and Mukidul Islam) who were trying to bring discipline and professionalism into the organisation. Major Wahid was "putting out fire with gasoline".

TESTING THE PHOENIX

BURO Savings and Credit Model (BSCM) 1990-91

Working with Technical Advisors, the BURO management team developed a savings and credit model that, if the assumptions held true, would result in profitable operations. In addition, a detailed and effective accounting system was designed and implemented to gather financial and management information on the progress of the five "model" branches where the new system was to be tested.

Under the BURO Savings and Credit Model (BSCM), BURO management elected to change several of the basic operational philosophies and practices of the organisation. In particular, the BURO decided to follow the more conventional target group identification and group formation.

1. *Target Group*: The target group was defined, in accordance with the Grameen Bank's policies, as people (primarily women) with < 0.5 acres of land (the functionally landless) or total assets of < Tk. 50,000.

2. *Group Formation*: A group size of ten was selected, and five groups of ten were to form *kendras* of fifty members. The choice of the group system was for several reasons:

   a. It allowed BURO to use social and group pressure to ensure prompt repayment, particularly since additional loans to other group members were made dependent on disciplined repayment patterns.

   b. It greatly facilitated the administration of the savings and credit aspects of the programme by bringing groups of members together in one place at a specified time. This saved the Village Development Workers seeking out and visiting each of the members individually as had been the practice before. In this way, the cost-effectiveness of the programme was greatly enhanced.

   c. It allowed BURO to use kendras for community development and extension activities and to train for group-managed projects.

   d. It brought BURO more into line with well-established theory and practice in Bangladesh, thus increasing the likelihood of the organisation attracting funds.

Extension and community development activities were still to be co-ordinated and undertaken with the VRDCs comprising representatives from all sections and classes of village society.

Under the BURO Savings and Credit Model members formed groups to save Tk. 5 per member per week. Interest of 10% was paid on members savings deposited with the organisation, and interest of 20% on principle was charged on loans. The real interest rate was increased through the introduction of the BURO levy (5%), which was designed to finance the training and administrative costs associated with a more professional and effective organisation. This increase was calculated as the minimum necessary to make the organisation viable.

Two additional levies were introduced :

1. *Emergency Fund* (10%) This fund was to be used in three ways:

   a. To pay off loans in the event of the loanee's death or permanent disability.

b. To issue supplemental loans in the event of loss of the loanee's income earning capability through loss or damage to the asset purchased with the original loan.

c. To recover loans overdue for more than six months.

2. *VRDC Levy* (5%) This levy was designed to link the funds that the VRDC had available to it for investment in the village social-development programs to the amount of money collected as loan repayment instalments. The levy was to be used to finance village social-development programs in conjunction with the VRDC levy of Tk. 1, collected in cash from the members each month.

While the VRDCs were to be formed to lead the community development process, and facilitate repayment the repayment of loans, the sanctioning of loans was centralised and to be performed at the district office level to strengthen control.

The Village Development Workers reported to the union level branch office, and were paid a salary of Tk. 150 plus 2.5% on all the savings deposits and the loan repayments collected from members. The Union Organisers received a salary of Tk. 250 and an additional 1.5% on all savings deposited and 0.25% of loan repayments collected. Thus these workers became salaried staff and therefore subject to direction (as opposed to suggestion) by the Branch Managers. Furthermore, the changes shifted the emphasis from rewarding exclusively for the collection of savings to a more balanced approach encouraging the full collection of loan repayments too. After some initial training, the BURO Savings and Credit Model was implemented in five branches in Tangail covering 82 villages on a test basis on 1st November 1990.

After the initial implementation efforts, the model branches were given insufficient guidance from the head office or district office staff. Head office staff were primarily engaged in internal power struggles and/or trying to assist/prop-up activities in other districts despite repeated advice from the Technical Advisors to close them. This was indicative of the deep philosophical divide that had opened up within the organisation, with the Executive Director clinging to the old BURO philosophy and mode of operation as the rest of management team tried to implement the new model. As a result, the limited number of follow-up assistance and monitoring field trips to the model branches was inadequate. District office level staff had no funds from which to pay salaries or for transportation into the unions, which resulted in limited ineffectual monitoring activities at this critical level. As a consequence, the union branch staff received little or no guidance, assistance or supervision, and in many respects, lapsed into the in-discipline that characterised the old BURO systems.

Meanwhile, the internal politics of the organisation were coming to a head. The Executive Director called all the District Organisers to a meeting with the Islami Adolnon (the Islamic Republican Movement - IRM) without consulting the National Executive Council or the Board of Directors. The District Organisers were requested to approve the merger of BURO with the IRM in an attempt to access some funds alleged to be in Pakistan. The District Organisers, desperate for any cash to prop up their ailing operations, agreed to merge with what was clearly a political organisation with dubious connections. The majority of the head office management and support team, unable to work any more with Major Wahid, then resigned and expressed the desire to work with the five BURO Savings and Credit Model pilot branches in Tangail. At this stage, PACT/PRIP was compelled to intervene - clearly its funds could not be associated with such a politically motivated organisation.

The philosophical and political divides within BURO had finally lead to a split in the organisation in June 1991, and BURO, Tangail was established to continue to implement the model. However, in the process, nearly a year's precious time had been lost.

After eight months of operation an internal evaluation was conducted to identify the success or otherwise of the implementation of the model, and the problems being faced by the organisation. As a result of this internal evaluation, BURO, Tangail management and the Technical Advisors made some key revisions to the model.

1. *Self-Financing Principle*: When the model was initially conceived, it was hoped that it would be feasible to create an entirely self-funding system that, over six years, would generate all its capital requirements through the savings of members. The original BURO the BURO Savings and Credit Model showed members joining and saving Tk. 5 per week to build their future in a spirit of patient co-operation and independence. If feasible, this approach would have represented almost total "*shawnirvar*", requiring only a small amount of institutional support during the

inception period. However, the first eight months of work in the five model unions demonstrated that while it is feasible to set up and run a self-financing savings and credit system, this is not possible without significant inputs of capital at the beginning. This conclusion was also reached by all the teams working on the second internal evaluation, and confirmed Rural Finance Experimental Project's observation on the basis of their analysis of savings performance, that the target group could not themselves provide the funds needed for lending.

The organisation was working in areas where larger well-funded NGOs (such as Grameen Bank, BRAC and CARE) were also active. While these larger NGOs were by no means able to fulfil all the needs for capital in the villages, their activities had given rise to a series of side-effects that made alternative approaches difficult to implement. In particular, traditional systems of pooling funds, and patiently saving to generate a small capital base (well documented in Maloney and Ahmed, 1988), had been replaced by high expectations of fast and frequent credit.

BURO, Tangail management and the Technical Advisors agreed on the need for an injection of capital of a minimum of $10,000 per branch if the membership's expectations were to be fulfilled, and if the groups were to be maintained and strengthened. This represented another fundamental departure from the BURO philosophy, which had held that the member's savings alone could generate the capital fund for the organisation's credit programme.

2. *Dissolution of the Village Resource Development Committees (VRDCs):* The VRDCs were envisaged by BURO as a way to oversee loans and to organise and harness the potential for self-development in the villages. However, few of the VRDCs ever worked properly, particularly since they tended to become dominated by the local elite. While the high rates of interest charged by the BURO Savings and Credit Model discouraged the local elite from seeking credit, the VRDC levies were aggravating the problems caused by the "capture" of the VRDCs by the elite by generating funds for them. Accordingly, the VRDCs were dissolved, and the *kendras* became the operative unit for village-

based development activities to be planned and implemented by *kendra* members.

3. *Group Size*: The group size in the BURO Savings and Credit Model system was ten members. This proved to be too large for several reasons:

   1. Finding ten members living in close proximity but without family members was difficult.
   2. Maintaining discipline and cohesion in groups of ten was difficult.
   3. Decision-making at the group level was hampered by the size of the groups.

The groups were reorganised in conformity with the Grameen Bank and most other systems, to comprise five members each. The *kendras* were then to comprise a maximum of ten groups of five, giving a total of fifty members. This was expected to facilitate group formation, enhance savings and loan repayment collection, and improve decision-making and cohesion among the members.

BURO, Tangail Revised Savings and Credit Model (BTRSCM) 1991-92

Working with Technical Advisors, the BURO, Tangail management team developed a revised savings and credit model that, if the assumptions held true, would result in profitable operations. Under BURO, Tangail Revised Savings and Credit Model (BTRSCM), BURO, Tangail members formed groups to save Tk. 5 per member per week. Interest of 10% was paid on members savings deposited with the organisation, and interest of 25% on principle was charged on loans.

In response to the observations and requests of members and Village Development Workers, BURO, Tangail management made some additional changes to the loan repayment instalments of the BURO Savings and Credit Model. The BURO Levy was subsumed into the interest rate, the VRDC levy replaced with a lower *kendra* levy, and the Emergency Fund contribution reduced to 2.5% of loan principle. The *kendras* were to plan and implement community development process, and facilitate repayment the repayment of loans. The sanctioning of loans remained centralised and performed at the district office level to strengthen control.

The Village Development Workers reported to the branch office, and were paid a salary of Tk. 300 plus 2.5% on all the savings deposits and the loan repayments collected from members. The Union Organisers (UO) received a salary of Tk. 400 and an additional 1.0% on all savings deposited and 0.25% of loan repayments collected.

After a prolonged programme of training in the classroom and in the field, the BURO, Tangail Revised Savings and Credit Model was implemented effective August 1, 1991. To bring the organisation's operations into line with the model, the number of Village Development Workers working in each branch was halved. This rationalisation allowed BURO, Tangail to screen out the Village Development Workers who were unable to perform their work effectively. With the printing and introduction of the prepared forms necessary to run the system late 1991, the Management Information System was generating monthly financial statements, ratio analysis and graphs of the ten critical indicators used by BURO, Tangail to monitor its programme implementation. The Tangail district office was converted into the head office, and from September 1991 top level staff operated at the district level. This, together with the training programme resulted in a remarkable improvement in the performance of staff. In order to maintain and build upon this field-based orientation, from April 1, 1992, the Dhaka Office in Mohammudpur was shut down, and the organisation operated out of its Tangail head office.

An intensive programme of village-level motivation was undertaken in the second half of 1991. As a result, the level of group formation improved and the results showed that members were still saving money and repaying loans regularly. Nonetheless, as noted in the Second Internal Evaluation Report, to maintain group cohesion, the organisation required capitalisation. Previously, the loan recovery rate had fallen beneath the minimum 90% required by both the BURO Savings and Credit Model and the BURO, Tangail Revised Savings and Credit Model. The head office staff made strenuous efforts to ensure overdue loan-recovery, and by 1992 the loan recovery ratios were as follows:

	January	February
1) Atia	93%	92%
2) Dewali	96%	97%
3) Mogra*	105%	104%
4) Pathorail	73%	75%
5) Silimpur	86%	85%

* >100% due to advance loan repayments

In December 1991, BURO, Tangail initiated the drive to raise the funds necessary to capitalise the organisation, and to maintain the head office for the next two years, with the clear understanding that the programme's ultimate objective was to become self-sustaining over a period of circa 8 years.

A Project Proposal was prepared for Phase I and II, and initial analysis of the costs and timing of Phase III was initiated at donors' request. Several donors visited BURO, Tangail in the field, and there was a growing consensus that the programme was important because of its explicitly self-financing nature, but that it required capitalisation as soon as possible to preserve the confidence of the members and the cohesion of the groups. Capitalisation would have several immediate and necessary effects:

1. Satisfy the demand for loans, thus increasing confidence in the organisation.
2. Further improve loan recovery rates through enhanced the confidence among the members.
3. Increase the savings through the compulsory savings for loanees.
4. Increase voluntary savings as a result of the increased confidence in the organisation.
5. Provide money for the *kendras'* development activities and the emergency fund through levies on loans issued; and thus
6. Improve the cohesion of the *kendras*.
7. Raise the remuneration of the Village Development Workers and branch staff, thus improving motivation, morale and performance.

After all by this stage, the older (more patient, naive or optimistic) members had been faced with four different systems and a variety of promises. The table below shows clearly the evolution of BURO to BURO, Tangail; from a development organisation attempting to involve the entire community to one using the "target group" approach more common in Bangladesh. As part of the evolution, the organisation also moved to a banking system operated through groups - groups which were also expected to be the locus for collective decision-making and community development activities.

	BURO Village Resource Development Programme	**BURO Small Savings Scheme**	**BURO Savings and Credit Model**	**BURO, Tangail Revised Savings & Credit Model**
Implementation Period :	1985-89	1989-90	1990-91	1991-92
Target Group :	None	None	< 0.5 acres of land or <Tk.50,000 Total assets	<0.5 acres of land or < Tk 50,000 total assets or < Tk. 15,000 annual income
Community Development Decision-making Locus :	VRDC	VRDC	VRDC	*Kendra*
Local Office Level	District	Union	Union	Union
Admission Fee: Membership Dues:	Tk. 10	Tk. 10	Tk. 20	Tk. 20
Share *	Tk. 200	Tk. 200		
Life**			Tk. 100	Tk. 100
Withdrawal Slip Cost:	Tk. 0.2	Tk. 0.2	Tk. 0.5	Tk.0.5
Loan Application Fee:	Tk. 15	Tk. 15	1.0% of loan principle	1.0% of loan principle
Levies:				
Savings			Tk. 1 pcm	Tk. 1 pcm
BURO			5% of loan principle	
VRDC			5% of loan principle	
Kendra				2.5% of loan principle
Emergency Fund			10% of loan principle	2.5% of loan principle
Repayment Schedule: Tk. 1,000 loan	Tk.20 Weekly for 10 Weeks	Tk. 20 Weekly for 50 weeks	Tk. 28 Weekly for 50 weeks	Tk. 25 Weekly for 50 weeks
VDW Salary: VDW Commission :			Tk. 150	Tk. 300
Savings	7.5%	7.5%	2.5%	2.5%
Loan			2.5%	2.5%
UO Salary: UO Commission			Tk. 250	Tk. 400
Savings	2.5%	2.5%	1.5%	1.0%
Loan			0.25%	0.25%

*   = Refundable   ** = Non-refundable

THE PHOENIX RISES

Phases I - III: Consolidation and Expansion

In Phase I of its expansion, BURO, Tangail continued to offer voluntary savings facilities unique in NGO programmes in Bangladesh, allowing members to withdraw their savings whenever they did not have a loan outstanding. Furthermore, also unlike many of the NGOs operating in the country, members were not compelled or pressured into accepting loans. With a view to creating a sustainable organisation, BURO, Tangail continued to charge 25% on principle to enable the members to further capitalise their organisation through branch level "profits". In addition, Phase I was used to strengthen the five existing "model" branches, increase the level of lending, and refine the management, training, audit and implementation systems of the organisation.

The five Phase II branches were opened at the end of 1992. The 1992 Annual Report showed that, despite the relatively low levels of external capitalisation ($10,000 per branch), three of the Phase I branches were turning profits (used to add to the revolving loan fund), and that the members had deposited $158,000 savings and made withdrawals (largely for productive purposes) of $118,000.

The Phase II branches were capitalised with $10,000 each in 1993 and BURO, Tangail commenced preparatory work in an additional three branches. During the year, the members deposited savings of $92,292, and made withdrawals of $36,797. By December 31, 1993, members' voluntary savings were providing over a third of the organisation's loan capital. The importance of this is discussed further in the chapter "Savings: Services for the Client or Capital for the Institution?"

The external evaluation team appointed to review BURO, Tangail's operations in May 1993 concluded:

"Based on the collective experience of the evaluation team in assessing the overall merits of small rural credit programs in Bangladesh, the team is of the view that, overall, BURO, Tangail is an organisation deserving of donor support. Its program is well-conceived, its organisation suited to carrying out the overall mandate, and, most importantly, its staff is dedicated, motivated and prepared to take on the responsibilities and challenges presented by the proposed extension project."

Phase III, which ran from July 1993 to December 1995, had opened an additional 10 branches, raised the revolving loan fund for each branch to $15,000, and provided $156,790 training and implementation costs. By the end of December 1995, 20 branches were operating. The Phase I and II branches were turning average profits of $2,654 and $1,330 a month respectively. The other 10 branches were also turning small-scale profits. All profits were re-invested in the branches' revolving loan funds. As of December 31, 1995, the donors (AusAid, Canadian Fund for Local Initiatives, ODA, PACT/PRIP, SIDA and South Asia Partnership) had contributed $308,380 to capitalise and fund the organisation, and the members had matched this with $105,895 from branch profits, and $198,055 in savings.

But, as BURO, Tangail management had pointed out in the donor support group meeting held in February 1995, problems and opportunities had arisen. The competition among NGOs offering financial services in Tangail was mounting, and while members greatly valued BURO, Tangail's voluntary open access savings programme (further discussed in the chapter "Savings: Services for the Client or Capital for the Institution?") and "Optimising Systems for Clients and the Institution" below), they continued to find the 25% interest rate too high. Indeed some began to leave BURO, Tangail for competitors, while others were saving with BURO, Tangail but taking loans from other organisations.

The external Mid Term Review Team, appointed by the donors' support group, concluded in July 1995 that:

"BURO, Tangail [BT] represents an interesting and important experiment in savings and credit programs. It has made significant progress and is worthy of continued attention and support."

"There are many NGO quasi-banks in Tangail and real if partial competition has now set in between them which makes BT anxious about a potential decline in demand for loans. BT is proposing to lower its interest rate on loans as a pricing strategy designed to increase demand and thereby volume of loans, and the team endorses it".

"The Team recommends that BT should compete not only on cost but also in quality and range of loan services, and should begin to experiment with alternative loan terms and repayment schedules."

"BT's customers use the savings services in a wide variety of ways and not just to build up investment capital. The Team recommends that

BT should offer at least two savings schemes: an open-withdrawal system and a fixed deposit with higher return."

Phase IV: The Quest for Sustainability and Quality Financial Services

BURO, Tangail took the recommendations of the Mid-Term Review Team to the staff and members in a programme of participatory consultation, which guided the formulation of the organisation's "Response to the Mid Term Review" by management with inputs from the Technical Assistance consultants (Graham Wright and Iftekhar Hossain) appointed by the donors' support group. This "Response" defined the guiding principles for the development of the new financial plan for the organisation to expand and achieve sustainable independence by the year 2001.

The Financial Plan included in the "Response to the Mid Term Review", was developed with the Technical Assistance consultants using sophisticated modelling in Lotus 123, and was thoroughly tested prior to being used to review different approaches to achieving BURO, Tangail's mission, and the organisation's goals. The result was an ambitious, but feasible, plan of expansion to provide better financial services to increasing numbers of members, while conducting operations research with the aim of broadening the range of financial services offered by the organisation. One additional substantial change was made to the implementation methodology. The *kendra* levy was not proving successful in promoting community development, and as had been hoped "allowing members to participate in, plan and initiate development activities appropriate for their village". In recognition of the limited impact of the *kendra* levy, BURO, Tangail decided to abolish the levy commencing January 1, 1996 - thus further reducing the effective interest rate on the loans. BURO, Tangail thus moved to becoming exclusively a financial service provider.

Under the plan, BURO, Tangail is to expand its operations to open 30 more branches, and to raise membership to 90,600 by 2001 and 100,000 by the year 2004. By the year 2000, the members will match the donors' capital contributions to the revolving loan funds. This will be done through a mixture of their savings and their contributions to the revolving loan funds through retained profits at the branch level after meeting head office costs. The branches will meet all recurring head office costs after the year 1999. By the end of the year 2001, BURO, Tangail plans to be financially independent and sustainable, able to offer financial services to its members without further recourse to donor funds.

Of the US \$14.359 million total project financing requirements for the five years from 1997 to 2001, the members will finance US \$9.956 million or 69%, and donors will finance US \$4.403 million or 31%. Of the US\$4.403 million, 82% [\$3.612 million] is for revolving loan funds, and 18% [\$0.791 million] is for branch establishment, programme implementation etc. costs. At the end of this period, BURO, Tangail will not require any additional financing from outside sources. All additional capital and operating requirements will be met from savings, borrowing from commercial sources, and members' contributions to capital funds.

BURO, Tangail believes that this can offer a cost-effective (at around \$50 per member) and equitable form of development for the rural poor Bangladesh. Through the supplementary programme of operations research to develop and introduce more flexible financial services, BURO, Tangail is providing important information for the increasing numbers of NGOs offering savings and credit services to the poor.

Through its work from 1991-95, BURO, Tangail believes that it has developed and tested a sustainable rural savings and credit model. Once an initial revolving loan fund (RLF) has been established, each branch is capable of not only financing itself, but also of remitting contributions to meet the head office costs. By charging interest rates that reflect the real cost of delivering the banking services to its members, BURO, Tangail has responded to the donor's challenge to offer *sustainable development in Bangladesh.*

The BURO, Tangail system represents a significant opportunity to establish compact sustainable savings and credit operations based in one district with a small Dhaka liaison office. This would create a sustainable savings and credit organisation of a manageable size, with circa 100,000 members and 50 branches.

The system is currently being financed by DFID, SDC and SIDA.

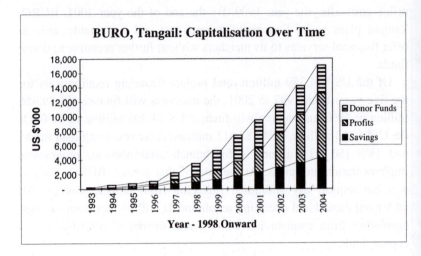

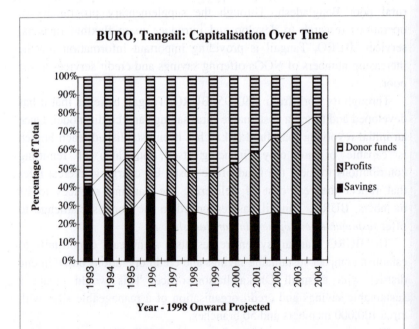

Rekha Basak Left Behind To Build Anew

Rekha Basak's simple but secure life came to an abrupt halt during the communal disturbances in 1992. Her brother-in-laws sold their six handlooms and left for West Bengal for good, but Basak and her husband could not leave. Unfortunately, they had spent all the money they had treating her husband's typhoid fever. The helpless Basak went to everybody she knew for help, but nobody responded. Finally, she sold all her jewellery and purchased a handloom so that she could start to weave again - but for lack of money, she could not buy yarn, and so was not able to operate the loom. She went from door to door to ask for a little working capital, but received none. She even went to a moneylender for help, but he refused: she was too high a risk. "My sari was in tatters, I had no blouse, and still despite the shame, went from house to house looking for help - but no-one believed that I had a future," Basak recalls.

As she made her rounds looking for someone to lend her some yarn or a little money to buy some, she heard that many of her neighbours had changed their fate by joining NGO "banks". Inspired by this, she also joined an NGO called RDS, even though it was hardly known to anyone. Like the other NGOs RDS had weekly meetings where members saved, and with much difficulty, Basak saved Tk. 200 in a little less than a year. But the RDS workers never seemed to have the money to give loans, and Basak desperately wanted a loan to use her handloom. Just as her hope was fading, the RDS workers stopped coming to the village, never to return ... and never to return Basak's precious savings.

Tears rise in her eyes as she remembers those dark and desperate days, "People warned me that some NGOs collected savings and then absconded, but I never believed that it would happen to me - I needed to believe that there was hope, and the RDS workers were very persuasive. When they left my husband was furious ..."

It was at this time, when all seemed lost, Basak, talked to her neighbour called Sarashati, who was a field worker of BURO, Tangail. Sarashati, moved by Basak's plight, encouraged her to form a new group, join the Centre in village and start saving. Of course, Basak's husband was extremely doubtful when she told him of the plan, but he had heard of BURO, Tangail and seen the Centre meeting in the village for some years, and so relented and let her join.

contd.

Continued from : Rekha Basak

Inspired and once again full of hope, Rheka Basak organised a group under the No. 16 Centre of Pathrail. She also motivated many others like her, who had been destitute and helpless, to join. Soon the life of Basak took another new direction. First, she took loan of Tk. 1,000, and finally managed to buy the yarn she needed to operate her handloom. Then she took another loan of Tk. 2,500 to buy some more yarn of better quality, before taking a third loan to buy another handloom. Now she has just taken Tk. 20,000 as her seventh loan. Today Basak has three handlooms, housed in a new, large tin shed and employs three of her distant relatives in the business.

Rekha has the greatest confidence in BURO, Tangail - "It changed my life", she says with a heart-warming smile.

BURO, Tangail - An Overview
As Of December 31, 1998

Organisation: BURO, Tangail has been operating since 1989, and is dedicated to the economic development of the poor, primarily in Tangail district, with the Mission Statement: "To establish an independent, sustainable organisation dedicated to providing effective flexible and responsive financial services to promote self-reliance among the rural poor in Bangladesh."

Through years of careful operations research, BURO, Tangail has developed and implemented a programme which emphasises the importance of savings as well a credit, and has become one of the more innovative and influential NGOs operating in Bangladesh.

Savings and Credit Activities: BURO, Tangail encourages potential clients drawn from the poorer "target" section of the community to form groups, encourages them to save, and provides credit to capitalise their income generation activities. By charging rates of interest designed to cover implementation costs and contribute to the capitalisation of the organisation, BURO, Tangail has developed a cost-effective and sustainable savings and credit system that by 2001 will provide financial services to around 100,000 members in a geographically compact area.

contd.

Continued from BURO, Tangail-An Overview

Members' Participation: The BURO, Tangail system encourages the members to participate in the planning, implementation and monitoring of the financial services and village development activities provided by the organisation, through participatory workshops, PRA and the Customers' Consultative Groups.

Scope of Operations: BURO, Tangail provides flexible financial services to 1,362 villages in Tangail district through 41 branches, which are managed from a head office located in Tangail town. There are a total of 448 staff who undergo regular classroom and on-the-job training.

Savings: In the year to December 31, 1997, net savings, including members' emergency funds increased by 105% to US$ 797,858, and the weekly savings rate in mature branches continued to rise, and was significantly above (usually more than double, often triple) the projected/budgeted rate of US$ 0.125. In the year to December 31, 1998, net savings including members' emergency funds increased by 14% to US$863,915. The declining rate in the rise in net savings arose from the lifting of the requirement to hold 15% of loans taken in savings account and the members' need to withdraw savings to meet emergencies in the wake of the disastrous 1998 floods.

Loans: As of December 31, 1998 US$ 12,242,543 in loans had been disbursed, and US$ 8,106,841 had been recovered. The loan recovery rate further improved over previous years to 98.08% loanees with up-to-date repayment records (with only 1.03% of loans with repayment instalments more than 26 weeks overdue).

Capital Funds: As of December 31, 1998, donors had contributed US$ 2,210,180 (59%) of the total capital funds, and the 71,479 members had matched this with US$ 647,508 (17%) from branch profits and US$ 863,915 (24%) in their savings and emergency fund accounts.

Profitability and Cost Analysis: In 1998, BURO, Tangail made a profit of US$ 376,219 (excluding grants of US$ 272,680 (reflecting the high rate of expansion at present) and the cost of donated capital (imputed at 10%): US$ 193,377), and this brought the organisation's retained earnings to US$ 647,508. Total expenditure for 1998 was 12.7% of the loans disbursed.

For details of this financial data, see
"BURO, Tangail At A Glance 1993-98"

BURO, Tangail Operations Research:
Philosophy and Methods

BURO, Tangail is unique in Bangladesh since (unlike the other better known NGOs) it has always offered its members access to all of their hard-earned savings. BURO, Tangail is committed to further enhance and improve the flexibility and responsiveness of its savings and credit facilities to meet the needs of its members.

BURO, Tangail has developed a programme of operations research to improve the flexibility of the financial services offered by the organisation, and to ensure that these are responsive to the members' needs. The operations research agenda is guided by:

1. the results of the organisation's attempts to improve the members' participation in its organisational and financial services development, including the Customers' Consultative Groups, PRA-based monitoring and evaluation techniques, and workshops with members and staff - i.e. client-based, or demand-driven, market research;

2. the reviews of external consultants; and

3. examination of successful products offered by other informal and semi-formal financial services providers.

Detailed design, costing and pricing of new products is undertaken by the Finance Director and his staff in collaboration with the Programme Implementation staff prior to the start of pilot testing. Pilot testing of new financial service products is conducted in well-established branches close to the head office in order to facilitate effective training, intervention and monitoring. Staff from these branches are trained in the new products and the accounting systems necessary to track them, and the pilot testing begins.

Senior staff from the Programme Implementation and Finance sections of head office then make regular visits to review the progress of pilot testing in the field. They examine staff, implementation, accounting and organisational issues and make any necessary recommendations on product design. The Customers' Consultative Groups are designed to allow clients to provide feedback on product design. Once the pilot has been running for a while, staff in the pilot Branches work with senior staff from the Finance section to examine

contd.

Continued from : BURO, Tangail Operations Reserach: Philosophy and Methods

profitability and liquidity issues, and to revisit the costing analysis and thus pricing of the product.

This process is further strengthened by an operations research review team of Microfinance experts (researchers, practitioners and accountants) drawn from outside BURO, Tangail, which conducts periodic reviews of the progress of the operations research programme, implementation issues, and clients' perceptions of the financial service products being offered, as well as ideas and options for further research.

Once pilot testing is completed (the period required to complete pilot testing of different products has varied with the complexity of the product, the success of the pilot test, the need for revisions to the design and pricing of the product etc.), successful financial service products are extended out to other branches as quickly as possible, in a phased approach.

BURO, Tangail Operations Research Programme

Until 1996, BURO, Tangail offered limited deposit (maximum Taka 50 per week) and limited withdrawals savings products (under which clients could only access their savings if they did not have a loan outstanding). The organisation also offered a traditional Grameen Bank-inspired loan programme, offering loans repayable in non-negotiable 50 weekly instalments. As part of its commitment to innovation and to offering the best possible services to its clients, BURO, Tangail is now developing and implementing new financial service products. New components of the programme proposed for testing and implementation include:

Savings Facilities

1. *Open Savings Deposits* - offering unlimited savings deposit opportunities (now introduced in all 40 branches*Open Savings Withdrawals System* - allowing open access to members' savings subject to maintaining 15% of the value of any loan outstanding (now introduced in all 40 branches).

2. *Total Open Savings Withdrawals System* - allowing open access to members' savings irrespective of whether they have a outstanding or not (currently being pilot tested in 1 branch).

contd.

Continued from : BURO, Tangail Operations Research Programme

3. *Fixed Term Deposit Scheme* - offering higher rates of interest for longer term (2, 5 and 10 years) contractual savings agreements (currently being pilot tested in 2 branches).

Credit Facilities

1. *Supplementary Loan System* - offering additional loans to maintain members' working capital (currently being pilot tested in 1 branch).

2. *Simple Prepayment Facilities* - allowing prepayment of loans when members have excess liquidity (now introduced in all 40 branches).

3. *Line of Credit System* - offering an overdraft facility (thus overcoming the problems of rigid repayment schedules that are so unresponsive to many members' business cycles) (currently being pilot tested in 2 branches).

4. *Business Loans* - larger loans of Tk. 20,000 - 75,000 for the more successful entrepreneurs among BURO, Tangail's members (currently being pilot tested in 3 branches).

5. *Leasing Loans* - larger loans of Tk. 20,000 - 75,000 to finance the acquisition of fixed assets (currently being pilot tested in 3 branches).

6. *Flexible Loan Repayment System* - offering longer repayment terms for repayment of the business and leasing loans and to assist poorer members repay their normal "general" loans (currently being pilot tested in 2 branches).

7. *Short-term Providential "Hand" Loans* - offering 3 month loans for emergency needs (currently being pilot tested in 2 branches).

BURO, Tangail believes in the open exchange of information to further the development process. It seeks to disseminate the results and findings of the programme and operations research to other NGOs (through the Credit Development Forum an umbrella organisation of over 300 savings and credit NGOs in Bangladesh), and to donors and other interested parties (through the BURO, Tangail donor support group and CGAP) and regular publication of annual reports and working papers.

Contact **BURO, Tangail** at:

18/Ka Pisciculture Housing Society, Ring Road, Shymoli, Dhaka 1207, Bangladesh Tel. 880-2-815815   Fax. 880-2-9125492   E-mail. bt@bdmail.n

BURO, Tangail: AT A GLANCE

Particulars	Figure in BD Taka					
	1993	1994	1995	1996	1997	1998
A. INSTITUTIONAL PROFILE						
Operational Area						
# Branches	10	16	20	30	40	41
# Thana Covered	2	5	7	10	14	16
# Union Covered	21	42	45	89	98	119
# Village Covered	191	246	537	574	1,032	1,362
# Members	7,055	8,511	20,924	32,744	45,003	71,479
Male	1,226	1,226	1,226	395	395	395
Female	5,829	7,285	19,698	32,349	44,608	71,084
Percentage of Female Members	83%	86%	94%	99%	99%	100%
# Staff	95	140	198	312	424	448
Male	53	89	139	220	319	339
Female	42	51	59	92	105	109
Percentage of Female Staff	44%	36%	30%	29%	25%	24%
Total Assets	7,105,098	18,767,033	28,489,110	43,258,729	99,478,430	212,354,969
Average-Annual Growth to Total Assets		164%	52%	52%	130%	113%

contd.

Contd. from Table: BURO, Tangail: AT A GLANCE

Particulars	Figure in BD Taka					
	1993	1994	1995	1996	1997	1998
B. PROFILE OF SAVINGS SERVICES						
Cumulative Savings Deposit	8,751,174	11,189,472	15,646,486	25,095,402	44,562,779	75,180,670
Cumulative Savings Withdrawals	6,078,996	7,647,323	9,137,135	12,333,063	18,000,932	48,166,280
Net Savings Taka	2,672,178	3,542,149	6,509,351	12,762,339	26,561,847	27,014,390
Net Balance Savings Growth Rate	-	33%	84%	96%	109%	1%
Average Net Savings per Member	379	416	311	390	593	378
Yearly Savings Deposits	2,133,761	2,438,298	4,457,014	9,448,916	19,467,377	30,480,509
Yearly Savings Withdrawals	1,474,876	1,568,327	1,489,812	3,195,928	5,667,869	30,143,526
Net Deposit Savings Growth Rate						
C. CAPITAL ADEQUACY						
Equity as Percent of Total Assets	39%	47%	57%	66%	53%	34%
D. PROFILE OF CREDIT SERVICES						
# of Outstanding Loanee	1,254	2,410	11,771	12,684	25,652	55,21
Male	129	287	411	264	227	28
Female	1,125	2,123	11,360	12,420	25,425	55,38

contd.

Contd. from Table: BURO, Tangail: AT A GLANCE

Particulars	Figure in BD Taka					
	1993	1994	1995	1996	1997	1998
Outstanding Loan Balance per						
Active Member	3,587	3,227	1,735	2,434	2,571	3,12
Average Loan Size		2,928	2,864	3,863	4,913	5,396
Loans in Taka						
Loan Disbursed (Cum. Taka)	11,114,220	25,656,720	59,082,720	111,563,720	231,128,720	514,186,790
Loan Recovered (Cum. Taka)	6,615,962	17,880,372	38,657,903	80,696,641	165,168,317	340,487,337
Outstanding Balance Taka	4,498,258	7,776,348	20,424,817	30,867,079	65,960,403	173,699,453
Net Outstanding Loan Growth Rate		73%	163%	51%	114%	163%
Portfolio at risk: Past due by week:						
0 Payments	95.05%	94.74%	97.07%	98.05%	98.07%	98.08%
1-4 Payments	0.00%	0.02%	0.38%	0.13%	0.25%	0.25%
5-12 Payments	0.14%	0.00%	0.50%	0.16%	0.15%	0.15%
13-25 Payments	0.15%	0.06%	0.26%	0.16%	0.49%	0.49%
> 26 Payments	4.66%	5.18%	1.80%	1.05%	1.04%	1.03%
E. PROFITABILITY						
Cum. Opening of the Year	321,576	66,692	4,358,046	7,491,191	11,887,930	19,135,819
Cum. Closing of the Year	66,692	4,358,046	7,491,191	11,887,930	19,135,819	27,195,344

contd.

Contd. from Table: BURO, Tangail: AT A GLANCE

Particulars		Figure in BD Taka				
	1993	1994	1995	1996	1997	1998
Adjusted Net Profit for the Year	(254,885)	4,571,670	3,133,146	4,396,739	7,240,151	15,801,199
F. CAPITAL FUNDS						
FINANCED BY						
Revolving Loan Funds (Donor Funded)	4,334,597	9,935,197	12,335,197	14,648,697	42,966,197	92,827,571
Capital Funds (Members)	66,692	4,358,046	7,491,191	11,887,930	19,135,819	27,195,344
Members Savings	2,672,178	3,542,149	6,509,351	12,762,339	26,677,407	27,014,390
Members Emergency Funds	293,508	759,641	1,413,471	2,844,763	5,352,459	9,270,053
% of Fund Contributed By:						
Donors	59%	53%	445%	35%	46%	59%
Members	41%	47%	56%	65%	54%	41%
G. KEY RATIOS						
Savings/Loans	59%	46%	32%	41%	40%	16%
Total Deposits to Total Assets	36%	23%	28%	36%	32%	17%
Total Loans to Total Deposits	178%	181%	258%	198%	206%	479%
Quick Ratio (Liquid Assets / Liabilities)	66%	43%	73%	78%	73%	84%
Interest Income Ratio (Interest Income/Total Assets)	14%	15%	18%	24%	18%	17%
Return on Investment Fund (Net Profit/ Total Asset)	-4%	24%	11%	10%	7%	7%
Operational Self-Sufficiency	30%	63%	70%	103%	67%	98%
Prevailing Exchange Rate : US $1 = BD Tk.	37	38	38	39	40	42

CONCLUSION

> *"Successful rural banking is founded on analysis of rural markets and their interlinkages, understanding rural behavior under changing social and economic conditions, and knowledge of the financial requirements and aspirations of villagers who control different economic resources and whose households are at differing stages in the developmental cycle of domestic groups" (Robinson, 1994).*

In the last decade the Microfinance "industry" has made significant strides forward - both in terms of quantity and quality of services being provided. Millions of the world's poor are now being served by a wide variety of Microfinance systems: self-help groups, credit unions, solidarity group banking, "village banking", formal sector banking with deepened outreach and so on. The importance of a variety of savings and of differentiated credit facilities is being recognised, and in this context there is increasing interest in product development.

INDICATORS OF PROGRAMME IMPACT

Microfinance's ability to help the poor reduce their vulnerability to "downward mobility pressures", to develop their business and to increase their net wealth is well documented. Sadly, however, this has often been confused by using "increased income" as the sole indicator of "reduced poverty", without reference to the complex and dynamic nature of poverty. Implicit in this traditional analysis and the obsession with targeting the "poorest of the poor", (who incidentally are almost never reached by Microfinance programmes), is that poverty is a linear/static state. This simplified analysis overlooks the dynamic nature of poverty and the fact that today's vulnerable, not-so-poor may be tomorrow's very poor if they do not have access to financial services to help them manage the risks and crises that beset their households.

Some critics have also argued that few of the poor are entrepreneurs and therefore cannot use the credit facilities extended to them effectively - an argument that is particularly attractive to advocates of "Business Development Services". However, the argument is based on the illusion that all loans are used for entrepreneurial activities, which they are clearly <u>not</u> since households often face more pressing needs and opportunities. Furthermore this argument also fails to recognise that most households seek a risk-reducing, diversified portfolio of livelihood activities and that this is preferable to depending on exploitative employment.

The claims that Microfinance is addressing the symptoms rather than causes of "social oppression" are slowly fading away as the "community development" NGOs move from approaches and rhetoric to "empower the poor to break the chains" towards the provision of financial services. Financial services that allow the poor to better manage their household economies are proving more popular, more empowering and more effective than "class struggle"…and have enabled poor households to find much more effective, non-confrontational ways of achieving the same ends.

Western feminist commentators have accused Microfinance programmes of making women even more vulnerable to gender-based conflict on the basis that they sometimes pass on their loans to their husbands. When it occurs, the practice of giving loans to the husband to use is usually based on sound economics – in many cases men can generate a higher rate of return on capital invested than women. Furthermore, careful examination of the evidence and the intra-household dynamics suggests that participation in an MFI's programme also typically strengthens the position of the woman in her family. Not only does the access to credit give the woman the opportunity to make a larger contribution to the family business, but she can also deploy it to assist the husband's business and act as the family's banker–all of which increase her prestige and influence within the household.

There has been inadequate analysis of the effects of Microfinance on health and education indicators. What little analysis has been done suggests that it does have an important impact in terms of increasing family planning acceptance rates amongst clients. However, considerably more work needs to be done in this area, not least of all since there is increasing evidence that access to Microfinance services allows households to make important additional investments in health and education.

It is now clear that well designed Microfinance programmes can "stretch the development dollar" by generating profits that can be reinvested in the institution, and by attracting additional capital funding through savings and (ultimately) access to capital markets. The power of financial services to allow the poor to better manage their resources, and as an extremely cost-effective development intervention, has placed Microfinance towards the top of the international development agenda. But, as many have already noted, some of the zeal to sell the idea of Microfinance has meant that it has been seen to be promoted as a panacea, which it clearly is not, and cannot be.

INDICATORS OF PROGRAMME QUALITY

The effectiveness and poverty-focus of Microfinance programmes is often compromised by their lack of responsiveness to clients' needs. This is best illustrated by the relatively high level of drop-outs from some Microfinance programmes – something that costs MFIs dear. Careful analysis of the reasons for "drop-out" from the programmes suggests that it is generally driven by dissatisfaction with the services and products provided by the MFI, a phenomenon that has also lead to growing levels of "multiple membership" of two or more MFIs. Clients with multiple membership are absorbing huge costs in order to get access to the financial services they feel they need - a larger loan or open-access savings facilities. Indeed, MFIs offering more flexible financial services better tailored to meet clients' needs are likely to be able to charge a premium for these services.

In the past, MFIs attempted to "graduate" their clients, either on the basis that once they had taken a certain number of loans they would suddenly no longer have a need for financial services, or that they could go to formal sector banks. This, however, is changing in the face of the understanding that almost everyone, and certainly every business, has an on-going need for financial services, and that these more mature, established clients are the most profitable and valuable of all for MFIs dedicated to achieving institutional sustainability. It is therefore in the best interest of MFIs to design the quality financial services that they need, and thus retain them as clients.

"Group guarantee" has long been seen as central to the remarkable repayment rates of MFIs in Bangladesh and elsewhere. However, there is growing evidence that neither peer pressure nor peer support are as effective as their advocates suggest - particularly after the first two or three loan cycles have been completed. Thereafter, in the case of default, group guarantee is soon replaced by group <u>fund</u> guarantee, and individual follow-up by the MFI's staff. Indeed this is economically rational since it does not make sense to risk losing many high quality clients who have always paid on time because one client has missed a few repayments. On the other hand it has become increasingly clear that the single most effective deterrent for defaulters is the prospect of losing access to financial services - follow-on loans and savings facilities. It follows, therefore, that the better the quality of the financial services provided, the more clients want to maintain their access to those services, and the less likely they are to default on loans from that quality financial service provider.

As noted above, there is increasing acceptance that traditional Microfinance programmes are not reaching the "poorest of the poor" – indeed they are rarely reaching the bottom 10-15% of the population. This is largely driven by the nature of the financial services provided by the MFIs which force the poorer members of the community to choose not to join, and those who are required to guarantee or follow-up their loans to chose to exclude the poorest. An MFI's ability to attract the poorest depends on the financial services it offers, and whether they have been designed to be appropriate for the needs of the poorer members of the community.

In the light of all of the above, MFIs are now paying increasingly close attention to the nature and quality of financial services and products they offer. The trade-off between the quality of the services and cost of providing the services is a clear one. Nonetheless, there is evidence that, to date, MFIs have put too much emphasis on trying to implement standardised, inflexible, low-cost, credit-driven systems when their clients are asking (and willing to pay) for a better quality and broader range of financial services.

One of the most important short-comings of Microfinance services in Bangladesh, and in many places elsewhere, is the absence of poor-friendly savings facilities. Fortunately, savings have now risen to the top of the Microfinance community's agenda. In view of the clear evidence that the poor can and want to save, there are moves away from loan-linked, compulsory, locked-in savings systems to open-access, voluntary savings services that are available irrespective of whether the client is borrowing or not. Previously, most MFIs in Bangladesh lacked the facilities to allow the poor to save in a way that helped them to meet their current needs and opportunities, as well as to save for the future. The large MFIs have instead concentrated on providing credit facilities at the lowest sustainable interest rates, and on capturing compulsory savings in order to do so.

The demand amongst the poor for flexible, open-access savings facilities has now been well demonstrated and documented. However, the compulsory, locked-in savings balances provide substantial capital and collateral funds for the large Bangladesh MFIs and it is this that prevents them from introducing more appropriate savings facilities. Nonetheless, it is now clear that voluntary, open-access savings schemes can generate much more net savings per client per year (and thus greater capital for the MFI) than compulsory, locked-in savings schemes ... and provide a useful and well used facility for clients while doing so. Managing the transition between compulsory, locked-in savings systems and voluntary, open access savings services without facing temporary (but large) capital outflows is however, difficult.

Regulation and supervision is the other major issue facing MFIs seeking to introduce voluntary, open-access savings services. Trying to strike the balance between effective and not excessively restrictive regulatory systems is proving a difficult challenge for those involved ... and it is probably time to look beyond traditional, conservative, central bank-driven methods to alternative, industry-appropriate schemes. Poor clients' demand for savings services necessitate this and a degree of creative flexibility hitherto unseen.

INDICATORS OF PROGRAMME QUANTITY

Driven in part by the MicroCredit Summit, there has been a push to extend Microfinance to as many people as possible. In the resulting rush, quantity has received more emphasis than quality, and blue-print replication, without reference to the local situation and environment, is the norm. The design of Microfinance systems requires a thorough understanding of the "financial landscape" in which the MFI proposes to operate. This necessitates research into the existing financial services available, who has access to them, and what additional needs and opportunities are present. The results of this research should have significant implications for both the design of the MFI's system and the financial services it offers, as well as the ultimate impact it has on its clients.

Donors have been using apex funding institutions to support larger numbers of small MFIs, but this risks suppressing client responsiveness and innovation through the apex organisation's standardised operational norms and reporting requirements. However, the most dangerous form of "replication" is that driven by consultants, leaders or donors recommending systems they only partly understand, in environments which they only partially comprehend. With the success of the Microfinance industry, the growing international reputation of the Grameen Bank, and the drive to reach large numbers of the poor, there are many alarming examples of this happening.

Finally, there is also a trend towards using financial services as a way of encouraging clients to attend meetings centred on other activities such as family planning or literacy. This "part-time banking" overlooks the complexity of providing financial services, and ignores the fact that clients come to rely on permanent access to financial services, and therefore suffer when the programme finishes and the organisation "withdraws".

THE WAY FORWARD ...

The Microfinance industry has reached a critical time in its development, a time when decisions have to be made, and indeed are being made, about how best to build on the success to date. One camp seeks replication and quantity, the other emphasises research and quality first. The former risks trying to run before they can walk and of compromising the success of the industry to date in the rush to reach tens of millions of families without a full understanding of the principles of Microfinance or (often) even the blue-prints they are seeking to implement. In the long run, this is likely to lead to increasing numbers of high-profile MFIs failing ...possibly even in Bangladesh. Developing environment and client-responsive Microfinance systems is a complex task, and one that takes time.

Even once the initial system has been implemented, there is a need for an on-going programme of "product development" to seek to improve the quality of financial services being made available to clients. This is the challenge for the future. The eventual impact of Microfinance on poverty and the sustainability of MFIs will ultimately depend on organisations' systems and products. The more appropriate and the higher the quality of financial services on offer, the better business will be both for MFIs and for their clients.

REFERENCES

Abdullah, Tahrunnesa, Stuart Rutherford, and Iftehkar Hossain, "BURO, Tangail - Rural Savings and Credit Program - Mid Term Review: Final Report", Dhaka, 1995.

Adams, Dale W. and Fitchett, D, *Informal Finance in Low-Income Countries*, Westview Press, Boulder, Colorado, 1992.

Adams, Dale W., "The Decline in Debt Directing: An Unfinished Agenda", mimeo, USA, September, 1998.

Adams, Dale on the DevFin Discussion Group, On-Line Internet System at Ohio State University, 1998.

Ahmad, Razia S. *Financing the Rural Poor - Obstacles and Realities*, University Press Limited, Dhaka, 1983.

Alamgir, Dewan A. H., "Review of Current Interventions for Hardcore Poor in Bangladesh and How to Reach them with Financial Services" a paper presented at the Credit Development Forum Workshop On Dropout Features, Extending Outreach And How To Reach The Hard-Core Poor, BIDS, Dhaka, 1997.

Alamgir, Dewan A. H., *The Impact of Poverty Alleviation Programme of Palli Karma-Sahayak Foundation : A Case Study.* Unpublished draft report, Robert S. Mc Namara Fellowship Research, The World Bank, 1997.

Alamghir, Mohiuddin, *Contribution of Grameen Bank to Gross Domestic Product of Bangladesh*, Programme for Research on Poverty Alleviation, Grameen Trust, 1999.

ASA, *Dropout in Micro-Credit Operation*, ASA, Dhaka, 1996

ASA, *Hardcore Poor In MicroCredit*, ASA, Dhaka, 1997.

Berenbach, Shari, and Diego Guzman, *The Solidarity Group Experience Worldwide*, in Otero, Maria, and Elizabeth Rhyne, *The New World of Microenterprise Finance,* Kumarian Press, West Hartford, 1994, and Intermediate Technology Publications, London, 1994.

Blood, R.O. and D..M. Wolfe, *Husbands and Wives: The Dynamics of Married Living*, The Free Press, Glencoe, USA, 1960.

Bornstein, David, *The Price of A Dream*, Simon & Schuster, New York, 1996 and University Press Limited, Dhaka, 1996.

Burkett, P., *Group Lending Programs and Rural Finance in Developing Countries*, Savings and Development No. 4-XIII, 1989.

BURO, Tangail, *Sustainable Rural Savings and Credit Programme, Project Document, Phase IV (1997-2001)*, BURO, Tangail, Dhaka, 1996.

Carpenter, Janney, "Bangladesh" in *Regulation and Supervision Case Studies*, Manuscript, 1997.

Chaves R. and C. Gonzalez-Vega, "Principles of Regulation and Prudential Supervision and Their Relevance for Microenterprise Finance Organizations", in Otero, Maria, and Elizabeth Rhyne, *The New World of Microenterprise Finance*, Kumarian Press, West Hartford, 1994, and Intermediate Technology Publications, London, 1994.

Chaves, R. and C. Gonzalez-Vega, *The Design of Successful Rural Financial Intermediaries: Evidence from Indonesia*, World Development, 24 (1): 65-78, 1996.

Chowdhury, A.M.R. M. Mahmud and F.H. Abed, "Impact of Credit for the Rural Poor: the Case of BRAC", *Small Enterprise Development, Volume 2*, Intermediate Technology Publications, London, 1991.

Chowdhury, A.M.R., and Alam M..A., "BRAC's Poverty Alleviation Efforts: a Quarter Century of Experiences and Learning", in *Who Needs Credit ? Poverty and Finance in Bangladesh (eds.) G.D.* Wood and I. Sharif, University Press Limited, Dhaka, 1997, and Zed Books, UK, 1997.

Chowdhury, A.M.R. and A. Bhuiya, "Socio-Economic Development and Health: Some Early Tables from the BRAC-ICDDR,B Project in Bangladesh", *Paper presented at "Economic Development and Health: Status"*, Ottawa, 1997.

Christen, Robert Peck, Elisabeth Rhyne, Robert C. Vogel and Cressida McKean, *Maximizing the Outreach of Microenterprise Finance - An Analysis of Successful Microfinance Programs*, Centre for Development Information and Evaluation, USAID Program and Operations Assessment Report No. 10, Washington, 1996.

Churchill, Craig F., "The Shifting Paradigm in Microfinance - the Case of "Get Ahead's" Stokvel Lending Programme", *Small Enterprise Development, Vol. 8*, No.1, Intermediate Technology Publications, London, 1997.

Dawson, J., "Beyond Credit - the Emergence of High-Impact, Cost-Effective Business Development Services", *Small Enterprise Development, Volume 8*, No. 3, Intermediate Technology Publications, London, 1997.

Deeba Farah and Ishrat Ara, "A Note on Providing Access to Savings of VO Members", BRAC, Dhaka, November 1995.

Dixon, R.B., "Assessing the Impact of Development Projects on Women", USAID, Office of Women in Development and Office of Evaluation, Washington, 1980.

Dreze, J. and A. Sen, *Hunger and Public Action*, Clarendon Press, Oxford, UK, 1989.

Edgcomb, E. and J. Cawley, "The Process of Institutional Development: Assisting Small Enterprise Institutions Become More Effective", in Otero, Maria, and Elizabeth Rhyne, *The New World of Microenterprise Finance,* Kumarian Press, West Hartford, 1994, and Intermediate Technology Publications, London, 1994.

Evans, T.G., M. Rafi, A. Adams, A.M.R. Chowdhury, "Barriers to participation in BRAC RDP", *BRAC*, Dhaka, 1995.

Fuglesang, Andreas and Dale Chandler, *Participation as Process - Process as Growth - what we can learn from he Grameen Bank*, Grameen Trust, Dhaka, December 1993.

Gibbons, S.S. and S. Kasim, *Banking on the Rural Poor*, Center for Policy Research, Universiti Sains, Malaysia, 1991.

Gibbons, David S., "The Grameen Reader - Training Materials for the International Replication of the Grameen Bank Financial System for Reduction of Rural Poverty", Grameen Bank, Dhaka, 1992.

Gibson, Alan, "Business Development Services - Core Principles and Future Challenges", *Small Enterprise Development*, *Volume 8,* No. 3, Intermediate Technology Publications, London, 1997.

Goetz, A.M. and R. Sen Gupta, "Who Takes the Credit ? Gender, Power and Control Over Loan Use in Rural Credit Programmes in Bangladesh" IDS Working Paper No. 8, Institute of Development Studies, Brighton, 1994.

Gonzalez-Vega, Claudio, "Microfinance Apex Mechanisms: Review of Evidence and Policy Recommendations", mimeo for CGAP, Ohio State University, August 1998.

Grameen Bank, *1995 Annual Report*, Grameen bank, Dhaka, 1996.

Greeley, M., "Poverty and Well-Being: Policies for Poverty Reduction and the Role of Credit", in *Who Needs Credit ? Poverty and Finance in Bangladesh* (eds.) G.D. Wood and I. Sharif, University Press Limited, Dhaka, 1997, and Zed Books, UK, 1997.

GTZ, "Comparative Analysis of Savings Moblization Strategies - Banco Caja Social (BCS), Columbia, (Draft)", CGAP Financial Instruments (Savings Mobilization) Working Group, Eschborn, 1997a.

GTZ, "Comparative Analysis of Savings Moblization Strategies - Bank Rakyat Indondesia (BRI)" (Draft), CGAP Financial Instruments (Savings Mobilization) Working Group, Eschborn, 1997b.

GTZ, "Comparative Analysis of Savings Moblization Strategies - Rural Bank of Panabo (RBP), Philippines (Draft)", CGAP Financial Instruments (Savings Mobilization) Working Group, Eschborn, 1997c.

GTZ "Comparative Analysis of Savings Mobilization Strategies (Draft)", CGAP Financial Instruments (Savings Mobilization) Working Group, Eschborn, 1997d.

Hannig, Alfred and Sylvia Wisniski, "Mobilizing The Savings Of The Poor Experience From Seven Deposit-Taking Institutions", mimeo, GTZ, Eschborn, January 1999.

Hasan, G.M. and N. Shahid, "A Note on Reasons of Dropout from Matlab Village Organizations", BRAC-ICDDR,B Joint Research Project, BRAC, Dhaka, 1995.

Harper, M., "From the Editor", *Small Enterprise Development, Vol 8* No.4, Intermediate Technology Publications, London, 1997.

Hashemi, Syed M. and Schuler S.R., *Sustainable Banking with the Poor: A Case Study of Grameen Bank*, Draft Manuscript, Dhaka, 1996.

Hashemi, S.M. and L. Morshed, "Grameen Bank: A Case Study", in *Who Needs Credit ? Poverty and Finance in Bangladesh* (eds.) G.D. Wood and I. Sharif, University Press Limited, Dhaka, 1997, and Zed Books, UK, 1997.

Hashemi, S.M. "Those Left Behind: A Note on Targeting the Hardcore Poor", in *Who Needs Credit ? Poverty and Finance in Bangladesh* (eds.) G.D. Wood and I. Sharif, University Press Limited, Dhaka, 1997, and Zed Books, UK, 1997a.

Hashemi Syed M, "Dropout and Leftouts : The Grameen Targeting of the Hard-core Poor" a paper presented at the Credit Development Forum Workshop On Dropout Features, Extending Outreach And How To Reach The Hard-Core Poor, BIDS, Dhaka, 1997b.

Hedrick-Wong, Y, B. Kramsjo and A.A. Sabri, "Experiences and Challenges in Credit and Poverty Alleviation Programs in Bangladesh: the Case of Proshika", in *Who Needs Credit ? Poverty and Finance in Bangladesh* (eds.) G.D. Wood and I. Sharif, University Press Limited, Dhaka, 1997, and Zed Books, UK, 1997.

Hirashima, S and Muqtada, M., "Issues on Employment, Poverty and Hired Labour in South and South East Asia: An Introduction" in (eds) Hirashima, S and Muqtada, M., *Hired Labour and Rural Labour Markets in Asia*, International Labour Organisation, Asia Employment Programme, ARTEP, New Delhi, 1986.

Hollis, Aidan and Arthur Sweetman, "Microcredit: What Can We Learn From the Past ?", *World Development, Vol. 26*, No. 10 pp 1875-1889, UK, 1998.

Holt, S., "The Village Bank Methodology: Performance and Prospects", in Otero, Maria, and Elizabeth Rhyne, *The New World of Microenterprise Finance,* Kumarian Press, West Hartford, 1994, and Intermediate Technology Publications, London, 1994.

Hossain, M. *Credit for the Alleviation of Rural Poverty: The Grameen Bank in Bangladesh*, Research Report No. 55, IFPRI, Washington DC, 1988.

Hulme, D. "The Malawi Mudzi Fund: Daughter of Grameen", Journal of International Development, 3 4, 1991.

Hulme, D. and P. Mosley, *Finance Against Poverty*, Routledge, London, 1996.

Hulme, D. and P. Mosley, "Finance for the Poor or the Poorest ? Financial Innovation, Poverty and Vulnerability" in *Who Needs Credit ? Poverty and Finance in Bangladesh* (eds.) G.D. Wood and I. Sharif, University Press Limited, Dhaka, 1997, and Zed Books, UK, 1997.

Jackelen Henry R. and Elisabeth Rhyne "Toward a More Market-Oriented Approach to Credit and Savings for the Poor", *Small Enterprise Development Vol. 2 No 4, ITP,* 1990.

Jain, P. "Managing Credit for the Rural Poor: Lessons from the Grameen Bank", World Development, 24 (1): 79-89, 1996.

Johnson, S. "Report of a Workshop on Microfinance Schemes: Models for the Empowerment of women and Poverty Reduction", Manuscript, 1997.

Johnson, Susan, and Ben Rogaly, *Microfinance and Poverty Reduction*, Oxfam, Oxford, UK, 1997.

Kabeer, Naila, "Money Can't Buy Me Love ? Re-evaluating Gender and Empowerment in Rural Bangladesh", Discussion Paper # 363, Institute of Development Studies, Brighton , UK, 1998

Kamal, A., "Poor and the NGO Process: Adjustments and Complicities", in *1987-1994: Dynamics of Rural Poverty in Bangladesh* (eds.) H.Z. Rahman M. Hossain, and B. Sen, Bangladesh Institute of Development Studies, 1996.

Khan K.A, and A.M.R. Chowdhury "Why Do VO Members Drop Out ?", BRAC, Dhaka, 1995

Khan, S.A., *The State and Village Society: The Political Economy of Agricultural Development in Bangladesh*, University Press Limited, Dhaka , 1989.

Khandker, S.R., B. Khalily, Z. Khan, "Is the Grameen Bank Sustainable ?", Human Resources Development and Operations Policy Working Paper # 23, World Bank, Dhaka, 1994.

Khandker, S.R., B. Khalily and Z. Khan, "Grameen Bank: Performance and Sustainability", # 306, World Bank Discussion Papers, Washington DC, 1995.

Khandker S. R and O. H. Chowdhury, "Targeted Credit Programs and Rural Poverty in Bangladesh", World Bank, Washington DC, 1995.

Kobb, Daniel, "Measuring Informal Sector Incomes in Tanzania - Some Constraints to Cost-Benefit Analysis", *Small Enterprise Development, Vol 8 No.4*, Intermediate Technology Publications, London, 1997.

Kramsjo, B. and G.D. Wood, *Breaking the Chains: Collective Action for Social Justice Among the Rural Poor in Bangladesh*, University Press Limited, Dhaka, 1991.

Lovell, Catherine H . *Breaking the Cycle of Poverty: the BRAC Strategy*, University Press Limited, Dhaka 1992.

Lund, Susan , "Credit and Risk-Sharing in the Philippine Uplands", Social Sciences Division, International Rice Research Institute, Manila, 1996.

Maloney, Clarence and A B Sharfuddin Ahmed, "Rural Savings and Credit in Bangladesh", University Press Limited, Dhaka, 1988.

Maloney Clarence, *BURO: What it is; What We Can Learn From It*, Manuscript, PACT/PRIP, Dhaka, 1990.

Mansell-Carstens, C., *Las Finanzas Populares En Mexico*, Centro de Estudios Monetarios Latino Americanos, Editorial Milenio, ITAM, 1995.

Matienzo, R., "Loan Profitability and Impact in the RD-12 Project", Canadian Resource Team, Dhaka, 1993.

Matin, I., "The Renegotiation of Joint Liability: Notes from Madhurpur", in *Who Needs Credit ? Poverty and Finance in Bangladesh* (eds.) G.D. Wood and I. Sharif, University Press Limited, Dhaka, 1997, and Zed Books, UK, 1997.

Matin, Imran, "Informal Credit Transactions Of Micro-Credit Borrowers In Rural Bangladesh", mimeo, Dhaka, 1998a.

Matin, I., "Rapid Credit Deepening and a Few concerns: A Study of Grameen Bank in Madhupur", mimeo, Dhaka, 1998b.

Meyer, R.L., "The Viability of Rural Financial Institutions and the System as a Whole", paper presented at the Fourth Technical Consultation on the Scheme for Agricultural Credit Development (SACRED), FAO, Rome, 1988.

Miracle, Marvin P., Diane S. Miracle and Laurie Cohen, "Informal Savings Mobilization in Africa", Economic Development and Cultural Change, 28, 1980.

Mizan, A.N. *In Quest of Empowerment: The Grameen Bank Impact on Women's Power and Status*, University Press Limited, Dhaka, 1994.

Montgomery, Richard "Disciplining or Protecting the Poor ? Avoiding the Social Costs of Peer Pressure in Solidarity Group Micro-Credit Schemes", Working

Paper for the Conference on Finance Against Poverty, Reading University, March 1995.

Mustafa, S., I Ara, et al. "Beacon of Hope: An Impact Assessment of BRAC's Rural Development Programme", BRAC, Dhaka, 1996.

Mutesasira, Leonard, and Graham A.N. Wright, *Savings and Risks – An Infinite Variety*, forthcoming.

Otero, Maria, and Elizabeth Rhyne, *The New World of Microenterprise Finance,* Kumarian Press, West Hartford, 1994, and Intermediate Technology Publications, London, 1994.

Pahl, J., *Money and Marriage*, Macmillan, UK, 1989.

Pal, Mariam S. "Replicating the Grameen Bank in Burkina Faso", *Small Enterprise Development, Vol. 8,* No.1, Intermediate Technology Publications, London, 1997.

PromPT, *Financial Services for the Urban Poor - Users' Perspectives*, PromPT, Dhaka, 1996.

PromPT, *Financial Services for the Rural Poor - Users' Perspectives*, PromPT, Dhaka, 1996.

Rahman, A, *Micro-Lending Initiatives for Equitable and Sustainable Development: Who Pays ?,* World Development, forthcoming.

Rahman, H. and M. Hossain eds. *Rethinking Rural Poverty: Bangladesh as a Case Study,* University Press Limited, Dhaka, 1995.

Rahman, R.I. "Impact of the Grameen Bank on the Situation of Poor Rural Women", BIDS Working Paper No. 1., Bangladesh Institute of Development Studies, Dhaka, 1986.

Rahman R. I., "Impact of Credit for Rural Poor: An Evaluation of Palli Karma-Sahayak Foundation's Credit Programme", BIDS Working Paper No. 143., Bangladesh Institute of Development Studies, Dhaka, 1996.

Rahman, Rushidan Islam, "Rural Household's Attitude Towards Savings and an Assessment of Demand for Saving Services", BIDS, Dhaka, 1997.

Rashid, A.K.A., "The ASA Self-reliant Development Model", in *Who Needs Credit ? Poverty and Finance in Bangladesh* (eds.) G.D. Wood and I. Sharif, University Press Limited, Dhaka, 1997, and Zed Books, UK, 1997.

Ritchie A., and M. Vigoda - A Post-Project Impact Evaluation of the Women's Development Project, CARE,Bangladesh, 1992.

Robinson, M. "Savings Mobilization and Microenterprise Finance: The Indonesian Experience", in Otero, Maria, and Elizabeth Rhyne, *The New World of Microenterprise Finance,* Kumarian Press, West Hartford, 1994, and Intermediate Technology Publications, London, 1994.

Robinson, Marguerite S., "Introducing Savings Mobilization in Microfinance Programs: When and How ?" Microfinance Network, Cavite, Philippines, and HIID, USA, November 1995.

Robinson, M.S., "From Credit Delivery to Sustainable Microfinance", in "The New World of Microfinance - Conference Proceedings", Coalition for Microfinance Standards, Philippines, 1997.

Rock, Rachel, M. Otero, S. Saltzman, *Principles and Practices of Microfinance Governance*, ACCION International, Washington, August 1998.

Rogaly B., "Micro-Finance Evangelism, "Destitute Women", and the Hard Selling of a New Anti-Poverty Formula", Development in Practice, Volume 6, Number 2, 1996.

Rosenberg, Richard, *Beyond Self-Sufficiency: Licensed Leverage and Microfinance Strategy* (draft), World Bank, Washington, 1994.

Rural Finance Experimental Project, *Terminal Evaluation Report*, Manuscript, USAID, Dhaka, 1982.

Rutherford, Stuart, *The Savings of the Poor: Improving Financial Services in Bangladesh*, Binimoy, Dhaka, 1995.

Rutherford, Stuart, *ASA - The Biography of an NGO, Empowerment and Credit in Rural Bangladesh*, ASA, Dhaka, 1995a.

Rutherford, S, *Proshika Samities as Savings and Loan Clubs*, Unpublished Draft Evaluation Report, 1996.

Rutherford, Stuart   *A Critical Typology of Financial Services for the Poor*, ActionAid and Oxfam, London 1996a.

Rutherford, Stuart, *Financial Services and the Poor: The Family of Schemes*, Manuscript, Dhaka, 1996b.

Rutherford, Stuart, *The Savings of the Poor: Improving Financial Services in Bangladesh*, Journal of International Development Vol. 10, No.1,1-15 , UK, 1998.

Rutherford Stuart and Iftekhar Hossain, *BURO, Tangail's New Products: Preliminary Operational Research*, Manuscript, Dhaka, 1997.

Rutherford, Stuart, "The Poor and Their Money – An Essay About Financial Services for Poor People", mimeo, (advance copy) Dhaka, 1999.

Rutherford, S, "Mountain Money Managers - How Poor People Manage their Money in the Central Cordilleras, and How CECAP Might Help Them Do Better", Consultant's Report for CECAP, Banaue, Philippines, 1997.

Rutherford, Stuart *The Savings of the Poor: Improving Financial Services in Bangladesh*, Journal of International Development, London, 1997a.

Sharif, I. "Poverty and Finance in Bangladesh: A New Policy Agenda", in *Who Needs Credit ? Poverty and Finance in Bangladesh* (eds.) G.D. Wood and I. Sharif, University Press Limited, Dhaka, 1997, and Zed Books, UK, 1997.

Sharif, I. and G.D. Wood "Conclusion", in "Who Needs Credit ? Poverty and Finance in Bangladesh" (eds.) G.D. Wood and I. Sharif, University Press Limited, Dhaka, 1997, and Zed Books, UK, 1997.

Schuler, S.R. and S.M. Hashemi, "Credit Programmes Women's Empowerment and Contraceptive Use in Rural Bangladesh", Studies in Family Planning, 25: 2, 1994.

Schuler, S.R., S.M. Hashemi, and S.H. Badal, "Men's Violence Against Women in Rural Bangladesh: Undermined or Exacerbated by Microcredit Programmes ?", *Development in Practice, Volume 8, Number 2,* Oxford, 1998.

Sebstad J. and G. Chen "Overview of Studies on the Impact of Microenterprise Credit", AIMS Brief No. 1, USAID, Washington, 1996.

Steel, W. F. and E. Aryeetey "Informal Savings Collectors in Ghana: Can They Intermediate?" Finance and Development., March 1994.

Todd, H. *Woman At The Center: Grameen Bank After One Decade*, University Press Limited, Dhaka, 1996.

Van Greuning, Hennie, Joselito Gallardo and Bikki Randhawa, "A Framework for the Regulation of Microfinance Institutions", mimeo The World Bank, Washington, December 1998.

Vogel, R.C. "Savings Mobization: The Forgotten Half of Rural Finance", in *Undermining Rural Development with Cheap Credit*, edited by D.W. Adams, D. Graham and J.D. Von Pischke, Westview Press, Boulder, 1984.

Walton, J., "Review of Miners, Peasants and Entrepreneurs", *Contemporary Sociology*, 14,4:471-2, 1985.

White, S.C. "Arguing with the Crocodile: Gender and Class in Bangladesh", University Press Limited, Dhaka, 1992.

Wiig, A., "Micro-Credit Programmes: Methods For Solving Dilemmas For Credit Expansion", Working Paper WP1997:12, Christen Michelsen Institute, Bergen, 1997.

Wood, G.D. and I. Sharif, "Introduction", in *Who Needs Credit ? Poverty and Finance in Bangladesh* (eds.) G.D. Wood and I. Sharif, University Press Limited, Dhaka, 1997, and Zed Books, UK, 1997.

Wood G.D., "Breaking Out of the Ghetto: Employment Generation and Credit for the Poor", in *Who Needs Credit ? Poverty and Finance in Bangladesh* (eds.) G.D. Wood and I. Sharif, University Press Limited, Dhaka, 1997, and Zed Books, UK, 1997.

World Bank, "CARE Village Banks Project - Guatemala", *Sustainable Banking With The Poor,* World Bank, Washington, 1997.

Wright, Graham A. N. and Shahnaz Ahmed, "A Comparative Study of Urban Savings and Credit Non Government Organizations in Bangladesh", ODA, Dhaka, 1992.

Wright, Graham A. N., M. Hossain and S. Rutherford, "Savings: Flexible Financial Services for the Poor (and not just the Implementing Organization)" in *Who Needs Credit ? Poverty and Finance in Bangladesh* (eds.) G.D. Wood and I. Sharif, University Press Limited, Dhaka, 1997, and Zed Books, UK, 1997.

Wright, Graham A.N., Deborah Kasente, Germina Ssemogerere and Leonard Mutesasira, "Vulnerability, Risks, Assets And Empowerment - The Impact Of Microfinance On Poverty Alleviation", mimeo report prepared for the World Development Report 2001, Kampala, 1999.

Yaqub, Shahin "Empowered to Default ? Evidence from BRAC's Micro-credit Programmes", *Small Enterprise Development, Vol 6, No. 4,* December 1995.

Yunus, M. "Credit for Self Employment, A Fundamental Human Right" in *The Grameen Reader* (ed. Gibbons), Grameen Bank, Dhaka, 1994.

Zaman, Hassan, Z. Chowdhury and N. Chowdhury, "Current Accounts for the Rural Poor: A Study on BRAC's Pilot Savings Scheme", BRAC, Dhaka, July 1994.

Index